THE AUTOBIOGRAPHY OF
LINCOLN STEFFENS

VOLUME ONE

THE AUTOBIOGRAPHY OF
LINCOLN STEFFENS

VOLUME ONE

A HARVEST/HBJ BOOK

HARCOURT BRACE JOVANOVICH
NEW YORK AND LONDON

TO
ELLA WINTER

ACKNOWLEDGMENTS

Chapters of this book have appeared in *The Pictorial Review, The Bookman,* and *Plain Talk.* Acknowledgments are made to these publications for permission to reprint.

CONTENTS OF VOLUME ONE

PART I. A BOY ON HORSEBACK

I. WHEN I WAS AN ANGEL   3
II. MY SAVAGE STAGE   11
III. A MISERABLE, MERRY CHRISTMAS   17
IV. A BOY ON HORSEBACK   24
V. THE SPORTING AGE   34
VI. A PAINTER AND A PAGE   42
VII. THE NEELY FARM   51
VIII. A PRINCE AND A COWBOY   59
IX. I GET RELIGION   68
X. I BECOME A HERO, SAVE A LIFE   77
XI. I GET A COLT TO BREAK IN   86
XII. I BECOME A DRUNKARD   94
XIII. NAPOLEON   101
XIV. ALL THROUGH WITH HEROISM   106
XV. PREPARING FOR COLLEGE   111
XVI. I GO TO COLLEGE   117
XVII. I BECOME A STUDENT   124
XVIII. BERLIN: PHILOSOPHY AND MUSIC   129
XIX. HEIDELBERG: THERE IS NO ETHICS   134
XX. MUNICH: THERE ARE NO ARTISTS   140
XXI. LEIPZIG: MUSIC, SCIENCE, LOVE   146
XXII. OVER THE ALPS TO PARIS   153
XXIII. PARIS, LONDON—HOME   159

PART II. SEEING NEW YORK FIRST

I. I BECOME A REPORTER   169
II. WALL STREET   179

III. BULLS AND BEARS   187
IV. THE POLICE   197
V. CLUBS, CLUBBERS, AND CLUBBED   208
VI. DR. PARKHURST'S VICE CRUSADE   215
VII. THE UNDERWORLD   221
VIII. BOSSES: POLITICAL AND FINANCIAL   231
IX. THE GHETTO   239
X. THE LEXOW POLICE INVESTIGATION   247
XI. ROOSEVELT AND REFORM   255
XII. SCHMITTBERGER: AN HONEST POLICEMAN   266
XIII. SAVING SCHMITTBERGER   274
XIV. I MAKE A CRIME WAVE   285
XV. I INHERIT A FORTUNE   292
XVI. I BECOME A CAPITALIST   302
XVII. REMAKING A NEWSPAPER   311
XVIII. A HAPPY NEWSPAPER STAFF   320
XIX. GETTING OLD BILL DEVERY   327
XX. THE CUBAN WAR AND T.R.   338
XXI. COLONEL ROOSEVELT AS GOVERNOR   344

PART I
A BOY ON HORSEBACK

I

WHEN I WAS AN ANGEL

EARLY in the morning of April 6, 1866, in a small house "over in the Mission" of San Francisco, California, I was born— a remarkable child. This upon the authority of my mother, a remarkable woman, who used to prove her prophetic judgment to all listeners till I was old enough to make my own demonstration. Even then, even though I was there to frown her down, she was ever ready to bring forth her evidence, which opened with the earthquake of 1868. When that shock shook most San Franciscans out of their houses into the streets, she ran upstairs to me and found me pitched out of bed upon the floor but otherwise unmoved. As she said with swimming eyes, I was "not killed, not hurt, and, of course, not crying; I was smiling, as always, good as gold."

My own interpretation of this performance is that it was an exhibit less of goodness than of wisdom. I knew that my mother would not abandon me though the world rocked and the streets yawned. Nor is that remarkable. Every well-born baby is sure he can trust his mother. What strikes me as exceptional and promising in it is that I had already some sense of values; I could take such natural events as earthquakes all in my stride. That, I think, is why I smiled then; that is why I smile now; and that may be why my story is of a happy life—happier and happier. Looking back over it now for review, it seems to me that each chapter of my adventures is happier than the preceding chapters right down to this, the last one: age, which, as it comes, comes a-laughing, the best of all. I have a baby boy of my own now; my first—a remarkable child, who—when he tumbles out of bed—laughs; as good as gold.

I was well-born. My mother, Elizabeth Louisa Symes, was an English girl who came from New York via the Isthmus of Panama to San Francisco in the sixties to get married. It was rumored about the east that the gold rush of '49 had filled California with men—self-selected, venturesome, strong young fellows who were finding there gold, silver, and everything else that they sought, excepting only wives. There was a shortage of women of the marriageable sort. My mother had highly developed the woman's gift of straight-seeing, practical intelligence which makes for direct action. She not only knew that she, like all girls, wanted a husband; she acknowledged it to herself and took steps to find one. There was no chance for her in the crowded east; competition was too sharp for the daughters of a poor family like hers. She would go west. A seamstress, she could always earn a living there or anywhere. She took one of her sisters, Emma, and they went to the easiest man-market in the world at that time, and there, in San Francisco, they promptly married two young men chums whom they met at their first boarding-house. They paired off, and each married the other's beau; otherwise it turned out just as these two wise maidens had planned. This on the authority of my father, who loved and laughed to tell it thus when my mother was there to hear; it annoyed and pleased her so. She was an amiable, teasable wife. He was a teasing, jesting father with a working theory that a fact is a joke.

My father was one of the sixteen or seventeen children of a pioneer farmer of eastern Canada, who drove west with his wife in a wagon to Illinois, where he bought, cleared, and worked his piece of wilderness, raised his big herd of tall boys and strong girls, and, finally, died in 1881, eighty-one years of age. He was a character, this grandfather of mine. I saw him once. My mother took me and my sister to visit him when we were very small, and I remember how, bent with age and brooding, he gradually looked up, saw us, said "Humph," and went back into himself and his silence. He came to life only one other time for me. I was looking at a duster made of horsehairs that was stuck in a knot-hole on a board fence. It looked just like a horse's tail, and I was peering through a crack to see the horse. My grandfather, watching me, said, "The horse was cut off the tail." I wondered, but he did not laugh, so I believed him.

Besides farming and breeding, my grandfather did some preaching, and when there was no regular teacher he taught the school. Also he raced horses and betted on them. Once, on a wager, he preached on the track between heats a sermon which was remembered long enough for me to hear of it. A favorite indoor winter sport of his was to gather the family around the fireplace and set my grandmother telling a story of some terrible night fight with the Indians. She described the approach of the savages so well that you felt the shivers creeping like Indians up your back, and at the attack, when the varmints broke out of the darkness with their tomahawks raised and ready, when the terror-stricken children turned to see the savages crash at them, a yell ripped the silence—my grandfather's. He chose the moment which he knew —which they all knew—"Mother" was working up to, and springing from his seat he shrieked, as he could shriek, the tearing war-whoop of the wild west. And my father said that though his father and mother played the game over and over, and always in the same way, so that the children not only knew what was going to happen, but were sure they could sit through it, the old folks collaborated so perfectly that, when the yell went up, they all were lifted by fright to their feet to fight, till the war-whoop turned into a laugh. It must have been thrilling; my father could not describe it without some of the old fear in his eyes, the terror which carried over to me, a little boy.

Because my father, the last child of the first "worn-out wife," was small and not strong, his father called him "the scrub" and told him that he probably would not live; and when he did live, the old man said that, anyhow, he was no use on a farm. He let him, therefore, do what he wanted to do: go to town, take a job in a store and courses in two commercial colleges. Working by day and studying at night, my father got his education and saved up enough money to go west. Horace Greeley had been preaching that to the young men of the east, but the old New York *Tribune* was read in the west also, and many a western boy grew up, as my father did, determined to go west.

My father traveled de luxe, for that day: on horseback. He joined a wagon train, led by Colonel Carter, and he and a chum of his, likewise mounted, served as scouts. They rode ahead or off on the flanks of the ox-and-horse train to look out for Indians.

They saw some. There were several skirmishes and one attack which became a pitched battle. When it was over, my father found his chum dead with an arrow in his breast. That arrow was kept along the front of a shelf in the bookcase of our home, and whenever it was referred to, my father would lay down his newspaper, describe that old fight, and show us the blood-stains on the arrow. If we would let him he would tell the whole tale of the long march across the plains, around the edge of the desert up through the Sierras, down into the Valley of the Sacramento River.

MY FATHER JOINED A WAGON TRAIN
From an old sketch by Theodore R. Davis, in *Harper's Weekly*

The overland approach is still an element in the overwhelming effect of a first impression of California. To me as a child, the State was the world as I knew it, and I pictured other States and countries as pretty much "like this." I never felt the warm, colorful force of the beauty of California until I had gone away and come back over my father's route: dull plains; hot, dry desert; the night of icy mountains; the dawning foothills breaking into the full day of sunshine in the valley; and last, the sunset through the Golden Gate. And I came to it by railroad, comfortably, swiftly. My father, who plodded and fought or worried the whole long hard way at oxen pace, always paused when he recalled how they turned over the summit and waded down, joyously, into the amazing golden sea of sunshine—he would pause, see it again as he saw it then, and say, "I saw that this was the place to live."

When the wagon train broke up and scattered, he went on to San Francisco. He was not seeking gold or land but a start in business, and in San Francisco he found it (Sept. 1862) as bookkeeper in the firm of Fuller and Heather, importers and dealers in paints, oils, and glass. That was his job when he married and I was born. But soon thereafter he was offered a quarter interest in a

SACRAMENTO IN 1851
From an old print

branch store which the firm was establishing in Sacramento. He went there, and that is where my conscious life began.

I can recall nothing of my infancy in San Francisco. My memory was born in Sacramento, where it centers around the houses we lived in. Of the first, in Second Street, I can call up only a few incidents, which I think I still can see, but which I may have constructed, in part at least, out of the family's stories of that time. I can see yet my mother with her two hands over her face, and several people gathering anxiously about her. A snowball had struck her in the eyes. It rarely snows in that part of California— once, perhaps, in four or five years—so that a snow fall would have excited those people, all from the east, and they would have rushed out of the house to play in the snow. This I infer from hearsay. But what I see now, and must have seen a bit of then, is my mother standing there in trouble. And the reason I am so sure I recall my own sight of her is that she looks pretty and girlish in this one memory. All my other mental pictures of her are older and—not a girl, not a woman, but just my mother, unchanging, unchangeable, mine as my hand was mine.

I think I see, as from a window, safe and without fear, a wild, long-horned steer, lassoed by three mounted vaqueros who spread out and held him till he was tied to a tree. No one else recollects this scene, but it might well have happened. Sacramento was a

"I THINK I SEE . . ."

center for ranches and mines. Lying in an angle of the Sacramento and the American Rivers, the town was the heart of the life, the trade, and the vice of the great valley of wheat and cattle ranches, of the placer mining of the foothills, of the steamboat traffic with San Francisco and, by the new railroad, with the world beyond. I remember seeing the mule teams ringing into town, trains of four or five huge, high wagons, hauled by from twelve to twenty and more belled mules and horses driven by one man, who sometimes walked, sometimes rode the saddled near wheel-horse. Cowboys, mostly Mexicans and called vaqueros, used to come shouting on bucking bunches of bronchos into town to mix with the teamsters, miners, and steamboat men in the drinking, gambling, girling, fighting, of those days. My infant mind was snapping wide-eyed shots of these rough scenes and coloring and completing them with pictures painted on my memory by the conversations I overheard.

I seem to have known of the gold strikes up in the mountains, of finding silver over the Range in Nevada, of men getting rich, or broke, or shot. I was kept away from this, of course, and I heard and saw it always darkly, under a shadow of disapproval. Other ideas and ideals were held up in the light for me. But secretly I was impatient to grow up and go out into that life, and meanwhile I played I was a teamster, a gun-playing, broncho-busting vaquero, or a hearty steamboat man, or a steamboat. I remember having a leaf from our dining-table on the floor, kneeling on it, and, taking hold of one end, jerking it backward over the carpet, tooting like a steamboat whistle. Three or four big chairs and all the small chairs in the house made me a mountain train of wagons and mules; a clothes line tied to the leader and strung through the other chairs was a rein which I could jerk just as the black-bearded teamsters did. And, of course, any chair is a horse for a boy who is a would-be vaquero.

Horses, real horses, played a leading part in my boyhood; I seem always to have wanted one. A chair would do on a rainy day, but at other times I preferred to escape into the street and ask drivers to "please, mister, gimme a ride." Sometimes they would. I was a pretty boy with lovely long blond curls. This I know well because it kept me from playing with the other fellows of my age. They jeered at my curls and called me a girl or a "sissy boy" and were surprised when I answered with a blow. They were taken off their guard by my attack, but they recovered and charged in mass upon me, sending me home scratched, bleeding, torn, to my mother, to beg her to cut my hair. She would not. My father had to do it. One day when the gang had caught me, thrown me down, and stuffed horse-droppings into my mouth, he privately promised me relief, and the next morning he took me downtown and had his barber cut off my curls, which he wrapped up in a paper as a gift for my mother. How she wept over them! How I rejoiced over them!

No more fighting by day, no more crying by night. The other boys accepted me as a regular fellow, but I got fewer free rides. I have no doubt the drivers liked my angelic locks. Anyway, before they were cut off, drivers used often to take me up in their seats with them and let me hold the reins back of where they held them and so drive real horses. My poor mother suffered so much from these disappearances that the sport was forbidden me: in vain. I went right on driving. I did it with a heavy sense of doing wrong, but I couldn't help going whenever a driver would take me. Once, when I was sitting alone holding the reins to let a team drink at a trough (the driver stood away off at the horses' heads), I saw my father come around the corner after me. I dropped the reins and climbed down off the wagon. My father took my hand and, without a word, led me home. There, at the door, my mother caught me up away from my stern father and, carrying me off into the parlor, laid me across her knees and gave me a spanking, my first. My mother! I had expected punishment, but from my father, not from her; I felt saved when she rescued me from him. And then she did it—hard.

This turned out to be one of the lasting sorrows, not of my life, but of hers. She told it many, many times. She said that my father stood at the door, watching her till she was done with me, and then he asked her why she did it.

"I did it," she said, "to keep you from doing it. You are so hard."

"But," he answered, "I wasn't going to spank him for that. He was having such a good time, he looked so proud up there on that old manure wagon, and when he saw me, he came right down, put his hand in mine, and came straight home, trembling with fear. I couldn't have spanked him. And you— Why did you do it? And why so hard?"

My mother cried more than I did at the time, and she always wept a little when she told it, explaining to the end of her days that she did it so hard just to show that he need not ever spank me, that she could do it quite enough. "And then," she'd break, "to think he wasn't going to do it at all!"

MY SAVAGE STAGE

THE world as I knew it in my angelic stage was a small yard, with a small house on one side of it and a wide, muddy street in front. The street was wonderful, the way to heaven. Astonishing things passed there, horses and wagons, for instance. It led in one direction to "the store," my father's place of business, where it was a rare privilege to go and be cheered and jeered at as the boss's boy. Across the street beyond some uninteresting houses was another street, called Front Street, which had houses only on one side. The other side was the reeling, rolling, yellow Sacramento River—a forbidden menace and a fascinating vision. That's where the steamboats plied, the great, big, flat-bottomed cargo and passenger boats, some with side wheels, some with one great stern wheel. I did not know, I did not care, where they went. It was enough that they floated by day and whistled by night safely on that dangerous muddy flood which, if it ever got a boy in its grip, would roll him under, drown him, and then let his body come up all white and still and small, miles and miles away.

But we moved from that Second Street house to a little larger one 'way over on H Street between Sixth and Seventh. A new and greater world. The outstanding features of it were the railroad, the slough, a vacant lot with four big fig trees, and school. The railroad had a switch line on the levee around the slough on Sixth Street, and I used to watch the freight cars shunted in there. I watched and I wondered where they came from. Unlike the steamboats those cars spoke to me of the world, the whole world. In my Second Street mind the steamboats just paddled up and down, as I did on my table-leaf; but those H Street trains of cars came from somewhere and they went somewhere. Where? I could not

read, but sometimes those box cars came in covered with fresh
snow, and snow was a marvel to me. All my picture books had
snow scenes, sledding and skating, houses alight in the dark
covered with glistening white. Not for me, any of this. The only
snow I ever beheld I saw from my schoolroom window, far, far
away on the mountain peaks. The snow-covered cars came, then,
from over the mountains, 'way, 'way over, and I wanted to know

MY BOYHOOD AND SACRAMENTO'S

The above and the three following illustrations are taken from the *History of
Sacramento County*, Thompson and West, Oakland, California, 1880

what was 'way, 'way over. They told me in scraps and I remember sitting by the railroad track, trying to construct the world
beyond out of the scraps of information people threw me till I
was called sharply to come home, and asked what in the world I
was mooning there at those cars for. Grown-ups don't understand
a fellow.

And they could not understand the fascination of that "filthy
old slough, which ought to be filled up" (as it is now). To me it
was a lonely place of mystery and adventure. Sometimes it was

high with water, and I could hunt mud-hens with my "slingshot."
Sometimes it was almost empty, and—sure it stank, but what of
that?—I could play scouts and Indians with the other boys in the
brush, dodging along the twisting trails made by the mechanics
going to and from the railroad repair shops on the other side of
the slough.

The lot with the fig trees was next door to us, and there I built
a nest and finally a house up among the branches—my savage stage,
which a kid has to claw and club his own way through, all alone,
he and his tribe. And there, in our hand-made hut in the monkey-
land of those fig trees, there I found out about sex.

Parents seem to have no recollection and no knowledge of how
early the sex-life of a child begins. I was about six years old when
I built that hut, which was a wigwam to me, a cache; it was a safe
place in which to hide from and watch the world below. Small
animals, birds, chickens, and sometimes people could be seen from
it, and it was fascinating to observe them when they were unaware
that I, a spy, an Indian, an army scout, could see all that they did.
The trouble was that they never did anything much and I never
did anything much. It was becoming a bore when one day a big
boy—eight or nine years old—came along under my tree looking
for figs. He saw my hut; he spied my two spying eyes.

"What ye think you're doing?" he demanded.

"Nothing," I answered.

He climbed up the tree, crept into my hut, looked it over, approving with his nodding head; then he looked at me. I shrank
from that look. I didn't know why, but there was something queer
in it, something ugly, alarming. He reassured me, and when I
was quiet and fascinated, he began there in that dark, tight, hidden
little hut to tell me and show me sex. It was perverse, impotent,
exciting, dirty—it was horrible, and when we sneaked down into
the nice, clean dust of the sunlit ground I ran away home. I felt so
dirty and ashamed that I wanted to escape unseen to the bathroom, but my mother was in the living-room I had to pass through,
and she smiled and touched me fondly. Horrid!

"Don't, oh, don't!" I cried, and I shrank away appalled.

"Why! What is the matter?" she asked, astonished and hurt.

"I dunno," I said, and I ran upstairs. Locking the bathroom
door, I answered no calls or knocks. I washed my hands, my face,

again and again till my father came home. His command to open I obeyed, but I would not let him touch me; and I would not, could not explain, and he, suspecting or respecting my trouble perhaps, let me off and protected me for a long period during which I could not bear to have my parents, my sisters—I would not let any one I loved touch me: all signs of affection recalled and meant something dirty, but fascinating, too. I could listen when the other boys (and girls) told one another about this dark mystery; I had to. It had the same lure that I felt in the hut that day. And I can remember a certain servant girl who taught me more, and vividly I can still see at times her hungry eyes, her panting, open mouth, and feel her creeping hands.

I do not remember what my first school taught me. Nothing like this, nothing of life. It was, at the beginning, a great adventure, then a duty, work, a bore that interfered with my boy's business. I can "see" now only the adventure. I was led to the schoolhouse by my mother, who must have known how I felt, the anxious confusion of stark dread and eager expectation that muddled me. She took me by the hand to the nearest corner. There I dismissed her; I must appear alone, like the other boys; and alone I trudged across the street up to the gate where I saw millions of boys playing as if nothing were happening. It was awful. Before I dived in I turned and I saw my mother standing, where I had left her, watching me. I don't remember that she made any sign, but I felt she would let me return to her. And I wanted to; how I wanted to! But I didn't. With more fear than I have ever since known, and therefore more courage than I have ever since had to rally, I walked into that Terror, right through that mob of wild, contemptuous, cruel, strange boys—grown-ups don't know how dangerous big boys are—I ran up the stairs and nearly fell, gasping, hot, but saved, into the schoolhouse. I cannot recall anything that happened there, only that we of the infant class were kept (probably to be registered) about an hour and that I came out and walked home with such a sense of victory and pride as I have never known since. I told everybody I met, even strangers, that "I've been to school."

I boasted my great boast all day and it was well received till, in the afternoon, after the "big classes let out," I repeated it to some big boys as a reason for letting me play ball with them.

"Yea," said the leader, "you bin to school, in the ABC class! Naw, ye can't play with us."

I have met that fellow since; everybody has. He is the killjoy that takes the romance out of life; he is the crusher that keeps us down on the flat; he is the superior person, as I well know. I have been that beast myself now and then. What makes us so?

And what makes grown-ups promise things to children and fail them? Charlie Prodger was the only man, except my father and Colonel Carter, who kept his word with me. He was something of a politician, and I was made to feel that there was something bad about a politician. I did not know what it was that was bad, but I did not care in the case of Charlie Prodger. I loved the sight of him coming dapper and handsome, smiling, toward me; and I had, and I have now, a deep, unreasoning respect for him. What grown-ups call good and bad are not what us boys call good and bad. Charlie Prodger was a good man to me then; he promised me a pair of stilts; other boys had them and could walk on them right through mud and water, over low fences and even up steps. Charlie Prodger did not say he would give me a pair; he was more wonderful than that. He said: "You'll get your stilts. Some day you'll find them on your front porch, and you'll never know where they came from." And sure enough, one day soon I found on the front porch the finest pair of stilts that any boy in our neighborhood ever had, and on them I climbed to heaven for a while—and for always to a belief in the word, not of all men, but of "bad" politicians like Charlie Prodger.

But Charlie Prodger never promised me a horse, and it was a horse I wanted, a pony. When he made good with the stilts I asked him to promise me a pony. I was sure that if I could get a promise out of him I'd get my pony. He laughed; he understood, but no, he said he could not give me a pony; so he would not give me the promise of one.

But there is another sort of fellow: the fellow that not only made promises and broke them, but probably never meant to keep them. A driver my father hired sometimes of a Sunday to drive us down Riverside Drive was, I thought, a great man and a good friend of mine. He let me sit up in the driver's seat with him and not only hold the reins behind his hands, but on a straight, safe piece of road he held behind and I held in front. One day he swung his whip at a pigeon, ringing it around the neck with his lash. That made a deep impression on me. He got down, wrung the bird's neck, and brought it to me. Poor pigeon! Yes. But I admired the driver's skill, and he boasted: "Huh, I can do it every time. I was a teamster in the mountains, and I got so I could snap a fly off the ear of my lead mule." No doubt he turned and winked at my fond parents, sitting in adult superiority on the back seat, but I saw nothing. I wanted and I asked my expert friend to catch me a pigeon—alive. He said he could; he said he would, but he didn't. He didn't on that drive, but he promised to on the next. He didn't. For years, I think, I asked that driver every time I saw him for my pigeon, and always he gave me, instead, a promise.

I must have pestered that poor, thoughtless liar, but the men I drove the hardest were those that I asked to give me a horse. And they were many, everybody that had anything to do with horses, and others besides—they all knew that I wanted a pony. My grandfather, Colonel Carter, my father, my father's partners, all received messages and, later, letters, asking for a pony; and most of them did not say they could not or would not give me one; most of them put me off with a promise. I had a stable of promises and I believed those promises. I rode those promises hard, once to a bad fall. One of my father's partners, who was coming from San Francisco on business, wrote that he was going to bring me either a velocipede or a pony—according as I chose the right one. Which did I want? I wrote that I preferred the pony, and when he came, he had nothing.

"You guessed wrong," he said. "I had no pony to give you. If you had chosen a velocipede—"

I stood there staring at him, and he laughed. He did not know the shock, the crushing agony that kept me still. I could not move. My mother had to pick me up and carry me to bed. I might have had a velocipede. I could use a velocipede. I could have made believe it was a horse, or a steamboat, or a locomotive, and it *was* a velocipede. My regret was a brooding sorrow, speechless, tearless, and that liar laughed.

III

A MISERABLE, MERRY CHRISTMAS

M Y FATHER's business seems to have been one of slow but steady growth. He and his local partner, Llewelen Tozer, had no vices. They were devoted to their families and to "the store," which grew with the town, which, in turn, grew and changed with the State from a gambling, mining, and ranching community to one of farming, fruit-raising, and building. Immigration poured in, not gold-seekers now, but farmers, business men and home-builders, who settled, planted, reaped, and traded in the natural riches of the State, which prospered greatly, "making" the people who will tell you that they "made the State."

As the store made money and I was getting through the primary school, my father bought a lot uptown, at Sixteenth and K Streets, and built us a "big" house. It was off the line of the city's growth, but it was near a new grammar school for me and my sisters, who were coming along fast after me. This interested the family, not me. They were always talking about school; they had not had much of it themselves, and they thought they had missed something. My father used to write speeches, my mother verses, and their theory seems to have been that they had talents which a school would have brought to flower. They agreed, therefore, that their children's gifts should have all the schooling there was. My view, then, was that I had had a good deal of it already, and I was not interested at all. It interfered with my own business, with my own education.

And indeed I remember very little of the primary school. I learned to read, write, spell, and count, and reading was all right. I had a practical use for books, which I searched for ideas and parts to play with, characters to be, lives to live. The primary school was probably a good one, but I cannot remember learning anything except to read aloud "perfectly" from a teacher whom I adored and who was fond of me. She used to embrace me before the whole class and she favored me openly to the scandal of the other pupils, who called me "teacher's pet." Their scorn did not trouble me; I saw and I said that they envied me. I paid for her favor, however. When she married I had queer, unhappy feelings of resentment; I didn't want to meet her husband, and when I

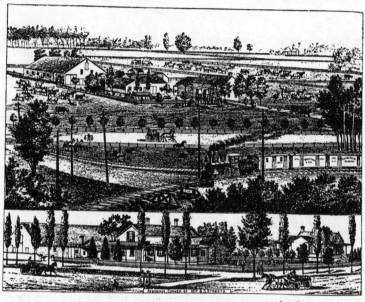

A TYPICAL SACRAMENTO RANCH IN THE '70's

had to I wouldn't speak to him. He laughed, and she kissed me— happily for her, to me offensively. I never would see her again. Through with her, I fell in love immediately with Miss Kay, another grown young woman who wore glasses and had a fine, clear skin. I did not know her, I only saw her in the street, but once I followed her, found out where she lived, and used to pass her house, hoping to see her, and yet choking with embarrassment if I did. This fascination lasted for years; it was still a sort of super- romance to me when later I was "going with" another girl nearer my own age.

What interested me in our new neighborhood was not the school, nor the room I was to have in the house all to myself, but the stable which was built back of the house. My father let me direct the making of a stall, a little smaller than the other stalls, for my pony, and I prayed and hoped and my sister Lou believed that that meant that I would get the pony, perhaps for Christmas. I pointed out to her that there were three other stalls and no horses at all. This I said in order that she should answer it. She could not. My father, sounded, said that some day we might have horses and a cow; meanwhile a stable added to the value of a house. "Some day" is a pain to a boy who lives in and knows only "now." My good little sisters, to comfort me, remarked that Christmas was coming, but Christmas was always coming and grown-ups were always talking about it, asking you what you wanted and then giving you what they wanted you to have. Though everybody knew what I wanted, I told them all again. My mother knew that I told God, too, every night. I wanted a pony, and to make sure that they understood, I declared that I wanted nothing else.

"Nothing but a pony?" my father asked.

"Nothing," I said.

"Not even a pair of high boots?"

That was hard. I did want boots, but I stuck to the pony. "No, not even boots."

"Nor candy? There ought to be something to fill your stocking with, and Santa Claus can't put a pony into a stocking."

That was true, and he couldn't lead a pony down the chimney either. But no. "All I want is a pony," I said. "If I can't have a pony, give me nothing, nothing."

Now I had been looking myself for the pony I wanted, going to sales stables, inquiring of horsemen, and I had seen several that would do. My father let me "try" them. I tried so many ponies that I was learning fast to sit a horse. I chose several, but my father always found some fault with them. I was in despair. When Christmas was at hand I had given up all hope of a pony, and on Christmas Eve I hung up my stocking along with my sisters', of whom, by the way, I now had three. I haven't mentioned them or their coming because, you understand, they were girls, and girls, young girls, counted for nothing in my manly life. They did not mind me either; they were so happy that Christmas Eve that I caught some of their merriment. I speculated on what I'd get; I hung up the biggest stocking I had, and we all went reluctantly to bed to wait till morning. Not to sleep; not right away. We were told that we must not only sleep promptly, we must not wake up till seven-thirty the next morning—or if we did, we must not go to the fireplace for our Christmas. Impossible.

We did sleep that night, but we woke up at six A.M. We lay in our beds and debated through the open doors whether to obey till, say, half-past six. Then we bolted. I don't know who started it, but there was a rush. We all disobeyed; we raced to disobey and get first to the fireplace in the front room downstairs. And there they were, the gifts, all sorts of wonderful things, mixed-up piles of presents; only, as I disentangled the mess, I saw that my stocking was empty; it hung limp; not a thing in it; and under and around it—nothing. My sisters had knelt down, each by her pile of gifts; they were squealing with delight, till they looked up and saw me standing there in my nightgown with nothing. They left their piles to come to me and look with me at my empty place. Nothing. They felt my stocking: nothing.

I don't remember whether I cried at that moment, but my sisters did. They ran with me back to my bed, and there we all cried till I became indignant. That helped some. I got up, dressed, and driving my sisters away, I went alone out into the yard, down to the stable, and there, all by myself, I wept. My mother came out to me by and by; she found me in my pony stall, sobbing on the floor, and she tried to comfort me. But I heard my father outside; he had come part way with her, and she was having some sort of angry quarrel with him. She tried to comfort me; besought me to come to breakfast. I could not; I wanted no comfort and no breakfast. She left me and went on into the house with sharp words for my father.

I don't know what kind of a breakfast the family had. My sisters said it was "awful." They were ashamed to enjoy their own toys. They came to me, and I was rude. I ran away from them. I went around to the front of the house, sat down on the steps, and, the crying over, I ached. I was wronged, I was hurt—I can feel now what I felt then, and I am sure that if one could see the wounds upon our hearts, there would be found still upon mine a scar from that terrible Christmas morning. And my father, the practical joker, he must have been hurt, too, a little. I saw him looking out of the window. He was watching me or something for an hour or two, drawing back the curtain never so little lest I catch him, but I saw his face, and I think I can see now the anxiety upon it, the worried impatience.

After—I don't know how long—surely an hour or two—I was brought to the climax of my agony by the sight of a man riding a pony down the street, a pony and a brand-new saddle; the most beautiful saddle I ever saw, and it was a boy's saddle; the man's feet were not in the stirrups; his legs were too long. The outfit was perfect; it was the realization of all my dreams, the answer to all my prayers. A fine new bridle, with a light curb bit. And the pony! As he drew near, I saw that the pony was really a small horse, what we called an Indian pony, a bay, with black mane and tail, and one white foot and a white star on his forehead. For such a horse as that I would have given, I could have forgiven, anything.

But the man, a disheveled fellow with a blackened eye and a fresh-cut face, came along, reading the numbers on the houses, and, as my hopes—my impossible hopes—rose, he looked at our door and passed by, he and the pony, and the saddle and the bridle. Too much. I fell upon the steps, and having wept before, I broke now into such a flood of tears that I was a floating wreck when I heard a voice.

"Say, kid," it said, "do you know a boy named Lennie Steffens?"

I looked up. It was the man on the pony, back again, at our horse block.

"Yes," I spluttered through my tears. "That's me."

"Well," he said, "then this is your horse. I've been looking all over for you and your house. Why don't you put your number where it can be seen?"

"Get down," I said, running out to him.

He went on saying something about "ought to have got here at seven o'clock; told me to bring the nag here and tie him to your post and leave him for you. But, hell, I got into a drunk—and a fight—and a hospital, and—"

"Get down," I said.

He got down, and he boosted me up to the saddle. He offered

to fit the stirrups to me, but I didn't want him to. I wanted to ride.

"What's the matter with you?" he said, angrily. "What you crying for? Don't you like the horse? He's a dandy, this horse. I know him of old. He's fine at cattle; he'll drive 'em alone."

I hardly heard, I could scarcely wait, but he persisted. He adjusted the stirrups, and then, finally, off I rode, slowly, at a walk, so happy, so thrilled, that I did not know what I was doing. I did not look back at the house or the man, I rode off up the street, taking note of everything—of the reins, of the pony's long mane, of the carved leather saddle. I had never seen anything so beautiful. And mine! I was going to ride up past Miss Kay's house. But I noticed on the horn of the saddle some stains like rain-drops, so I turned and trotted home, not to the house but to the stable. There was the family, father, mother, sisters, all working for me, all happy. They had been putting in place the tools of my new business: blankets, currycomb, brush, pitchfork—everything, and there was hay in the loft.

"What did you come back so soon for?" somebody asked. "Why didn't you go on riding?"

I pointed to the stains. "I wasn't going to get my new saddle rained on," I said. And my father laughed. "It isn't raining," he said. "Those are not rain-drops."

"They are tears," my mother gasped, and she gave my father a look which sent him off to the house. Worse still, my mother offered to wipe away the tears still running out of my eyes. I gave her such a look as she had given him, and she went off after my father, drying her own tears. My sisters remained and we all unsaddled the pony, put on his halter, led him to his stall, tied and fed him. It began really to rain; so all the rest of that memorable day we curried and combed that pony. The girls plaited his mane, forelock, and tail, while I pitchforked hay to him and curried and brushed, curried and brushed. For a change we brought him out to drink; we led him up and down, blanketed like a race-horse; we took turns at that. But the best, the most inexhaustible fun, was to clean him. When we went reluctantly to our midday Christmas dinner, we all smelt of horse, and my sisters had to wash their faces and hands. I was asked to, but I wouldn't, till my mother bade me look in the mirror. Then I washed up—quick. My face was caked with the muddy lines of tears that had coursed over my cheeks to my mouth. Having washed away that shame, I ate my dinner, and as I ate I grew hungrier and hungrier. It was my first meal that day, and as I filled up on the turkey and the stuffing, the cranberries and the pies, the fruit and the nuts—as I swelled, I could laugh. My mother said I still choked and sobbed now and then, but I laughed, too; I saw and enjoyed my sisters' presents till—I had to go out and attend to my pony, who was there, really and truly there, the promise, the beginning, of a happy double life. And—I went and looked to make sure—there was the saddle, too, and the bridle.

But that Christmas, which my father had planned so carefully, was it the best or the worst I ever knew? He often asked me that; I never could answer as a boy. I think now that it was both. It covered the whole distance from broken-hearted misery to bursting happiness—too fast. A grown-up could hardly have stood it.

A BOY ON HORSEBACK

M Y LIFE on horseback from the age of eight to fifteen was a happy one, free, independent, full of romance, adventure, and learning, of a sort. Whether my father had any theory about it or was moved only by my prayers I do not know. But he did have some ideas. He took away my saddle, for example. My mother protested that I had suffered enough, but he insisted and he gave me reasons, some for himself, some for me. He said I would be a better horseman if I learned to ride without stirrups and a saddle-horn to keep my balance. The Indians all rode bareback, and the Comanches, the best horsemen on the plains, used to attack, clinging out of sight to the far side of their horses and shooting under their necks.

"We had to shoot a Comanche's horse to get the fellow," he said, "and even then the devil would drop behind his dead pony and shoot at us over the carcass."

I consented finally to having my beautiful saddle hung high in the harness room until I could sit my horse securely. The result was that I came to prefer to ride bareback and used the saddle only for show or for games and work that needed stirrups and a horn, as in picking up things off a box on the ground or handling cattle (calves) with a rope.

That, however, was but one detail. I had begun about that time to play boys' games: marbles, tops, baseball, football, and I can see now my father stopping on his way home to watch us. He used to wag his head; he said nothing to me, but I knew he did not like those games. I think now that he thought there was some gambling in them, and he had reason to dread gambling. It was a vice that hung over from the mining days in California, and the new business men were against it. They could not have it stopped

24

because "Frank" Rhodes, the political boss, was the keeper of a famous gambling-house; he protected business men, but also he protected his own business. They could not fight Frank too openly, but they lost money and they lost clerks and cashiers through the gambling hells. My father had had to discharge a favorite book-keeper on account of his heavy play at the gaming-tables. He may have given me the pony to keep me from gambling games or to get me up off the streets and out into the country. There was another result, however, which he did not foresee.

After that blessed pony loped into my life, I never played those trading games which, as I see them now, are the leads not merely to gambling but to business. For there goes on among boys an active trade in marbles, tops, knives, and all the other tools and properties of boyhood. A born trader finds himself in them, and the others learn to like to trade. My theory is that those games are the first lessons in business: they cultivate the instinct to beat the other fellows on 'Change and so quicken their predatory wits. Desirable or no, I never got that training; I never had any interest in, I have always had a distaste for, business, and this my father did not intend. I remember how disappointed he was later when he offered to stay in his business till I could succeed him and I rejected the "great opportunity" with quick scorn—"Business! Never."

My pony carried me away not only from business but from the herd also and the herding habits of mind. The tendency of the human animal to think what others think, say what the mob says, do what the leaders do or command, and, generally, go with the crowd, is drilled in deep at school, where the playground has its fashions, laws, customs and tyrannies just as Main Street has. I missed that. I never played "follow the leader," never submitted to the ideals and the discipline of the campus or, for that matter, of the faculty; and so, ever since, I have been able to buy stocks during a panic, sell when the public was buying; I could not always face, but I could turn my back on, public opinion. I think I learned this when, as a boy on horseback, my interest was not in the campus; it was beyond it; and I was dependent upon, not the majority of boys, but myself and the small minority group that happened to have horses.

I began riding alone. When I mounted my pony the morning

after I got him I knew no other boys that had horses, and I did not think of anybody else. I had a world before me. I felt lifted up to another plane, with a wider range. I could explore regions I had not been able to reach on foot. Sacramento is protected from high water in the rivers by levees which send the overflow off to flood other counties. I had visited these levees on foot and wondered what was beyond them. Now I could ride over them and the bridges to—anywhere, I thought. The whole world was open to me. I need not imagine it any more, I could go and see.

I was up early to water, feed, and clean the pony before breakfast. That meal, essential for the horse, was of no importance to me. I slighted it. My father, cautioning me not to work a horse till he had fed fully, said I had plenty of time to eat myself. But I could not eat. I was too excited, too eager, and when I was free to rise from the table I ran out to see if the pony was through his breakfast. He wasn't. I watched him; he was in no hurry. I urged him a bit, but he only lost time looking around at me curiously, and then slowly resumed his meal. My sisters came out to see me off, and one of them rebuked my impatience with a crude imitation of a grown-up.

"The *pony* eats like a gentleman," she said, as if I cared about gentlemen. Something my father had said hit me harder. He said that teamsters, vaqueros, and Indians fed more and longer when they were in a hurry to get off on a long, hard run than on other days; they foresaw that they must be "fortified with food." It took nerve, he admitted, to eat that way, but those fellows had nerve. They could control their animals so perfectly because they had self-control. They didn't force a horse, even in a pursuit. They changed the gait often and went long stretches at a walk. And they could shoot straight, especially in a fight or a battle, because they never became fidgety.

I didn't know it then, but I can see now, of course, that my father was using my horse to educate me, and he had an advantage over the school teachers; he was bringing me up to my own ideals; he was teaching me the things my heroes knew and I wanted to learn. My mother did not understand that. When she came out to the stable, I was anticipating the end of the pony's meal by putting on his saddle blanket and surcingle, and telling my sisters where I was going.

"Don't ride too far the first day," she said. "You will get hungry and sore."

Awful! But I got away at last, and I rode—in all directions. Intending to do one levee that day, and the others in succession the next two days, I rode over them all that morning. I rode over the first one to the American River, and I was disappointed. The general character of the earth's surface did not change much even in that great distance and the change was for the worse—sand and muddy brush. I turned back and rode over the opposite levee, and I could hardly believe it—the land on the other side was like the land on this side. I rode into town again and went across the bridge over the Sacramento River to Yolo County, and that was not different. By that time I was hungry, very hungry, and I came home. Also I was a little hot and uncomfortable in the seat. I was late for lunch, but my mother had kept things warm for me, good things, and she did not ask me very bad questions. Where had I gone? I told her that. What had I seen? I could not tell her that. I had gone to the horizon and seen nothing new, but I did not know that myself well enough to report it to anybody else. Nor could I answer her inquiry for the cause of my depression. Only I denied that I was sore, as she suggested. No, no, not that. I had fed my horse and rubbed him down; when I had eaten I went out and watered and walked him. Then I cleaned him till my sisters came home, and then we all cleaned him.

The next day I was sore, so sore I could hardly sit or walk, but having lied about it, I had to prove it; so I rode off again, in pain, but bravely as a cowboy or an Indian taking torture; only I did not go far. I stopped, dismounted, and let my pony feed on some grass under the trees of East Park. I lay there, and no, I did not think; I imagined things. I imagined myself as all sorts of persons, a cowboy, a trapper, a soldier, a knight, a crusader—I fancied myself as the hero of every story I had read. Not all on this one day. From the day my pony came to me I seem to have spent many, many hours, playing around in my imagination, which became the most active faculty of my mind. For, as I say, I was alone much of the time. I learned to like to be alone, and that pleasure I come back to always, even now. When I am tired of the crowd I go off somewhere by myself and have a good time inside my mind.

As a boy I would ride far, far away to some spot, give my pony a long rope to swing round on, and let him feed on the grass, while I sat and did nothing but muse. I read a great deal. Finding that books fed my fancies, I would take one along, and finding a quiet nook, I read. And my reading always gave me something to be. I liked to change the hero I was to the same thing on horseback, and once wholly in the part, I would remount my pony and be Napoleon, or Richard the Lion-hearted, or Byron, so completely that any actual happening would wake me up dazed as from a dreaming sleep. Dream people lived or lay in wait for me in the brush across the river, so that the empty spaces beyond my old horizon, the levee, became not only interesting but fascinating with dread or glory, and populated with Persons.

"Hey, kid! Don't swim the river there. The rapids'll sweep you clean to San Francisco."

I looked up. It was the bridge-tender, the man that walked the trestle over the American River after every train to put out fires started on the dry sleepers by live coals dropped from the locomotives. I respected a man that filled a responsible place like his, but I slid into the water, swam along shore, came out, and dressed. I could not tell him that Byron swam the Hellespont, which was harder to do than to cross the American at that point; and I did not like to confess that I had a trap set on the other side where the Chinamen had their peanut farm and represented the Saracens to me. When I was dressed, the trestle-walker bade me meet him at the end of the trestle. I did, and a friendship was well started. He didn't scold me, he praised my swimming, but he said that the current was strong at that place and that it wasn't brave, it was foolish, to go in there. "A boy oughtn't to do what a man wouldn't do." He asked me some questions, my name, age, where I lived, where my father's business was. He felt over and approved my pony. I asked him how he could walk so fast on the trestle, having no planks to go on, and stepping from one sleeper to the other.

"Oh," he said, "I can walk 'em fast now because I walked 'em slow at first."

I wanted to try. He took my hand and made me walk slowly, one by one, until I was over my nervousness. When I could do it alone, he invited me to his watchman's cabin, about one-third of the way across. I went, he following. When we reached his little house we sat down, and we had, man to man, a nice, long talk, which became so confidential that I trusted him with the information that I was a trapper and had my traps set for beavers all up and down the river. And my faith was not misplaced. He didn't say that there were no beavers in that river; we both knew there weren't, and we both knew that that didn't matter. All he said was that he was a gold miner himself—and expected to strike it rich some day.

"I don't work at it much," he admitted. "Mostly I tend bridge. But in between trains, when I ain't got a thing to do, I think about it. I think how I came west to find a fat claim and work it and get rich, so I write home that that's what I'm doing, prospectin', and I am, too, and sometimes I play I have struck it and I go home and I spend my money."

After that I caught more beavers, and he and I spent my profits my way. Yes, and after that he struck it richer than ever, and him and me, we went back east and we just blew in his money his way. It was fun. I got a bad name from this. There were grown-ups who said I was a "fearful liar," and no doubt I was unconvincing sometimes. My father asked me questions, and I told him about my bridge-tender. I said that my bridge-tender could run as fast as a train on the trestle, and my father gave me a talking-to for telling such a whopper. I felt so bad about it that I told the bridge-tender.

He thought a moment and then he said, "The next time your father is to take a train out this way, tell me, and tell him to be on the rear platform."

The next time my father was to take a train that crossed the trestle, I told him what to do, and I went out to my bridge-tender. He climbed down off the trestle, disappeared into the brush, and came back with a few ripe cantaloupes. We waited till the train came. Now trains had to go slow on that trestle, and as the locomotive passed, the bridge-tender held up a melon to the engineer and said something about "easy does it." So when the train passed, the bridge-tender jumped out after it and ran and ran; and he caught up to the rear car and he handed that melon to my father, who waved to him and then took off his hat to me.

The bridge-tender and me, we were awful proud. We talked about it and laughed. "That'll fix him," the bridge-tender said, and he wished we could get just one beaver to show 'em. "I'd give good money if I could buy one somewheres."

But I had no trouble about the beavers. Men scoffed, and some boys did at first, but I soon had all my crowd setting and watching traps in the river. And we had a war, too. There was that peanut farm run by the Chinamen who were Turks and Saracens. We boys were crusaders, knights. So when we used to swim over to steal the peanuts, we either got peanuts, which were good, or we had a battle with the Saracens, which was better. They came at us with clods of earth, which they threw. We fired back, and when they came too near we dived into the river, and ducking and diving, swam home to the Christian shore.

My crowd was small and of very slow growth. They were all fellows I met on horseback, an odd lot. First—and last—there was Hjalmar Bergman, a Swedish boy. His father, a potter, and his mother lived in a hut out on the outskirts of the town; they spoke no English and were very poor. Hjalmar had a horse because his father, who had received it in payment of a debt, had no use for it. Black Bess, as I renamed her, was a big mare, high spirited, but well trained in the cattle game. Whenever any dangerous work had to be done the vaqueros would borrow Black Bess, and we boys would go with her and see the fun. Jake Short, who was the best cowboy in town those days, knew Bess well; and she knew him or his business. Once there was a "loco" (mad) steer in a field that had to be shot. We sat on the fence and watched Jake ride out on Bess with his big Colt revolver ready. When Bess caught sight of the steer coming head down at them, she halted, braced herself, and stood fast, moving only to keep facing the crazy beef. Jake dropped the reins, settled his hips to the left in his saddle, and leaned far forward on the right side. The steer came madly on till he was within ten feet of them; then Jake fired and Black Bess leaped bodily to the left, letting the steer fall upon the spot where she had stood. Jake jumped down and finished the steer, and there stood Bess just where he had left her.

"That's what I call a hoss," he said to Hjalmar, and I was proud. Bess was Hjalmar's hoss, but she was in our crowd.

There were other boys with horses, all sorts of boys and all sorts of horses, but mostly they were boys and horses that belonged in one way or another to the cattle and the butchering business. Will

Cluness, the doctor's son, had a pony "just to ride," but he didn't go with us much; he preferred marbles, tops, and the other games on the ground. I invented or adapted games to horse play; Will liked some of them. Hide-and-seek, for example. We found a long, straight stretch of road in old East Park, with paths and brush and trees beside it. There, at the end of a run of, say, an eighth of a mile, we drew a line across the road. The boy who was "it" held his horse on the line while the rest of us scattered into the woods. "It" called out now and then—"Ready?"—until there was no answer; then he rode where he thought we might be. He took care to keep behind him a clear run to the home line, but he had to hunt for us or the sight of us on our horses. Our game was to ride out of sight around him and make a dash for home. If he saw one of us or a horse he recognized he shouted the rider's name, pointed, and, turning, ran his horse for home base. The named rider would start at the same instant, and there was a race.

The horses soon learned this game and would start for home so suddenly at the sight of "it" that their boy was sometimes left behind. I was hiding under a tree one day when my pony saw the white horse of Ernie Southworth, who was "it"; he leaped forward, banging me against a limb of the tree; I clutched the limb, and the pony darted out of the woods, met "it" on the road, raced him, and won. We had a dispute whether the rider had to be on his horse at the finish, and it happened so often that the horse came in alone that we made a rule: a horse, with or without his rider, won or lost the race.

But Will soon tired of this and our other games. He could not fight Saracens that were really only Chinamen, and he held it in great contempt to set traps for beavers that did not exist. There were other boys like that. They were realists, I would say now; practical men. I learned to play with such boys, too, but I preferred the fellows that were able to help create a world of our own and live in it.

I took men into my crowd, too; especially horsemen. The other fellows did not; they said that grown-ups laughed at and spoiled every game. And that was true in the main. But I knew men like the bridge-tender who could play, and there was Jake Stortz, a German who lived and had his barn on the block back of my stable. Jake had the city street-cleaning contract, and he was a fireman and a truck-man. He had lots of horses. His wife, a bare-footed peasant woman, took care of the horses, and she and Jake were my advisers in the care, feeding, and handling of my pony. Jake let me be a fireman. He put a bit on my pony's halter, as he did on one of his own horses, arranged it so that you could with one movement snap it into the horse's mouth, untie, clear, mount him bareback, and so start for a fire the moment the whistle blew. At first I had to ride to the fire with Jake, and he would not wait a second for me, but I soon learned the signals and where to head for. I beat Jake to the fire sometimes, and the firemen knew it. "Where's Jake?" they'd call to me when I dashed up alone.

The first time there was a fire when I was at the dinner table, I upset my chair and frightened the whole family, but I got out and away so fast that nobody could say a word till I came home an hour or so later. Then I had to explain; my father spoke to Jake, and there was no trouble. I could go to fires any time except when I was in school or in bed, and my mother made me a fireman's red shirt.

But there was some unnecessary trouble about a stallion. Mrs. Stortz, who had charge of all the breeding of their animals, took me into all the technique of having colts. I held the mare while she steered the stallion. It was difficult work. The stallion got excited; he never wanted to wait till the mare was ready, and Mrs. Stortz had to hold him off. If the mare was restive and kicked, I had to hang on and make her stand. But we did this so often that we soon had it all down pat. And I had to "watch out" when the foal was due. Mrs. Stortz was responsible but busy, so I had to help; keep my eye on the mare who was left in the pasture field, with instructions to call her at the first sign of the birth.

One day as I was riding out on my pony I saw a mare down and the colt half out, and I couldn't make Mrs. Stortz hear. I let my pony go home; I ran to the mare, and she seemed to have given up. I patted her head, urged her to try again, and then ran and myself pulled out the baby horse. I did it all alone. Meanwhile I had been calling, "Mrs. Stortz, Mrs. Stortz." She came, and when she saw that all was well, she kissed me. And she told Jake and everybody. Jake was so glad. He said that that colt was to be the best horse he ever had and he'd name him after me. And he did. And I watched my colt grow with great impatience. Which was all

all right. My father heard of it, and he spoke of it, but while there was some doubt about something—he wagged his head over it—he did not forbid anything. A couple of years later he came home with a handbill in his hand, and he was very angry. I didn't see why. I had seen the bill myself; it was posted up on Jake's barn; I had one in our stable; and it was in every blacksmith's shop and at the race track. It carried a picture of my colt, full grown and with my name. It was an announcement that "this splendid, high-bred stallion Lennie S. would stand the season for all mares at $50 a throw." My father had a talk with Jake and the handbills were all called in; another bill, with the same horse and the same price, but another name, was put out.

V

THE SPORTING AGE

THE range a horse gives a boy is wide enough—for a while. I was content—for a while—with the ground I could cover in half a day's riding on a Saturday and from three till six on a school day. If I left home promptly after breakfast on a no-school day and right after school on the other days, I could see a good deal of the world. When I had seen all within that circle I had to repeat; intensive exploration was the result. I discovered then the race track.

The county fair grounds were not far away from our house. I had gone there with my father afoot to see the cattle parades and watch the races. Between the fairs there seemed to be nothing doing. I speeded my pony a quarter of a mile on the fine, but deserted, track—and it was fun to play I was a jockey, ride like one all bent over, and then walk my victorious racer down the stretch before the grandstand, which I refilled with a cheering crowd.

One morning, when I turned in there early, I found out that the fair grounds were not deserted. A string of race horses was being exercised, blanketed, by grooms and jockeys. I tagged on behind. Some of them hooted at me, called me a "kid," and ordered me to keep away. One of them, a colored boy called Smoke, riding the last of the string, turned his head and told me not to listen to them. I listened to him, and when the others bade me again to "sneak," he answered them.

"Ah, leave him be," he said.

On the back stretch I rode up beside him, and he explained that there were some stables open all year round on the fair grounds and that more would soon be arriving to train. I might come to his stable whenever I wanted to.

34

"You jes' as' for Smoke," he said, "say ye're a pal o' mine, an' that'll be enough an' a plenty."

I accepted Smoke's hospitality often after that. The other boys soon were used to me—even the trainers spoke to me. One trainer saw a use for me. Smaller and lighter than any of the jockeys and able to stick a horse without a saddle, he asked me to ride a trotter of his. I was delighted; it was a way to get inside. He brought out his big, fast mare, blanketed and bitted, tossed me up on her back, and ordered me harshly to "trot her a mile, just as hard as she'll trot. And, mind this now, kid," he added like a threat, "don't you let her break. See?"

I did it. I lay 'way back on the small of my back, lifted my knees, and so, balancing with all my weight and strength on the reins, put that heavy trotter around the mile in good time. Fine—for the trotter; for all trotters, and especially for colts. No weight, no harness, as free as in the pasture, and yet held down to a trot. And no wages to pay. Other trainers took me on. It was hard on me; some of the horses were heavy-gaited; they shook me pretty badly, but I could not complain, could I?

STEFFENS, JOSEPH, merchant, Sacramento; was born in York township, Upper Canada, January 15, 1837; his parents removed to Carroll county, Illinois, arriving in May, 1840, where his father, stepmother and two children still reside; he was deemed physically weak, and at the age of nineteen was by his parents advised to leave the farm, attend the Rock River Seminary, Ogle county, Illinois, and Bell's Commercial College, Chicago, to prepare for a mercantile life. After leaving those institutions, and teaching school two or three terms, in 1859 he engaged with G. M. Clayton & Bro., paints and oils, Freeport, Illinois, at $20 per month, where he remained three years. In the summer of 1862 he crossed the Plains, with Levi Carter, now of Stockton, arriving in Sacramento and San Francisco September 9. The last of the same month he secured the position of bookkeeper with Fuller & Heather, paints and oils, San Francisco, at $50 per month; remained with them until the house consolidated with that of Cameron, Whittier & Co., same business, in 1869, under the name of Whittier, Fuller & Co. After one year there he came, in February, 1870, to Sacramento, to take charge of the firm's branch here. He was admitted as partner in this firm in January, 1874, being still a partner in the Sacramento house. January 15, 1865, at San Francisco, he married Miss E. Louisa Symes, of Hoboken, New Jersey, who arrived in that city by the " Moses Taylor" November 27, 1862. They have four children— Joseph Lincoln, born in San Francisco, April 6, 1866; Lulu, in same city, August 24, 1868; Lottie, born in Sacramento, October 26, 1872, and Laura, in same place, June 18, 1874. Store, Orleans Building; residence, southeast corner Sixteenth and K streets.

MY FATHER'S "WHO'S WHO"

Smoke said it was an imposition, and the other jockeys called me a fool of a kid. But the trainers told me that if I kept small, ate little, and worked hard, I might become a jockey some day.

Being a jockey became what being a knight or a poet or a vaquero used to be. I worked hard. I used to do four and five miles a day on four or five horses. I studied and adopted the language, manners, and stubby gait of the jockeys, and I made my way; I was rising fast in racing circles. There was some trouble sometimes at home. I did not eat at all at some meals; others were modified fasts, and—I was hungry. My mother was worried. She couldn't make out what the matter was and appealed to my father, who, as was his wont, eyed me, wagged his head, and said nothing for a week or so. He saw me break my fast now and then, eat ravenously, and, filled up for once, resume my "training." At last he took me aside and spoke.

"What are you trying to do?" he asked. "Fast? I see you refuse all your food, then break down and eat like a pig. That isn't the way to fast, you know. The way to fast is to eat nothing—and that is all right. But what's it all about?"

I told him all about what it was all about: how I was the best bareback rider of fast trotters on the turf and had a great future before me, if I could keep down my weight, as a jockey. He heard me out, asked a few questions: the names of my stables, of the trainers, and of my favorite jockey, Smoke.

"All right," he said. "If you are going in for racing, do it well. But the way to keep down your weight is not to eat nothing, but to diet, taking moderately of plain, simple foods; no sweets, no fats, none of the heavy dough-like things you have always eaten too much of. I'll help you choose and limit your foods, and you tell me from time to time how you are getting on at the track."

That ended my troubles at home. My mother fretted some; not much; a look from my father saved me from eating even the cakes that she made to tempt me. And, as always, she helped adjust my clothes to my new occupation. She changed the fireman's shirt she had made me for the fires to a close, high-necked jockey's shirt, and had high heels put on one pair of shoes. I was a jockey at home, and at the track I was an institution, and not only as a rider and trainer of trotters.

I went to all the races, of course. They let me in, free, at the stable entrance. I used to be sorry for my father and friends, who had to leave me there and go on themselves by the ordinary gate for the public and then sit on the grandstand, while I had the run of the paddocks, the stretch, and the betting-ring. But these were places for between heats. When the horses went up the stretch to start, I climbed up to my post, one of the pillars that held up the grandstand, the one directly opposite the judges' stand, to which the wire was fixed. There, in an angle formed by the pillar and one of its braces, I sat and had the best view of the track on the whole course. It was better than the judges'. I could see as well as they which horse passed first under the wire. The gamblers and touts soon saw that; they knew that I knew the rules, the horses, the jockeys, and so, when it was a close heat and the judges were consulting, the horsemen would call up to me for the result.

"Hey, kid, who takes the money?"

And, promptly and certainly, I would tell them and, climbing down, run off up the track to watch the grooms strip, scrape, sponge, and blanket the horses. Racing was to me what I had heard it called, the Sport of Kings and the King of Sports. I idealized it as I idealized everything, and consequently I had my tragedy of disillusionment—as always—young.

Being in with the stables, I soon began to hear about "fixed races." What were fixed races? The first answer was a laugh, a chorus of hoots from the jockeys. "Say, the kid wants to know what a fixed race is!" I was hurt. Smoke may have seen my humiliation; he came up to me and said, "Never you mind, kid, I'll tell you some day."

"Yes, he will," said another boy. "He knows all right."

And another said: "A fixed race, kid, is a good thing. That is when we get ours, see?"

It was Smoke who explained it to me: that usually at every "meet" there were some races prearranged to have an unexpected horse win over the favorite. Since they, the jockeys, grooms, trainers, and owners, were all betters, they could make "big killings" when they were "in on the know" of a fixed race. Sometimes one crowd knew, sometimes another, and sometimes everybody got in, and then—sometimes—the "fix" was "unfixed" at the last moment and "everybody lost" but the owner, trainer, and jockey.

I didn't bet. I had no wages, and therefore I had no compensation for the heartbreak of this information. I had only the suffering due to the crash of my faith. It was sad to see a rider I knew and liked hold back a favorite that I loved and knew could win. I could cry—I did feel tears in my eyes whenever such a thing happened.

Smoke took it the way I did, and yet one day he told me he had to pull the horse he was to ride, a gelding that the nigger had talked so much about that we both adored the animal. He was a "sure thing," this horse, young, but a coming favorite. All the stables knew that, and they knew how Smoke could get the best out of him. When Smoke told me the stable had sold out this horse he smiled. I was sorry for the horse and ashamed for Smoke. I looked away till I heard Smoke say, "Well, anyway, I've put up a pile of money on the race, all I've got, all I could beg, borrow, or steal."

From my post under the wire I watched that race, and having been "put wise," I saw Smoke pull the horse. He had to. That horse had the habit of winning, and he meant to win again. It became almost a fight between the horse and the jockey. I was afraid others—maybe the judges—would see what Smoke was doing. He got a bad start, which the horse made up on the outside of the first turn, when he took the lead and held it, going slow, all along the back stretch. The quarrel broke out on the far turn. The horse's head flew up twice as if to catch and take the bit, but Smoke kept it and at the beginning of the home stretch he was riding in the ruck. There his horse broke free for a moment and sailed up, easy, to the leaders, only Smoke had him inside against the rail and he couldn't get through. And when he moved out to go around, it was too late. With Smoke holding him hard he could not go, and under the wire he was third. The horse fixed to win was first.

I didn't want to go up the track to see the horses after that race. I sat still, and I saw our favorite come back, champing and angry, I thought, and dazed, to the judges' stand. When Smoke raised the butt of his whip to the judges and got his bid to dismount and came up to be weighed, he jumped down and, do you know, his horse turned his head and looked at him? It was just one glance, and I noticed that Smoke did not return it; he turned his back and ran with his saddle and all up to be weighed. He was ashamed before the horse. And the horse was ashamed, I was sure, before the crowd. He went home, head down, champing, and when the grooms started to rub him down, he kicked at them.

After a while, when I could, I went back to the stables to find Smoke. He was nowhere in sight, but a hostler, seeing what I was up to, winked and tossed his head over toward the rear; and there back of the stables was Smoke, crying.

"It's all right," he blubbered when I came up to him. "It's good business for white folks, an' a nigger don't matter, but—de hoss! A hoss is a gen'leman, kid. It hurts him to lose a race, it breaks him —permanent—to sell a race. You ought to 'a' seen de look he done give me when I got down off'n him. I had to sneak out o' his sight, and I don't see how I kin ever look 'im in de face again."

I began to lose interest in the race track. Racing wasn't what it was cracked up to be, and the bridge-tender, whom I consulted, could not help me much.

"You mustn't feel so bad about things," he said when he had heard the whole story. "The nigger was all right, as men go, and, as he said, the horse is a gentleman. There's something to hang on to in racing, as in everything. This railroad, for instance. It's a crook in politics, but—there's some of us keeps it going straight enough to carry freight and passengers."

He went on to tell me a lot about "the road" and life that I did not understand. All I gathered was that nothing is as it seems, but it's all right somehow. He put the blame on what he called "the suckers": the outsiders that bought stock in the road and bet on the races—blind.

My father noticed that I was cold on the track; I ate all sorts of food and talked of other things. I did not go to the races, except now and then when he took me, and finally I would not go even with him. The reason for this was that the last time I went with him and some of his business friends, he and they were suckers. I left them in the grandstand, went down to the stables, and the boys told me that the principal event of the day was a fixed race, and how, and who was to beat the favorite. Returning to my father's party, I found them betting on the favorite. I felt like warning them, but they thought they knew all about the horses, their records, their pedigrees, owners, jockeys—everything. They were sure the favorite would win. I waited therefore till the horses were started and the books closed. Then I told them which horse would win. They seemed not to hear me, but they remembered when my horse came in first. They turned on me and asked me how I had guessed it. I answered them as I heard a jockey answer such a question once.

"Well, not by pedigree and performance."

"Why didn't you tell us?" they demanded.

"I dunno," I said. I could not tell them that it was because they were suckers and that I did not care for suckers, only niggers, horses, and other gentlemen, like the bridge-tender. My father was angry or thoughtful; he waited till we were alone at home, and then to his questions I answered with the truth, not only about that race, but racing: the whole story of my experience on the track. He did not say much. He just sat there and thought. He often did that: just sat and brooded. I remember how it used to trouble my mother, those long silences. This time he was only an hour or two. I had to go to bed, but when I was almost asleep, he came up, sat on the edge of my bed, and said: "I wouldn't give up racing entirely, if I were you. Horse racing is a fine sport, but bad men get into it as they do in other things, and they try to spoil it all. But they can't spoil it if we who play fair do our part. We have bad men in business, too, but business is all right. No. Drop in on the track once in a while. Don't overdo it, as you did; don't be a jockey, but go on and know all about horses."

This advice struck me as man to man. I took it. I did not go to the races often, but I did go to the track now and then till two incidents came together to stop me. One morning as I was riding a trotter, my knee breeches worked down, leaving the lower part of my body free, and, as it bobbed up and down with the horse's hard trot, I had a most delicious local sensation, so entrancing that I loosed the reins, relaxed all my muscles, and rolled off the horse, which broke and ran, leaving me on the back stretch. I was not hurt. I was bewildered, and, bewildered, I walked across the fields to the stables. There the trainers and jockeys gathered around me, demanding angrily why the deuce I had turned the horse loose that way. I tried to tell them what had happened, and, after some moments of puzzling, somebody seemed to understand. I didn't, but the crowd passed some key-word that unlocked their minds and their mouths. They burst into a queer sort of jeering laughter, slapped their thighs, and hooted—all but the trainer of the horse. He flew into a rage. "No more of that on my horse," he declared, and the other trainers agreed that I couldn't be trusted to exercise trotters any more. I was a joke. I slunk off on my pony, humiliated and perplexed.

And then came the fall of Smoke. He was the only jockey who did not laugh at the sight of me. He never referred to my humiliation. Smoke had troubles of his own, and shame, too. It seems that he had pulled his horse that day so well that he was called an expert at losing a race and was put up on other favorites to keep them from winning. He who hated it most had to do it most. He came under suspicion, was watched, caught, and ruled off the track.

Poor Smoke! He came to my stable to tell me about it. A little fellow, no bigger than I was, he could not understand. "White folks ain't fair," he said. They told him to pull their horses. They had influence. Any one of them could have gone to the front for him and got him off with a fine. They wouldn't do it. Not a man would speak up for him. "Didn't want to get mixed up into it." No. They asked Smoke not to give them away, and he didn't; and it was partly because he would not confess and betray his stable that he lost his license.

Smoke disappeared. I never saw him again. But my father saw me right after Smoke told me his story. I was sitting on the fence back of the stable, looking into the alley, thinking.

"What are you doing there?" my father asked me gently. "Your mother says you have been sitting up there for an hour or two."

"I was just a-thinking," I said.

"What about?" he asked.

"Smoke was here today," I said. "He's fired off the track."

"For pulling his horse?"

"For doing what his trainer told him to do."

My father stood there, and he thought too. Neither of us said a word. We just thought and thought till my mother called us to supper.

"What's the matter with you two?" she asked.

"Oh, nothing," I answered, and my father backed me up.

"Nothing much," he said, and my mother turned upon me sharply.

"Don't you be like your father," she said. "Don't think, and think, and think—nothing."

VI

A PAINTER AND A PAGE

MY FATHER brought home to dinner one Sunday a painter, W. M. Marple, an artist from "the City," as we called San Francisco. I was excited. I had read about the famous painters; art was one way of being great; and I had been taken to the Crocker Art Gallery in Sacramento. All very interesting, but there was some mystery about pictures. Those that I liked best were scenes in mining-camps or on ranches and, generally, from the life about me. I could not discover anything very great in them. It seemed to me that they weren't even true; they didn't see things as I saw them. It was evident that in art, as in everything else, there was something to learn. And this visiting artist was my chance to learn it.

"I can't tell you anything about art," he said when I put to him at table my eager questions. "Nobody can. But I can show you."

He proposed after dinner to go out and make some sketches. He meant that he was going to paint a picture! And I could watch him at it! Where? What was there to paint in Sacramento? I guessed that he would paint the Capitol; that was the greatest thing in town. But no, I had a triumph, but it was not on my guess of the Capitol.

My father, mother, and others always wondered why I spent so much time over on the American River bottom: a washed-out place, where no one else ever went. Why not ride in the streets or the good country roads? I could not explain very well. The river bottom was all gravel and sand, cut up by the seasonal floods and left raw and bare of all but dead, muddied brush and trees. I remembered how it disappointed me the first time I saw it, the day I rode over there on my new pony. Since then I had filled it up with Indians, Turks, beavers, and wild beasts and made it a beautiful scene of romance and adventure. But I could not tell everybody that! I was ashamed of my taste in natural scenery.

And yet that was Mr. Marple's choice. He asked my father to take him there. He said he had passed by it on a train one afternoon and had seen something he wanted to paint. To my father's astonishment and mine, we had to lead the great painter to my playground. I was the guide, of course, a troubled, but a very proud leader; I could not think myself what Mr. Marple would like to see and paint there. A hole, where I swam because the water was warm, did not suit him. He pushed on deeper into the brush and, forgetting us in a most fascinating way, he moved about, here, there, till, satisfied at last, he unpacked his stuff, set up his easel, put a small square of boarded canvas on it, and went to work without a word.

How I watched! His first movements I could imitate, and I did, to the bridge-tender the next day. That painter looked at the scene in which I could see nothing to paint; nothing; just brush, miles and miles of mud-stained brush and leafless, drowned scrub willows. He studied this with one eye, held up the handle of his brush, and measured something which he dabbed off on his canvas. Then he looked some more, long, hard, while he pinched paints in little piles on his already mixed-up board of many colors. What was he doing? I asked. "Getting the colors right," he said, and with that, he began suddenly to paint. Fast. I lost track of what he was doing, though I did not take my eyes off that easel and the scene. I could not make out what was going on. Whatever it was, he was quick about it, so quick that in a very few minutes he had the whole canvas covered, and then, as he stepped back and I looked, suddenly it became a picture, a picture of the scene; only—

"What is it?" I asked him.

"Oh, the name of it when the sketch is painted," he said, "will be, say, 'A sunset.'"

Yes, that was right. The sun was burning a golden hole in the top line of the brush and the brush under and around the hole was gold, too, old gold; the whole was a golden picture. But— He was looking at it himself, squinting, with his head on one side, then on the other; he touched it here, there, and finally, backing far away, he said, "Not so bad, eh? Not bad."

It was beautiful, I thought, but it wasn't good; it wasn't true. It was bad of the brush; it wasn't brush at all. And I said as much. He laughed, and he answered me with a saying I never forgot.

"You see the brush and the baked mud. All right. They are there. Many things are there, and everybody sees what he likes in this and in every other scene. I see the colors and the light, the beautiful chord of the colors and the light."

Now I did not see the brush either; it was not the baked mud that made me come and play over there; and I told him so. I admitted that I had seen that the first time I rode out there, but after that—after that—

"Well," he encouraged me, "what did you see after that?"

I was caught. I owned up to the Indians, Saracens, elephants, and—he did not laugh. My father did; not the painter. Mr. Marple said that if I were an artist, I should paint Indians or wild animals—"You should paint a princess in the brush if you see her there." I could understand that.

"But your golden light is really there," I said, "and my Indians aren't."

"Your Indians are where my gold is," he answered, "where all beauty is, in our heads. We all paint what we see, as we should. The artist's gift is to see the beauty in everything, and his job is to make others see it. I show you the gold, you show me the romance in the brush. We are both artists, each in his line."

My father bought that picture, and my mother arranged to have me take drawing lessons. I was going to be a great painter for a while and fill the American River bottom with—what I saw there. But my drawing teacher did not teach me the way Mr. Marple did; I could not learn to copy other drawings; all I ever did that was called good was a group of horses' heads. My mother held me to it; she made me take drawing lessons as she made me take music lessons long after I had lost all desire and interest in them. That was her guiding principle of education: that her children were to have a chance at everything; no talent was to be overlooked in us. None.

The proper fruit of Mr. Marple's visit was of another, a similar sort. I was to have a lesson, not in drawing, but in seeing. Mr. Marple's son, Charlie, came to live with us. Maybe that was the purpose of the painter's visit. Anyway, after him came Mrs.

Marple, and from her I learned that her son, a boy a little older than I was, had a promise of an appointment to be a page at the next session of the Legislature. She was looking for a place for him to live, a house where he would be cared for. "Would I like a playmate?"

Would I? I was delighted. I could show him all the places I knew, and he could show me the Legislature. But what was a page? There were pages in my books; they were little boys at court or in the service of knights and ladies. But a page in a Legislature, what was that? A messenger, they said, a boy that carried bills and letters and notes from one member to another on the floor of the House or Senate. I became interested in the Capitol, the Legislature, the government. I read up on, I asked everybody questions about these things, I visited the Capitol, and as always with me, I formed some sort of picture of the machinery of government. Yes, and I had made in my mind also a portrait of Charlie Marple, made it up out of what I had read of stories and pictures of pages at court.

When Charlie came he was no more like my picture than his father's sketch was like my river bottom, and as for the Legislature . . . Charlie was a homely fellow—and weak, physically— not graceful and pretty, and he wasn't so eager for politics as he was to use my pony. He had been told about that; he had been looking forward to riding it; and when we went together out to the stable, his expectations were satisfied. He put his hand cautiously on the pony's rump, and the face he turned to me was alight with pleasure.

"But," he said, "I can't ride; never was on a horse in my life."

"It's easy," I reassured him, and I boosted him up on the pony's back there in the stall. When he found that easy, I untied the horse and led him out around the yard until Charlie learned to sit him without hanging on too hard to his mane. A happy boy he was at the end of his first lesson, and I was proud. I got on and showed how I could ride, up and down, around the block, at any gait. "Easy, see?"

We had to go to the Capitol and to the hotel lobbies to inquire about his appointment, which was only promised; and I worried: I knew what promises were. I went with him and it was his turn to show me things. He seemed to know as much about politics as

I did about my riding, but he was more interested in riding than he was in that Legislature. He made me tell him over and over where he would ride: down the river, up the river, out in the country, to the trestle bridge, to the beaver traps. There was a long delay of his appointment, and I wondered why. The legislators were in town; Sacramento was filled with them; and the Legislature did not meet. Why?

Charlie explained indifferently that they were "organizing." There were committees to "fix up" and a lot of fat jobs to be distributed; not only pages to appoint, but clerks, sergeants-at-arms—everything; hundreds of them, and yet not enough to go around. There were, for instance, three times as many boys promised pageships as there were pages; and a pageship was a petty job. The page got only $10 a day. Some places paid much more than this in salaries, besides what you could make out of them.

"It all depends on who gets the speakership," said Charlie. "Let's go riding."

"But aren't you afraid you'll get left?" I asked anxiously.

He wasn't. His "member" was the San Francisco leader of the Republican railroad crowd which was sure to capture the speakership and thus the whole organization of the House. They could fill any job, but of course they had to give something good to the Democratic railroad gang and "chicken-feed" to the opposition Republicans. That was "good politics."

So we went riding, both of us on the one horse. I rode in front, Charlie holding on to my waist behind. He was glad of the delay. Until the sessions began, we could play all day every day together, and his salary was cumulative—$10 a day! The amount of it impressed me. A boy getting $10 a day was a wonder to a boy like me, who never had more than a dime at a time. Charlie hardly thought of it. His thoughts were on the pony, on learning to ride, seeing the rivers and the country, or playing Indians and crusaders, and trapping beavers.

I wish I could recall all that I went through that winter. It was a revelation; it was a revolution to me. Charlie was appointed a page; we all went to the opening session, where, with a formal front, the Speaker was elected (just as if it had not been "fixed"), speeches made (just as if spontaneously), and the committees and the whole organization read off (just as if it had not been "settled" days and nights before). Then I saw why Charlie wasn't interested in his salary: he got none of it; it all went home; and he had no more money in his pocket than I had in mine. But also I saw that the Legislature wasn't what my father, my teachers, and the grown-ups thought; it wasn't even what my histories and the other books said. There was some mystery about it as there was about art, as there was about everything. Nothing was what it was supposed to be. And Charlie took it as it was; my father took it as it seemed to be; I couldn't take it at all. What troubled me most, however, was that they none of them had any strong feeling about the conflict of the two pictures. I had. I remember how I suffered; I wanted, I needed, to adjust the difference between what was and what seemed to be. There was something wrong somewhere, and I could not get it right. And nobody would help me.

Charlie was forever for getting away from the Capitol. So were the legislators. They kept adjourning, over every holiday, over Sundays, over Saturdays and Sundays, over Saturdays, Sundays, and Mondays. We could ride, therefore, and we did. We made long trips out to the ranches, up and down and across the rivers. Charlie never wearied; he never got enough of our exploration and of our romance. He entered into the spirit of my games of "playing" knight or cowboy. He learned to ride; he could go off alone, but I liked riding, too, and he preferred that we stay together. It was more fun to talk and think together about dangers ahead; it was safer to meet them shoulder to shoulder. I enjoyed our many, many days of free play.

But I enjoyed also the sessions of the House when Charlie had to be on the floor. He found me a seat just back of the rail where I could sit and watch him and the other pages running about among the legislators in their seats. Charlie used to stand beside me, he and the other small pages, between calls, and we learned the procedure. We became expert on the rules. The practices of debate, quite aside from the legislation under consideration, fascinated me. I wished it were real. It was beautiful enough to be true. But no, speeches were made on important subjects with hardly any one present but the Speaker, the clerks, and us boys. Where were the absent members? I did not ask that question often; not out loud. The pages laughed; everybody laughed. Charlie explained.

"The members are out where the fate of the measure debated here is being settled," and he took me to committee rooms and hotel apartments where, with the drinks and cigars, members were playing poker with the lobbyists and leaders. "The members against the bill are allowed to win the price agreed on to buy their vote."

Bribery! I might as well have been shot. Somewhere in my head or my heart I was wounded deeply.

Once, when the Speaker was not in the chair and many members were in their seats, when there was a dead debate in an atmosphere of great tension, I was taken down a corridor to the closed door of a committee room. There stood reporters and a small crowd of others watching outside. We waited awhile till, at last, the Speaker came out, said something, and hurried with the crowd back to the Assembly. Charlie held me back to point out to me "the big bosses" who had come "up the river" to "force that bill through"; they had "put on the screws." I was struck by the observation that one of the bosses was blind. We went back to the House, and quickly, after a very ordinary debate of hours, the bill was passed on the third reading and sent to the Senate, where, in due course, it was approved. It was a "rotten deal," the boys said, and I remember my father shook his head over it. "The rascals!" he muttered.

And that, so far as I could make out from him and from all witnesses—that was the explanation. The Legislature, government—everything was "all right," only there were some "bad men" who spoiled things—now and then. "Politicians" they were called, those bad men. How I hated them, in the abstract. In the concrete—I saw Charlie Prodger often in the lobby of the Legislature, and I remember that some one said he was "one of them," a "politician." But I knew Charlie Prodger, and I knew he was not a "bad man."

And the sergeant-at-arms, who was called "bad"—one of the San Francisco gang—he was one of the kindest, easiest-going men I ever met. He looked out for me; he took care of all the boys. Many a time he let Charlie Marple off to have a free day with me. And there were others: every "crook" I met seemed to me to belong in a class with the bridge-tender, Mr. and Mrs. Stortz, and all the other grown men and women who "understood a fellow"

—did not stick at rules; did not laugh at everything a boy said and frown at every little thing he did.

When the Legislature closed and Charlie Marple went home, I was left to ride around the country alone, thinking, thinking. I asked questions, of course; I could not think out alone all that I had been learning that winter; I could not easily drop the problem of government and the goodness and badness of men. But I did not draw from my friends any answers that cleared my darkness. The bridge-tender said that all Legislatures were like that. And Jim Neely said so too. Ah Hook was not interested. "What for you askem me fool question," he said. "Chinaman he findee out long time allee government allee samee—big clook."

But there was an answer of a sort about that time, an answer to one of my questions: Why didn't somebody challenge the rascals —if they were so bad? The boss of Sacramento, Frank Rhodes, the gambler, was having one of his conventions of the local ring-leaders in a room under his gambling-house. It was at night. There were no outsiders present, none wanted, and the insiders were fighting, shooting men. During the meeting Grove L. Johnson, a well-known attorney in the town, walked in with his two sons, Albert and Hiram, both little more than boys, and both carrying revolvers. They went up to the front, and with one of his boys on one side of him, the other on the other, Mr. Johnson told those crooks all about themselves and what they were doing. He was bitter, fearless, free-spoken; he insulted, he defied those politicians; he called upon the town to clean them out and predicted that their power would be broken some day. There was no answer. When he had finished, he and his sons walked out.

Something in me responded to that proceeding. It was one way to solve my problem. There was no other response, so far as I could see or hear. People said unpleasant things about Grove L. Johnson, and the Rhodes ring went right on governing the town. Later, much later, the boss disappeared, and still later Grove L. Johnson himself was one of the bosses of the Legislature. Albert Johnson died. But Hiram Johnson became a reform Governor of California and a United States Senator.

What struck and stunned me at the time was that this courageous attack by the Johnsons—especially by the boys—had no effect upon the people I knew. I was trying to see the Legislature and government as Mr. Marple saw the sunset through the brush in the river bottom; not the mud but—the gold, the Indians—some beauty in them. The painter said there always was something beautiful to see. Well, Mr. Johnson and his two boys—their defiance was beautiful; wasn't it? I thought so, and yet nobody else did. Why? I gave it up, or, better, I laid the question aside. I had other things to think of, wonderful things, things more in my line.

VII

THE NEELY FARM

WHEN the romance began to fall off the race horses, I looked around for a new interest and there was none within my old range. I had about exhausted the resources of the world within a quarter of a day's ride of home. My circle must be widened; I must go off for all day. What held me? Not my parents; they let me go wild. Not my pony: he was a tough little cayuse. The noonday meal was the stake I was tied to. If I could ride away out into the country till noon, eat there somewhere, and ride back in the afternoon, I could cover miles and miles, see new things, new people. The problem was where to eat and feed my pony.

I tried nowhere at first. I rode half a day, dismounted on the edge of a vineyard, and ate grapes, but there is no grass when grapes are ripe; my pony had to nibble stubble. That was not enough for him, and the grapes were too much for me. I came home with a stomach-ache. My mother, who did not understand a boy at all, said it was the grapes, and she proposed that I take my lunch with me. "Your father does," she argued. Yes, but teamsters, scouts, knights, and vaqueros did not carry a lunch—and I wasn't going to. When my mother insisted and made up a lunch parcel for me I hid it in the stable or ditched it. I would not be weak. I would "find" myself, as my kind of people did.

I consulted the bridge-tender about it. He said l might share his meal whenever I wished, and his fare was good regular food: ham and eggs with black coffee and brown sugar. He could not provide for a horse, however, and the bridge was not far enough out of town. I used his hospitality only for breakfasts when I rose early and could get out to his place by six-thirty A.M.

I made friends with Ah Hook, a Chinese farmer a little farther

51

out. He was hostile at first. Having a patch of melons and another of peanuts, he was suspicious of a boy.

"What for you come catchem eat here?" he asked. "What for you no go home?"

I explained, "Too far," and he asked, "What for you go too far?"

That was an easy question. I had to see what was beyond. He laughed.

"Melican boy, he go lookee see—what? No ting, no ting. China boy, he no go lookee see. He know all-leadee, notting, allee samee."

I answered that: "What for you Ah Hook come allee way China lookee see—Sacramento?"

"Me no come lookee see Sacramento," he replied. "Me come catchem dollar, go home China."

"Yes," I argued, "you come catchem dollar to catchem eat allee samee me."

Ah Hook liked that. He chuckled and surrendered.

"All li," he said. "All li, you come eatee lice here."

And I did once or twice, and Ah Hook put up my pony to feed with his old skeleton of a horse. But his bill of fare was always the same "lice" and tea, both made Chinese fashion, and I didn't like rice. I had to find another road-house.

As my custom was, I made a business of the search, and I turned the business into a game. My youngest sister has turned this trick into a philosophy. "Why work?" she says whenever any one complains of the labor of something. "Make a game of your job and then—play."

I played that I was a fugitive from justice in search of a friend, but I became so absolutely a hunted criminal that I was too cautious. I ran away from the people who might have helped me. I found nothing, and another day was wasted because I was after an enemy and forgot that it was actually a friend I wanted. I avoided everybody. The next Saturday I was more sensible. I was the trusted scout of a general who sent me out to find a base, an advance post where he could quarter and supply his troops; and he ordered me to hunt till I got what we must have. Riding up on a low eminence on the Stockton road, I folded my arms and reconnoitered, and I saw several places that would do. I was judging by appearances; I preferred neat farms. The Duden Farm was spick and span. It was small, but all the buildings were painted; the fences were well made and the fields well tilled. Mr. Duden had a blacksmith's shop on the corner of the main road and a cross road. There he himself always worked; his sons kept the farm. That was an objection. Country boys had an uncomfortable way of looking a city boy contemptuously up and down, asking technical questions, and laughing at the answers. I was desperate, however; the troops must be provided for; the general was a fine chief but a martinet. I considered the Duden place.

Riding on to the blacksmith's shop, I stopped and stared at Mr. Duden. He looked up from his anvil, asked me if I wanted my pony shod, and when I said I didn't, he went on with his work, hammering red-hot irons and spattering the sparks all over everything, even his leather apron and—to my wonder—his own bare, hairy arms. It was a fascinating sight. I wouldn't mind being a blacksmith who shod horses. The glowing splinters burned black spots on the floor, but they didn't burn Mr. Duden. Why? I asked him.

"They know me," he answered, but he did not look up. He went on beating the red-hot irons, ducking them sizzling into water and poking them back in the open fire, just as if I wasn't there. I rode on, therefore, and the Dudens lost for a year or two the chance to know and feed me.

The Duden place was five miles out. Two miles farther there was a cross road that led left to Florin, a railroad station, now the center of a Japanese colony which has been written about many times as an example of the failure of the whites to hold land against the cleverest of the yellow races. In my day the farms were almost ranches in size and the houses few. There was no building between Dudens' and the cross road, none beyond for miles. It was all open fields of wheat, shining hot in the sun. You could see the heat radiating like white flames over the land. I turned down the Florin road because I saw off to the left of it an oasis, a white cottage, with a flying windmill in a small, fenced garden of young trees, and near it a big, unpainted barn. Pretty good. A lane opened off the road; I jogged along it between the yellow wheat and the great, light green vineyard irrigated by windmills, up to the house. I saw that there were flowers in the garden, kept fresh by tiny streams of water, carried all through and around it by a perfect little system of ditches. The whole place was neat, cool, shady, and quiet; and not a sign of a human being till I arrived opposite the cottage gate. There I saw, with a start, a woman standing, wiping her hands on her apron and staring hard at me. It was Mrs. Neely.

Mrs. Neely was the New England wife of William Neely, a

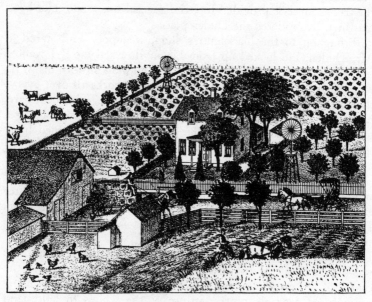

THE NEELY RANCH

tall, straight, gentle man from Mississippi. This I learned later, and indeed a good deal of what I have to tell now of her and me is her story, told afterward to my mother, and all mixed up hopelessly with my own recollections. But I can see still the picture of her at our first meeting; I can feel the straight line of her tight, silent lips, and the gleeful, dancing look out of her watching, inquiring eyes. She drove all thought of my troops out of my head.

"How de do?" I began anxiously.

"How do you do?" she answered.

"I'm Lennie Steffens," I explained, "and I'm looking for some place where I can get lunch for us when I'm off on long trips in the country."

"Us?" she repeated. "Who are us? You don't mean you and your pony?"

"Yes," I said, "and my father says it's more important to feed my pony than me, but he can eat grass, if you have no hay."

"Oh, we have hay," she answered, "but why should we feed a boy and a horse whenever they happen along?"

"I don't know," I said, and I didn't. I was often asked the question; I had even asked it myself; and I never could answer it.

"Where do you and your pony live?" she questioned. "And what do you two do for a living? What are you doing now 'way out here?"

I told her where I lived. I could not tell her what I did for a living, except that I went to school. And as for this trip, I had explained that, but I repeated a little more fully. I was hunting for a place where I could always be sure of regular meals when I was out on the Stockton road.

"Does your mother let you range the country wild like this? And your father! Do they know where you are today?"

"No." I blushed for them. "They don't know where I am to-day. They hardly ever know till I get back. But they don't mind. They let me go anywhere I want to, as long as I am with my pony."

"Umph, I see," she said. "They trust the pony." And she called, "Jim, Jim."

A man stuck his head out of the barn. "Hallo?" he answered.

"Here, Jim," she said. "Come and take this useless boy's good-for-nothing pony; put him in the barn and feed him. Hay, no barley. And you"—she turned to me—"you climb down off that horse and come with me."

Jim came and took the pony with a wondering look at me. I went with Mrs. Neely, who led me to her kitchen and bade me "wash up." She said I was dirty. She went on with her cooking, and when I had washed, we had a long talk. I don't remember what it was all about, but I do recall her interest in my sisters, who did not interest me. They weren't boys and could be used, so far as I had discovered, only on rainy days, when they served pretty well as brakemen and better still as passengers on a train

of chairs or a steamboat. Yes, and she asked me about school, which
bored me. The only good thing I could tell her about school was
that Friday was a short day, closing at two o'clock instead of three,
and there was no school from then till Monday. Two days and a
half free. In order to use them, however, I had to find places
where I could stop and feed up.

She saw, she said. "And when you decide that we will do for
one stopping-place, you will go on and look for others farther out."

"Ye-e-e-s," I agreed. I had not thought so far ahead as that,
but the moment she mentioned it, I could see it would be well to
have other stations. Also I could see that Mrs. Neely could understand—some things; which is very important to a boy, whose life
is one long search for people who have some insight; intelligence
is so rare, especially among grown-ups.

Dinner was a long time preparing. I thought Mrs. Neely would
never stop putting things on the table—wonderful things: cakes
and jams, honey and milk and pickles. Long after there was
enough even for me she kept baking and cooking and pulling
things out of cupboards, cellars, and the oven. And I wasn't the
only impatient one. Before she was ready Jim came up to the
house.

"Always first—to meals," Mrs. Neely said uncomfortably, but
Jim answered her back. "It's late," he said. "That noon train went
by long ago." Her reply was a blast on a horn that brought Mr.
Neely up to the door. Both men wiped their boots carefully on
the door-mat outside the kitchen door, and that made me notice
that the house was very clean.

I was introduced to Mr. Neely as "a good-for-nothing boy who
has come here on a useless pony for a square meal for both, and he
proposes, if the board is satisfactory, to come often, whenever he
is passing by—at meal times."

"Then," said Mr. Neely, "I hope that you have a good dinner
for him." He said this charmingly, with a polite bow to me, and he
gave me a warm handshake. I liked Mr. Neely right then and
there. Of Mrs. Neely I could not be sure; she was queer. As for
Jim, Mr. Neely's brother—I ranked him where Mrs. Neely put
him, at the foot of the table; he was just a regular fella.

"Yes," Mrs. Neely repeated when the men had washed up and
we were seated at table, "I have done my best, as you see, with

the cooking of this first—a sample meal. For I infer from what he tells me that he won't come to us again unless he is suited, though he says his father says that it is more important that Jim feed his pony well." It was true that I had said all that; only the way Mrs. Neely said it made me feel very uneasy. It was always a puzzle to me why people took what I said and gave it a twist that made it sound preposterous or ridiculous.

I was hungry, however. So were the other men, and the food was not only abundant, it was good. I had chanced upon the best cook in the county; so I ate; we all ate, all but Mrs. Neely, who kept at me with questions, funny questions. How was the election going to go? Who would be our next President? What was playing at the theater? And the opera? (Sacramento had no opera.) When would the next ball be? What were the latest fashions? I didn't answer the questions; didn't have to; nobody did. We just ate and ate, and she asked questions without waiting for answers till I was full, very full, and then Mrs. Neely got me started telling the story of my life—to come. That seemed to interest them all; they sat around listening to what I was going to be, until Mrs. Neely said it was time to go to work. Then Mr. Neely shook hands with me, said good-by, and told me to come again whenever I wanted to.

"That settles it so far as we are concerned," said Mrs. Neely. Mr. Neely was head of the house, and if he said I might come again, I could be sure of a welcome from her.

"But how about you?" she asked me. "Do you want to come again? Does the board suit you?"

I told her it did; I was very sincere on that point, and she was glad. She liked to have a visitor now and then from the great world; liked to hear the news. She complained that some visitors, especially boys, did not know much, had no idea what was going on; and some boys were a lot of trouble, banging around and breaking fences and things, making noises that scared the cattle and fowls. I wasn't like that. She was pleased that I was different. And she seemed to have a grievance against a boy that came, not by himself, but with a horse that had to be fed and cleaned. What would I do with a boy like that? What could such a boy expect? To be taken in and coddled and— I was troubled. It sounded just like me, this part, and Jim grinned. She turned on him and drove him out. "You go on to your work," she commanded angrily, and when he obeyed and was gone, she grabbed and squeezed me.

"You darling," she said, "you darling," and she kissed me, several times, hard, the way my mother did till I had put a stop to the practice. I couldn't stop Mrs. Neely. I saw what looked like wetness in her eyes, and besides, all of a sudden she pushed me out of the house and slammed the door.

Jim was waiting for me. He took me out to the barn. He kept snickering a suppressed laugh while he showed me that the pony had fed well. He put on bridle and blanket, boosted me upon the pony.

"Now, boy," he said, "you come often. We get better meals when you do. The Missis doesn't strain herself every day the way she did today. And Will, he likes you."

"But how about Mrs. Neely?" I asked. "Does she really want me to come?"

"Want you?" Jim exclaimed. "*Want* you! She has wanted a boy like you all her life."

VIII

A PRINCE AND A COWBOY

A BOY's life is pestered with problems—hard ones, as hard as any adult's. There is the whole world to get into your head. You have to make a picture of it; that's easy, but the picture has to correspond somewhat with the world outside, which keeps changing. You have the sun going fine around the earth, and then all of a sudden you learn something more and the earth starts whirling around the sun. This means a complete readjustment. It happens often. Every time I had everything all right and working harmoniously inside so that I could leave it and mind my own business, some fact would bob up to throw it all out. I remember how, when the earth was flat, I had to put China and the Far East to the west of me, no easy task for a boy; and then when I had that done, I studied a book which made the earth round like an orange. Where was one to put China then?

I consulted some of the other boys about that, and they looked dazed for a moment; but they soon turned to the ball and bats and bade me do likewise.

"Ah, play ball," they said in effect.

Our cook, a Chinaman, was contemptuous. "What for you go lookee see find China? China no lost. Fool boy lost, yes, but China all li."

And this, the construction of the universe as a whole, was only the main business of life. There were minor problems. It took me and my crowd days of exploration to discover and map in our minds the confluence of our two rivers, the American and the Sacramento. It took longer to make out how the river steamboats and the railroad trains could start from Sacramento at right angles and arrive both at the same place, San Francisco. Also there were the inhabitants of the earth to understand, the grown-ups who do and say such queer things. They say they love you and yet they balk you like enemies. They tell you to be good and you'll succeed, and the next thing you know they will be chuckling about how dishonest some successful man was. Nor will they explain anything, not seriously. They laugh at a fellow's questions. Or if they pretend to throw a light, they only cast a shadow that darkens and complicates the puzzle. They don't seem to realize how painful your need is to find out just where you are at in a mixed-up world. Sometimes it seemed to me almost as if they didn't know where they were at themselves.

As I was leaving the Neely farm that day I was wondering what Jim Neely meant by what he said about Mrs. Neely wanting a boy like me and what Mrs. Neely meant by being so cross with me and then so soft. If she wanted me why couldn't she take me straight as a regular fellow would? I could not make it out. I thought and thought, but the sun was hot over me and the pony was hot under me. I did what I had to do with many, many questions: I gave them up, for the present; I laid them aside and hung on to the thought that anyhow I had a feeding-station seven miles out on the Stockton road. And before I reached home I had another feeding-station still farther out, and another problem.

Single-footing along the flaming road, I picked up the track of cattle going my way, and pretty soon there was a cloud of dust ahead. Hurrying as much as I could on such a day, I caught up with a cowboy driving a small herd of big calves and young steers to market. I asked if I might help him.

"You betcher life," he answered. "My horse is about in."

No wonder. It was a small drove, and, as the cowboy said, it's easier to handle a big drove. If there's a mob, cattle will herd like humans. But when they're a few, and of mixed ages, they are like a bunch of shooting stars. "Maybe we can do it together," he said. "I'll drive from behind here and you'll ride along the side of the next cross road, doing the dirty work."

It was dirty work. A calf would bleat and bolt. My pony would spring ahead and cut him off. Then a young steer, smelling water, would bellow and go, with others after him, down the road. I had to race to the front, stop short, and hold them. An open lane on one side was easy; the pony would of himself see and take and hold it, but when there was a cross road, open both sides, we had, us two cowboys, alternately to drive and head. I would shoot up, yelling, along one side, then fall back and drive as he galloped up the other side. By good team work we got by. I was sweating, my pony was in a lather, and the cowboy and his horse were caked with the mud of the damp dust. He was pleased, however, and, to keep me with him, he paid me a compliment (the way grown-ups do).

"You know the cattle game, don't you?" he said.

"No," I answered, "but my pony does, and I'm learning it from him. How long you been on the road?"

"All day," he said. "The ranch is about twenty miles out."

Twenty miles out! Just right. I began fishing for an invitation to visit him, asking him questions. The ranch was not a big one, he said; it was mostly a wheat farm, only part hay and cattle. He was one of five or six hands that worked steady on the place.

"Why don't you ride out and see us sometime?" he invited. "You like to work cattle. We'll let you have all you want of it."

I told him about my gang, and he laughed. "Five or six! All kids? Well, you may all come. Why not? Make a week-end of it." A week-end? What was that? He used lots of funny words, and he spoke them very English. And he suggested a date when there would be work for us to do, cattle work.

I liked the idea, accepted it, and I liked this fellow. I stared at him approvingly till he turned away as if embarrassed, and when he looked back at me, he asked me a diverting question.

"Why no saddle?"

I explained that my father wanted me to learn bareback, and that led to the Comanches. I told him all about them, how they rode, fought, and—I must have become so enthusiastic about those Indians that he suspected me.

"I see," he said, "you are a Comanche Indian chief."

This struck me at first as fresh. I did not like to have anybody walk right into my—my privacy, like that, sit down, and stick his feet up on the table. But my second thought was that maybe he was my kind of a fellow, like the bridge-tender. I decided to see.

"No," I said. "I used to be a Comanche chief's son, but that was long ago; several weeks back. I am—something else now. I'll tell you what I am if you'll tell me first what you are."

"Why," he said, "I am, as you see, a cowboy."

I was disappointed. He did not understand. I said as much. "Of course, I can see you're a cow-puncher, but that's only your job. I don't mean that. What I mean is, what are you really?"

"Really?" he echoed. "What's really? I'm a real cowboy."

"That's funny," I said, "I thought you'd tumble to what I meant, and you didn't."

I was about to give up, and he seemed to sense that. He looked almost ashamed, and I didn't care. If he wasn't my sort, if he didn't belong to our crowd, he didn't matter. We rode along in a silence that could be felt, like the heat, till a steer charged the fence. "Water," I called as my pony charged at the steer, and I was glad that the rest of the herd joined the attack on that fence. It kept us busy for a while. When we could fall back and ride together, the cowboy had decided to talk.

"I'll tell you about myself," he said. "My name, my cattle name, is Duke. That's what the cattlemen call me from Texas to the Pacific, only they pronounce it Dook. And they name me so, not because I am a duke. My father, as it happens, is a lord, but my older brother will inherit his title. I myself, I am nothing, as you see. I'm called by an English title because I am English, but as a matter of fact, I am a plain American cowboy."

I was thrilled. I had read about the English nobility, books on books, and here for the first time I was seeing one.

"Is that what you mean by 'really'?" he inquired.

"Maybe," I answered, and it was his turn to be disappointed. I was sorry now. It was my turn to talk. I told him about me, to explain what I meant.

I had been reading Scott's novels lately, I said, and lots of other English stories about knights and gentlemen and ladies. I knew what a younger son was and had even thought I'd like to be one.

"Really?" he said, only he said it differently from me.

"Yes-s—" I hesitated. But I decided to trust him. "Yes," I confessed. "I wouldn't have minded being the son of a lord, and, as a matter of fact, I was—not exactly that, but I've been something like that for a good while lately."

"But why?" he asked. "You are in the way of being what I wanted to be when I was a boy, and yet here you are—"

"Nothing," I interrupted, and I poured out my woes.

Here I was, a boy, just an ordinary boy. I wasn't a poor boy, like the boys I had read about in stories, the fellows that started with nothing, no father, no mother, no home. They starved in the streets, picking up now and then a crust of bread to eat, and finding here and there a dark hallway to sleep in, but they begin by selling papers and shining shoes; they are smart, industrious, honest, and brave; so they rise slowly but surely and by and by they are a success. They own the paper they sold or—whatever it is they are at.

"That's great," I summed up. "They are heroes of books. I'd like to be the hero of a book."

But, I grieved, I could not be that. My father and mother did not die when I was young. They are both still living, and they had a home for me. I didn't have a chance; I could not go out and suffer, strive, and become a success.

The Duke saw my predicament. He tried to be encouraging. There were other things I might do.

"What?" I demanded. "I can't be one of those rich men's sons or the son of a duke and do what they do." There were stories about them, too. They had boats and rivers they could row on; not like the Sacramento and the American Rivers: not swift floods or all dried up. They had snow and ice and parks. They could go sledding, and skating, and they had places to go riding in, made on purpose for saddle horses, and grooms to follow them. Not like me. I had to ride over to the river bottom or out on the plains, always with other boys, among farmers and—and—

I halted. I had almost said something that might hurt his feelings. He saw my embarrassment, and like a duke, he bridged it gracefully (the nobility is very graceful, you know).

"And cowboys," he suggested.

"Yes," I said, and to make it easy for him, I explained gracefully that I didn't mean him. I was glad I had met him; I was certainly coming out to his ranch with my crowd to help with his cattle. I had to do something to fill up my time.

"But you can see, can't you," I said, "that working cattle on a ranch isn't what a fellow with ambition would choose to do if he had his choice."

A team was coming toward me. "I'll head 'em," I said, and I rode up and turned our cattle off to the right side of the road. After that there were two cross roads in succession; both the Duke and I were busy, and by that time, the city limit was near. There were other things to think of.

What butcher were his calves for? When he told me, I told him that all would be well. Loony Louie was that butcher's ranchman; he would be on the look-out for us, with the bars down, and there was a pond in his corral. The cattle would turn in of themselves for the water. And this happened. We had a couple of miles of very hard work. The herd split, and half of them got away up one of the many lanes. My pony brought them back, and—well, we worked the whole tired, famished drove to the butcher's place. There was Louie standing out in the middle of the road with his gate wide open. The cattle rushed in, and our horses followed— one mad rush for the pond, and there they all waded in up to their bellies and sank their heads in up to their eyes. And Louie, closing the gate and running after us to the pond, stood and danced there; he laughed and yelled like a maniac at the sight of the drinking animals.

I saw Duke looking astonished at him.

"What's the matter with that man?" he asked, as we rode up out of the water and headed for town. I saw my chance to explain what I meant by "really."

"Well," I said, "Loony Louie is called crazy, but he isn't. He is all right, only he loves stock. You saw how he was glad when your thirsty calves wallowed in the water and drank their fill? Well, he loves that; he loves to see 'em drink and feed. He'll cry if he sees them slaughtered; sure. That's why they say he's crazy: because he loves animals and goes crazy when he sees them drink when they're thirsty and eat when they're hungry; and—and when they're killed he goes crazy too."

"Poor devil!" the Duke muttered.

"No," I corrected, "Louis was in prison once for stealing cattle and once he was in the insane asylum for the same thing. But I know him, and I knew what he wanted: knew he didn't want to own cattle but only to take good care of them, so I got him a job here to take care of the butcher's cattle. It would have been better to put him on a ranch where cattle aren't killed, but no rancher would take a loco cattle-lover. Only this old German butcher could understand about Louie. He gave him the job of priming up his cattle, and he keeps him away as much as he can from the slaughter house."

"Really!" the cowboy exclaimed, and I answered, "Yes, really. And there you have said it yourself."

But he didn't see it even yet. We rode along the city streets, quietly; all you could hear was the flap of his chaps and the clink of his spurs.

"Come again, kid," he said at last.

"Why, don't you see?" I said. "That butcher's man, who has the job of feeding up cattle to be killed, he is really—he is playing he's the friend of those calves of yours, and he'll take 'em into the barn, feed them a lot, pet them, talk to them, and he will listen to them, and—and—"

"And?" the cowboy boosted, and I told him straight how Louie could sit up on a fence with you and tell you how a young calf feels when it is separated from its mother and what a wild steer would like to be—really.

"He does to me," I said. "He has told me stories that are—real about what the cattle tell him."

"Really?"

"Yes," I said, and I told him about the bridge-tender, whose job was to tend the American River trestle. A good job, and dangerous, and he did it up brown. But he didn't care for it. "He's really a prospector who strikes it rich and goes home where his people live, and the girl that wouldn't marry him, and—and—"

"And—" the cowboy said, and I saw he was understanding, so I went on.

"And I go out there and sit in his cabin, and him and me, we go back home rich and spend the money; he just blows it and he makes his folks proud of him, and—and—"

"And—"

I had to go back and explain that the bridge-tender's troubles all came from a certain preacher in his home town who, because the bridge-tender got to dancing and raising the dust, denounced him to his face in a sermon in the church. The bridge-tender was with his girl, and it so shamed her that she wouldn't have him 'round any more.

"See?" I said, and he saw that much; so I trusted him with the whole truth, how, when the bridge-tender and I are alone on the trestle and there is no train due, we make his pile, we go back east to his home. We walk into that church—everybody's there, the girl, too, of course—and the bridge-tender, who has been the talk of the town for a week, he walks up the middle aisle of the church, draws his gun, and makes that preacher come down out of his pulpit, kneel down, and apologize to the girl.

"And she marries the bridge-tender?" the Duke asked.

"Sometimes," I answered. "Sometimes we take her, and sometimes she begs to be took, but we scorn her."

We had come to the corner where there was a small drovers' hotel with a stable next door, the Duke's hotel. We stopped; since the Duke did not seem to see it, I pointed it out to him: "Your hotel," I said.

"Yes, yes," he said. "But let's finish this. Your butcher's man is —really—a cattle-lover; your bridge-tender is a rich miner. Any others like that?"

"Yes," I said. "You know Hank Dobran, the gambler, that runs this hotel and bar where you are stopping tonight? Well, he —this is a secret, of course—when Hank has made enough to be independent—he tells me he is going to turn in and clear up the dirty politics of this town and make a fine, grand town that all the other cities all over the world can copy."

"Any more?" he asked after a while, and I looked at him and he wasn't joshing me. He believed. I answered him, therefore:

"Every fellow I get to really know is that way," I told him. "Every one of them is playing he is really something else besides what his job is. And that's what I mean by really," I said, "and—and that's why I asked you what you were, really."

The Duke did not answer. He just sat there on his horse in front of the hotel stable. We were so quiet that the stableman came out and looked at us—and gave us up. But his wonder brought the Duke to. He spoke.

"I was that way, kid," he said. "I was like you. I read books, as a boy; I read and I wanted to go and be what I read. Only I read stories about the far west, Indians, scouts, cowboys. I read about knights, too, and lords and ladies, kings, queens, and princesses. Yes, but I saw that sort. I knew them as—as you know cowboys. So I didn't want to be a prince or the son of a—duke. I played I was a cowboy. I could ride; I had horses, yes, and—but I hated to ride on our silly little saddles on bridle paths in our fancy parks with a groom behind me—and my sister. I wanted to go west and be a cowboy among cowboys—and really ride—really. And—well —as you see—I did. That's what I am now and have been for ten years. It isn't what I imagined it to be. It is no more what it is cracked up to be than a lord is or the son of a lord. But no matter, here I am, Dook the cowboy—really a cow-puncher."

He seemed to be sad about it, and his sadness put up a problem to me, the hardest puzzle of that day.

"Funny!" I said. "You're a cowboy really—and I—I don't know what to be now, but for a long time lately—weeks—when I rode up to you, I was a prince, the son of a lord, the Black Prince in the Middle Ages."

The Duke didn't laugh the way some men would. He thought and thought, and at last he looked as if he was going to say something. He didn't. He changed his mind, I guess. For all he did was to put out his hand, take mine, and shake it hard, once.

"Good-by, Prince," he said. "It is time to go home. It's time for both of us to go home—really."

"Good-by, Duke," I said, and I rode off home puzzling and puzzling.

I GET RELIGION

D URING the morning recess at school the next Monday, I
gathered my crowd (of horse-boys) on the school steps,
and while we watched the other boys playing leap-frog,
I reported the Duke's invitation to visit his ranch some weeks
hence and my plan to start on a Friday afternoon, stay somewhere
out in the country that night, go on early the next day to the
cattle ranch, and work and play with the cowboys till Sunday afternoon or Monday morning. They were delighted, but where were
we to stay Friday night? I told them all about the Neely farm
for me and they asked me to "ring them in on that." Since there
were five or six of them at that time, I hesitated. They pressed me
to try it. They gave many, but different, reasons for thinking Mrs.
Neely would take us all in.

Hjalmar Bergman said she would because his mother would.
Charlie Raleigh, who was the oldest of us, argued that my account
showed that Mrs. Neely liked me so much she would do anything
I asked. Will Cluness held that she would if we paid her, but that
was no use because we never had any money. Another fellow
thought we might offer to work out our board and lodging; another that we might fix it up with Jim Neely to let me sleep in
the house, and say nothing about the others but sneak them into
the barn, trusting to luck to swipe enough food for supper and
breakfast. By the time school "took in" again, I had promised to
ride out to the farm the next Saturday and see what I could do.

I did that, and all I got was another pretty problem. Jim saw
me coming up the lane. He hailed me from the barn, and he was
so friendly that I felt encouraged to consult him at once, before
I dismounted.

"How many boys did you say?" he asked.

"Oh, from five to six or eight—depends on how many can get off."

He grinned. "Wall now," he said, shaking his head, "I think that if I was you, I wouldn't put that up to the old lady."

"Why not?" I appealed. "They are all all-right fellows."

"Sure thing," he said. "The boys are all right, but what's the color of their horses?"

I told him: white, gray, black, etc., and two bays besides mine. He asked for the markings on the other bays. None, I said, all red.

"Um-hum," he reflected. He looked critically at my pony, and he answered in a very peculiar way. "No. It won't do. Mrs. Neely is very particular. She is one of those rare women that likes a boy that rides a bay pony with a white star on his forehead and one white forefoot. She would be furious if you brought her any others."

Now, what could you make of that? I leave it to anybody that that was a puzzle. I sat there on my pony puzzling and puzzling, till Jim called me down, took my pony, and sent me into the house to see Mrs. Neely.

NEELY, W. F.; Post Office, Florin; lives one mile west of that place, and seven miles from Sacramento; was born in Mississippi, in 1821, and lived there until 1852, engaged in merchandising; he came to California in that year and settled in this county; followed teaming until 1868; since then he has been farming; owns eighty acres, worth, with improvements, about $4,000. He was married, in 1867, to Miss Martha Whitten, a native of Maine. A view of Mr. Neely's place may be seen on another page.

MR. NEELY'S "WHO'S WHO"

"So," she greeted me, "here you are again. Out for another square meal? All right. This time you have brought me all the news from town, no doubt; the answers to all my questions. Of course. You go and find Mr. Neely; he's ditching in the vineyard; and don't come back till I blow the horn. Then we'll hear the news you have collected for me."

I had no news. I had forgotten her old questions. I never thought of anybody but myself, my mother would say; I could hear her saying it. Maybe it was true. I was ashamed of myself. But Mr. Neely received me gladly, a little too polite; he shook hands with me and said, "How do you do?" which is a strange question to put to a fellow who doesn't know or care how he is. I said I was all right, and I asked him how he was. "Pretty well,"

he said, of course; you could see he was well. I told him about
Mrs. Neely's questions, how I had forgotten them and didn't
know what I would do when she asked them at dinner. He only
laughed a little and looked away.

"Never mind," he said. "Her questions are for me, not you.
She misses theaters, music, church, and her relatives, out here on
a farm in the west. Thinks we should have stayed east and lived
in a city. And maybe we should; maybe I shouldn't have listened
to the tales about California and the golden west. Maybe—"

He was quite sad, like Dook was and the bridge-tender sometimes, and I was sorry, but I couldn't see how it had anything to
do with me, the Neelys' coming west. I asked Mr. Neely what I
could do, but he only handed me a hoe and showed me how to
clear the ditches, opening one side stream and closing another.
And it was fine to do. I worked all morning and learned all about
irrigating, something about hog and hay raising, a farmer's sea-
sons, markets, and so on. It was very interesting. I had half a mind
to be a farmer myself. And why not? If being a prince isn't what
it's cracked up to be, why not be a farmer and be done with the
terrible problem of choosing a career?

But Mrs. Neely did not want me to be a farmer. She thought
it better for me to become a preacher. It was sudden, but I considered it. When she called us on the horn, I ran across fields to
water my pony; but I met Jim, who said he had done that; so I
came back to the house with him. I noticed how he walked, a
sort of plodding gait as if over a plowed field, and I could copy
it pretty well. He noticed it.

"You're walking like a regular farmer," he said.

Pleased, I told him I meant to be a farmer, and noted each
thing he and Mr. Neely did to prepare for dinner. I washed up as
they did, chucked my hat on the bench with theirs, and wiped my
feet as carefully on the mat. And at table—crowded with good
things—I ate in silence, hungrily. Mrs. Neely sat on the edge of
her chair, watching us, helping, rising to fetch us whatever was
wanted, without a word. She ate little, but she did not ask me
the questions I feared. No. We were at peace till Jim gave me
away.

"He's going to be a farmer, that boy," he said as he sat back,
sated.

"He is not," Mrs. Neely answered, just like that. I was startled. Mr. Neely smiled, Jim winked at me, but Mrs. Neely sounded so sure that I was convinced. The men left me with her. She had to clear away, and that, her duty, she did silently, quickly, and most thoroughly. She not only washed the dishes pans, knives and forks, as the Chinese servant did at home; she polished them. She set the whole dining-room-kitchen to rights, thoroughly; then she set herself to rights, took off her apron, and turned to me.

"What time do you start for town?" she asked. I told her about four. "Very well," she said, "let's go out in the garden and talk." We went into the garden and she worked, irrigating and picking flowers and—talking. I can see her now, a slight figure with small, tender, strong hands, kind brown eyes, and firm, straight little mouth, tending her flowers and saying, "I'm their pastor, and they need me as much as they need the sun. It is good to be needed." I can't remember all that she said, but pictures came up in her words, as flowers shine in shrubbery, and I got somehow the story of a little girl who dreamed of being needed in the garden of the world. She met as she grew older and she loved a tall, handsome man who was good, "the best man in the world": generous, kind, faithful. And this prince of simple men, he needed her; he said so, but, clearer still, she saw his need. She took him, gladly, and he took her—he took her far, far away. And it was a beautiful place where they went, a garden indeed, and he was good always. "That girl lived twenty years with that man and she never discovered in him a single fault. There is no other man like that." He was her ideal and "the novels are all wrong; they did not live happy ever after, those two. They lived only at peace for ever. That is what lovers have for ever, true lovers; not happiness, but peace." There could not be happiness for her because the garden was too big; it was a state, and no woman and no one man could tend it. Only many men and many women could irrigate and prune and bring up the flowers in so big a garden. And her man did his part of that. For he was a farmer. But it was not enough for her, because her dream was to be the princess of a prince who tended not land and cattle, but mankind; not wheat and grapes, but souls, the spirits of men and women and children. She could have served with her man in a garden of souls, and he, with his beautifulness, would have been a prince of peace to his fellow men as he had been to her alone and she would have been a gardener to the children of men instead of only to her flowers and her wonderful, wonderful man.

It was a sad, a very sad, happy story, and it had a moral. "Happiness comes from your work," she pointed. "Not from love and not from goodness, but from finding out what you like to do and doing it. And so—don't be a farmer," she snapped with her scissors. "Be a minister."

And because the story was so sad and so happy, I thought I might become a minister. But she wasn't through. She questioned me about what I wanted to be. I gave her the list: Indian chief, cowboy, knight, statesman, locomotive engineer, prince—I didn't tell her all my ideals. I suppressed the jockey stage, and the teamster, the steamboat, and a large number of other ambitions; she did not notice any omissions. She seized upon the prince. That was the thing to be, only not a royal but a spiritual prince. And she got out of me, too, some of my other problems: how the world was made, where children came from, where China was on a spherical globe. She discovered also that these problems troubled me deeply and were driving me to thought and study and worry. And she had the answers to all of them.

"If you will believe," she said—"if you put your faith in God and leave it all to Him, your troubles will be over and you will be at rest. Try it."

And I tried it. She told me the biblical story of the Creation more really than I had ever heard it, and so beautifully. I knew it very well. I had had church and Sunday school regularly, and I did believe in God and Christ. Of course. I had begun of late to have some emotional sense of religion. Religion, however, had been a duty, not a reality; church was, like school, like other requirements, a mere matter of the dull routine of life. My imagination, my emotions, had all gone into my own adventures, experiments, and play. She turned them into religion and made it a part, almost the whole, of my life—for a while. I had from that day's talk with Mrs. Neely a sense of comfort and clearness which she said I might, as a preacher, convey to all mankind.

When I went out to the barn for my pony, Jim, who came to help me, looked at me curiously.

"Going to be a preacher, eh?" he said. "How old are you?" I

told him. "Oh, well, that'll be all right." And he boosted me up on my pony and watched me ride off, as Mrs. Neely did, waving from the garden.

It was an ecstatic time for me. I rode out to the Neely farm whenever there was time. I had begun "going with girls" and to parties. My mother, noticing it, had me and my sisters take dancing lessons, and we had parties in our house. I fell in love. I really loved several girls, besides Miss Belle Kay, whom I called on often. I adored her, and I think now she understood me pretty well. She took me seriously, let me worship her, and played up her part perfectly. She let me tell her about my other girls, whom I merely loved at first; no adoration about that; she helped me to pick one out of the several and encouraged me to intensify my concentrated sentiment. This romantic period was coming to a head when Mrs. Neely discovered and turned it into religion. I still went to dances; I still called on my girl. I still enjoyed all the girls and the parties and the ice cream and cakes. I was happy in all this, but so was I happy at my beaver traps, hunting, swimming, and riding with my friends, men and boys. But happiest of all were the miserable hours I spent weeping over my soul in my bed, praying for it in corners, and going to church where the music was wet even if the sermons were dry. My father eyed me keenly as I developed my sudden interest in church-going; he had just seen me fasting as a jockey, but my mother accepted this, as she did all my conversions, without skepticism, with heartfelt sympathy. She assured me that Mrs. Neely was right, that my prayers would be answered. And the test came soon.

The time was coming for the week-end out on the Duke's ranch. All the boys were ready for it. When I reported that Jim said that Mrs. Neely would take in only boys on red ponies with certain white marks, they went out themselves on their off-colored horses and made other arrangements. Meanwhile I spent all my spare time on the Neely farm, talking religion with Mrs. Neely, farming with Mr. Neely, and life in general with Jim Neely. My father suggested that I change my address, live there, and visit my own family now and then; it would save the pony many a trip, and I said I would take up the subject with the Neelys and let him know. He got a look from my mother which made him snap his paper with his finger and turn to the news of the day.

Each of my parents thought the other did not understand me, and I agreed with both of them. And I preferred it so, because my sisters, who did understand me, abused the power of their intelligence.

"Let's see," said one of them, "you are going out to the Neely farm to work cattle on Saturday and then to the ranch for a Sunday of prayer. Is that the plan?"

We took our horses to school at noon on the Friday of our departure, our horses, guns, and all the dogs of our several neighborhoods. Leaving the animals hitched in the shade of the trees outside the grounds, we went to our classes for the hour and a half which, curiously, was longer than the whole two hours of other days. It was hot; the schoolroom was a bake-oven. The only cool thing in sight was the snow on the Sierras far, far away; the only interesting sight was the face of the clock. The teacher was cross, but hot too and prompt. She also watched the clock; I saw her look at it, and she saw me unlacing my shoes and unbuttoning buttons; she knew why I was undressing, and at 2:29, with a nod at me, she banged the bell and I was the first out of the room, the first into the street, where the dogs greeted me with yelps. The other fellows were close after me, but I was mounted when they arrived and with my dogs (mostly Jake Stortz's greyhounds) was galloping down the street toward the American River. The race was on.

Since Sacramento City is laid out in squares, you could ride out any street you chose and turn wherever you liked. I had my street alone for a while; we always took different streets for the start. But there were only a few places where you could cross the railroad track, and we met in groups at those places, and headed for one spot on the river where we all came together. This day we all crossed the track at the same place, and I was still first; my teacher had seen to that; but through the brush and over the sandy bottom of the river we were in a bunch, a bunch of undressed or undressing boys who dropped their clothes in heaps on the sand and rode naked into the river. As the horses plunged, hot, into the icy water, you had to dive off their backs and swim or wade back to beat them ashore, else they would get away; and so when you were out and had them standing in line, the race was over. I was first.

Tying our horses to the brush, we swam; that is to say, we dived in, swam a few strokes, and came out to roll in the sand—repeating this till we were "used to" the cold water. Then we usually swam across the stream and swiped peanuts and melons from the Chinese farmers, but this day they (the Saracens) were expecting us. There were several of them; we saw them hiding, in wait for us. And besides we had something more interesting than a war with the Saracens ahead of us. We dressed early, after only two hours of swimming, rode back to town, and took to the Stockton road. It was hot, the horses were sweating, the dogs panting, and we were uncomfortable from the sand in our clothes. But we raised a hare a few miles out, and as the dogs charged, we followed over the fence and had a hunt, short but fast. One of Jake Stortz's dogs picked up the hare; he was mine, therefore, and I hung him like a scalp from my belt.

As we approached Florin we separated one by one, each with his dogs for the place he was to stay the night. I rode up the Neely lane, my three dogs after me, and Jim and Mrs. Neely came out to greet me.

"What's this?" she demanded. "Dogs, too? You never said there would be dogs. What can we do with—"

Jim came to the rescue. "I'll find a place for them," he said. I leashed them for him, and he went off with the dogs and the pony. Mrs. Neely was grumbling about the dogs, but she gripped me by the shoulder, and when Jim was gone, she exclaimed at my appearance. A fellow never is neat after a swim, but she scolded me, ran her fingers through my hair, down my neck. "Sand," she discovered. "Sand everywhere. You come with me."

She pulled me over to the big irrigating tub in the garden, yanked off my clothes, and stuck me in the cold water. "You stay there," she commanded, and she shook out my clothes. Hanging them up on the branch of a tree, she darted into the house, and, coming back with soap and a brush, she washed, she scrubbed me, complaining all the time about boys and ponies, and dogs; savages, inconveniences, dirt, and dogs; selfishness, thoughtlessness, inconveniences, and dogs. "Dogs, too!" she would exclaim. But she got me washed, helped me dress in rolled-up clothes of her husband's, and it seemed to me as if she liked us all, boys, ponies, inconveniences, and dogs. She was putting on her indignation, I felt; I wasn't sure, because she was very rough. She would jerk me around; she wouldn't let me dress myself; she wanted to put on every garment, shirt, pants, shoes and stockings. And when I was fully dressed, she brushed my hair and took me by the hand to her kitchen, where I had to sit by the fire while she finished her preparations for supper, which I evidently had belated. Anyhow, Mr. Neely came in uncalled, and when she began to tell him indignantly about me and how I came to them full of sand and dirt and dogs, he smiled and interrupted.

"Yes, yes, but you. How are you?"

"Oh, I'll be all right," she answered impatiently. But he touched her cheeks, and I noticed that they were red. "That's the stove," she said, but he wagged his head and looked anxious.

We ate the hot supper with hot breads, in silence as usual, we three men, and Mrs. Neely hung over me and gave me selected morsels to eat. She ate not a mouthful, as Mr. Neely remarked at the end. "No, I can't," she said, and she rose, and went about clearing the table and the kitchen while we sat silent. There was something the matter, but I began to feel sleepy; I tried to keep awake, but my head nearly sprained my neck, and at last, I remember, Mrs. Neely, having finished her work, spoke up.

"Now, then, you dirty boy, you are tired," she said. "You'll be falling asleep in your chair. Come with me." Mr. Neely offered to take me to my room, but "No," she commanded sharply, "I'm going to put him to bed."

She put her arm around my neck and drew me into the parlor where she had all ready, on the sofa, a piled-up white bed. It looked good, all clean and cool, and I could have tumbled right into it myself, had she let me. But, no, she must undress me, put on me one of Mr. Neely's great nightgowns, and we kneeled together by the bed and prayed. I had no special request to make; so I said a regular prayer, the Lord's, and I hardly could say that, so heavy was I. But Mrs. Neely prayed something about being "spared sickness, which is idleness." Then she rolled me into the bed, drew the sheet close about me, and as I fell asleep, she seemed to be crying quietly. Still on her knees, with her arms out over me, I felt her sobbing.

There was something the matter.

X

I BECOME A HERO, SAVE A LIFE

ONE of the wrongs suffered by boys is that of being loved before loving. They receive so early and so freely the affection and devotion of their mothers, sisters, and teachers that they do not learn to love; and so, when they grow up and become lovers and husbands, they avenge themselves upon their wives and sweethearts. Never having had to love, they cannot; they don't know how. I, for example, was born in an atmosphere of love; my parents loved me. Of course. But they had been loving me so long when I awoke to consciousness that my baby love had no chance. It began, but it never caught up. Then came my sisters, one by one. They too were loved from birth, and they might have stayed behind as I did, but girls are different; my sisters seem to have been born loving as well as loved. Anyhow my first sister, though younger than I, loved me long before I can remember even noticing her, and I cannot forget the shock of astonishment and humiliation at my discovery of her feeling for me. She had gone to Stockton to visit Colonel Carter's family, and in a week was so homesick for me that my father and mother took me with them to fetch her. That was their purpose. Mine was to see the great leader of my father's wagon train across the plains and talk live stock with him. You can imagine how I felt when, as we walked up to the house, the front door opened and my little sister rushed out ahead, threw her arms around me, and cried— actually cried—with tears running down her cheeks, "My Len, my Len!"

I had to suffer it, but what would Colonel Carter think, and his sons? And as it was with my family, so it was with Mrs. Neely. I came to love her, as I did my mother and sisters, but only with great difficulty, because she loved me first, loved me when I was loving not her, but her delicious cooking, and worst of all she loved me as a regular fellow such as I was—a horseman, trapper, scout, knight—cannot afford to be loved. Hence my feelings that night, when, some time after Mrs. Neely prayed me to sleep, Mr. Neely called me. There was something the matter, and I was not sorry, I was almost glad.

"Mrs. Neely is sick," he said. "She has a high fever, and I have to ask you to get up quick and ride into town for the doctor. Will you?"

Would I? "Paul Revere," I thought, and I was up and dressing. No pony express rider ever dressed faster than I did. Nor more gladly. Mr. Neely was telling me what doctor to get, where to find him, what to say, and I heard his directions. Sure. But I was eager to be off on my long, hard night ride—seven miles to go, six, five, four, and so on till, panting and exhausted, the pony and I would knock up that doctor and—

Jim Neely came in. "Your horse is at the gate, ready," he said. Great! Jim said it right, and I answered, "So am I." Mr. Neely turned away. "I must go back to Mrs. Neely," he said, and his face looked anxious, frightened. It was evidently a real emergency. I dashed out, Jim following me to the garden gate, and I seized and jumped up on my horse.

"One moment," Jim called and took the pony by the bit and spoke; he spoke very slowly. "You know, don't you, how to ride fast and far?"

Of course I did, and I wanted to start, but no, Jim wasted precious time talking.

"You start off easy, a gentle lope to, say, the main road. Then you walk the pony a hundred yards or so, then you lope again to about Dudens' place. By that time the pony will be warmed, but a bit winded. Walk again till he's easy, then go it; gallop a mile or so. Walk him again, fast, but walk; then you can run him a bit; not far. Trot half a mile—"

It was awful. Jim was right. That was the way it was done; I knew that; but it was hard; it was not the way the Paul Revere poem did it, nor any of the other poems; all the books let a fellow run the whole way, and that was the fun of it, to run till your horse dropped. But the cavalry, the scouts, Indians, and cowboys, all hurried as Jim said, except when they were drunk. And Jim said I was not to get drunk even on excitement. I had to keep my wits about me and think of everything.

"About your dogs, for example," he said, "and the other boys. What am I to do about them?"

I was glad it was dark, so that Jim could not see that I was ashamed to have forgotten everything. He asked me if it would be right for him to drive down to Florin with the dogs to meet there the gang and tell them to go on alone to the ranch.

"Yes, that'll be all right," I said. "Let go."

But Jim didn't let go. He suggested that I go home after seeing the doctor, have my breakfast there, and come out to the farm again tomorrow, Sunday. Yes, yes, I agreed, only—

"How far can your pony run at full speed?" he asked, and I told him; a quarter of a mile. "Well then, remember that," he said. "He can run only a quarter of a mile, and you have seven miles to go."

By this time I was so dashed, so unheroic, that Jim may have seen my depression. He gave me a boost back up to the poetic. "Now go," he said; "you are going to find out that the hero business is hard work, requiring judgment and self-control, not merely whip and spurs. And," he added, "your friend Mrs. Neely needs you tonight, you and a doctor. Good luck to you."

So I got away, but of course Jim stood and watched me. I had to lope slowly down the lane to the cross road and so on to the main road. It was a faster lope than Jim meant, but I walked the pony halfway to Dudens', and—well, I followed instructions pretty nearly. It was a strain. The hero business was, like everything else apparently, not what it was cracked up to be. I had time to think that; I had time to think of a lot of things out there alone in the dark—pretty dark—on that road all alone. There were some farmers driving to market, but I passed them fast, and so really was out there alone most of the time. And I could not imagine much. Jim had spoiled the game, and my thoughts finished it. For the chief of my thoughts was that Mrs. Neely was really ill, needed me, and—and—this is what hurt: I had been glad she was sick so that I could make an unselfish dash to town for the doctor. What was the matter with me? Did I think only of myself, as my mother said? Was I incapable of love and devotion?

By the time I reached the city limits the light of dawn was breaking, outside and in. It showed up over the Sierras, and it showed up all over my conscience. The light brightened the mountains and the road; it was quietly beautiful outside, but inside it darkened my soul and agitated my ugliness. I was like the rest of the world; I was not what I seemed. I was a sham. And I didn't want to be a sham. No, I didn't.

Religion came to my rescue. As I thought of Mrs. Neely sick and praying, so good to me and expecting so much goodness from me, I remembered that I was to be a preacher, a shepherd of men. Well, here I was, a shepherd. With a wave of emotion, I cut out being a Paul Revere and became a minister, a country preacher, like my grandfather, riding on his horse to get a doctor to come and save a lost lamb or sheep, Mrs. Neely. That seemed to give a meaning to my night ride, an heroic meaning, and I galloped on into the city happy again, happy and sad, a combination which occurred often in my young life. The clatter of my horse's hoofs rattling along the sleeping streets, echoing from the dark, dead houses, gave me the thrill I liked. I met and flew past a milkman, wondering what he would wonder about me and my speed, but I didn't care, really. I bent over my pony's neck, held the reins low down like a jockey, and twisting and turning into the right street, darted at full speed up to the doctor's house. Throwing the reins over his hitching-post, I ran up the stairs, rang the bell, knocked at the door, again and again, till at last a sleepy Chinese servant came to the door.

"Wasser maller you?" he demanded.

"Doctor, quick," I said.

He turned, grumbling, and disappeared. He was gone a long time, and when he came slipping back, he bade me calmly "Come in." He led me upstairs and on into the doctor's bedroom, where the doctor lay deep in bed. When I sank my message down to him, he groaned, was still a moment; then up he came and out, and he dressed.

"Mrs. Neely," he said as he pulled on his boots. "Great, good woman that, a lady, the American gentlewoman. We must save her." And, quickly dressed, he came with me down the stairs. At sight of my horse he paused.

"Oh," he exclaimed. "No buggy. You came a-horseback. Must

have been a dark and lonely ride"—and looking at me—"for a boy." He asked and I told him who I was. "Good boy," he said, "brave boy. And you want to save Mrs. Neely. Well, we'll save her together. You've done your part. I'll go and get my rig, and I'll do mine. What'll you do now?"

"I'll pray for her," I said. "She wants me to."

"Oh, you'll pray, eh? I meant to ask if you'd drive out with me or go home?"

"Jim said I was to go home," I answered.

"Um-hm," the doctor said. "Good. You go home and pray for Mrs. Neely, and I'll drive out and do the rest. And maybe the best I can do will be to tell her you are praying for her."

As he went out to his stable, I remounted and rode home. It was full dawn when I reached the stable. I rubbed down and fed my pony, and that done, I knelt in the stall and prayed for Mrs. Neely. It was an exquisite pleasure, that prayer; so I prolonged it until I was lifted into a state of bliss. Thus moved, I went into the house, up to my room, and tried to sleep, in vain. I prayed some more. I had discovered something, the joy of prayer; and the light of it must have been on my face when I appeared at breakfast. Everybody looked up, and everybody but my father said something.

"Why—?" one sister began, and another, "How—?" "But what ails you?" my mother exclaimed. "Nothing," I answered, but after a while I broke down and told it all, Mrs. Neely's illness, my night ride, the doctor, and—and the prayers. There was universal admiration and sympathy, excepting, as I noticed, on the part of my father. He looked sharply at me for a moment, and he might have spoken if my mother had not caught his glance and warned him: "Now, Joseph." He obeyed. He snapped his morning paper and read it.

The next few days were wonderful. I was exalted. I was melancholy; I worried about Mrs. Neely's condition, which was serious. The doctor shook his head and told me so when he came back from his first visit. He had sent out a nurse with some medicines that afternoon and was going himself that (Saturday) night. I moped around Sunday morning, went mournfully to church, where I joined in the prayers with my whole heart and some tears.

"He's enjoying it," I heard my father blurt to my mother as

we were coming out of the church, and she was shocked, indignant, and shut him up. So was I hurt, and yet I gradually realized that it was true. What did that mean? I was unhappy, I was miserable, and yet—and yet I was happy. I prayed for Mrs. Neely's recovery, I wanted her to get well, and yet—and yet, I saw and I faced the fact that I would not for the world have had her not sick.

That afternoon I was to ride out to the farm. I called, first, on the doctor, who was really worried. "Very, very ill," he said, "but we must save her. We will. You are praying?" he asked. I was. "Good," he said, "I told her you were." And he gave me some medicines to take out, and I rode the long seven miles with the lifting sense that I was really of use to some one at last.

Jim was dressed in his Sunday town clothes and looked scared. Mr. Neely I did not see, nor the patient, of course. The nurse was in the kitchen and she didn't see me. She would not even look at me. I stayed with Jim, who fed and rubbed my horse. As we sat on the top board of the corral fence, he talked beautifully about Mrs. Neely.

"I thought she didn't like you," I commented.

"Huh," he said. "She always pretends to be down on a fellow. It took Will years to believe that she liked him, even him. And you. Remember how she pretended to resent your nerve in coming here just for meals? I tell you that woman is so full-up with love that she has to make out she is down on us, and she is so good and kind that she has to act bad and hard and cold. That woman is one of these here hypocrites, upside down—just the opposite from us."

He was watching the road, and by and by he got down off the fence. "Here they come," he said. I looked and saw Hjalmar Bergman on Black Bess, waving from the end of the lane. Jim explained that he had arranged to have the other boys stop there for me on their way home from the ranch.

He had my pony ready, and as he boosted me up on his back, Jim said: "There is one thing more. The nurse says the crisis will come for Mrs. Neely tonight. The doctor will be here for it, no doubt. I think it would be fine if you would do tonight what she asked you to do—pray."

"I've been praying all the time," I answered.

"I know," Jim said, "but a prayer tonight might be answered, and that would please Mrs. Neely if she gets well."

I promised. And then I almost forgot it. When I joined Hjalmar and he and I rode down to the main road to meet the other fellows, we got to talking about their time at the ranch. It must have been great. They had good hunting on the way out, landed there with fourteen hares and a lot of birds. They were well received; the cowboys messed around with them all afternoon, when they were cutting out some young steers for the market. Saturday night there was a great dinner, drinking and gambling by the gang, and on Sunday—games, racing, roping, shooting—everything. I had missed it!

But the news that hurt me most was that Dook was gone. I would never see him again, and "it was my fault." He had told the other hands about us boys; he had arranged for our reception and entertainment; and then, about a week before we were to come out to the ranch, he up and left. He had a chance to get a boat that was sailing from San Francisco to England, a boat that he knew the captain of; but when the other fellows asked him why he was going home so suddenly, he answered: "It was something that kid said."

"What did the kid say?" they asked him.

"Oh," he answered, "the kid said that there was romance everywhere, even at home."

I was dazed; so was Hjalmar; so were the other boys. "Did you say that?" Hjalmar asked.

I had not. I didn't even know what it meant. "What is romance?" I asked, and the boys didn't know either. We all puzzled awhile, then dropped the problem to pick up a buck hare that rose in the road; he bounded with the dogs and horses after him and twice jumped the fence before the dogs got him.

When we reached town it was dark, and I was late to supper. I was thinking. What did the Duke mean? What is that which is everywhere, even at home? That romance business? And why did the Duke sail for home? Why not a steamship? Why didn't he stop and see me on his way? Was he angry with me? But, chiefly, what is romance? I forgot all about Mrs. Neely and my promise to pray. I fell asleep thinking about the Duke and romance. On Monday I had school, and it was interesting that day; we had the ranch to talk over and over. We were invited to come again. But that afternoon I remembered with a pang that Mrs.

Neely needed me. I called on the doctor; he was not in his office, and he was not expected home till late; had a bad case out in the country that was coming to a crisis that night.

"So," I thought, "the crisis was not last night; it's tonight." I still could pray. And thinking about that, and thinking how thoughtless I had been, I worked myself up into a crisis of my own; I prayed, riding my pony; I prayed in his stall. I was in such a state of repentance and faith at supper that my mother was worried. She tried to have me tell her what the matter was. I wouldn't. I went off alone to my room and there, kneeling down, I prayed and wept for a long, long time, till I saw my mother peeping in at the door.

Indignant, I rose and was about to say something when she put her arms around me and disclosed her belief in me, in prayer, and especially in my prayers. She was so truly, so emotionally sympathetic that I told her what I was praying for: Mrs. Neely and her crisis that night. "Perhaps it is at this very hour," she suggested, and somehow that got me by the throat. I dropped back on my knees, and I prayed aloud, my mother beside me.

The next day I called on the doctor. He was hurriedly leaving his office on a case, another case. "Mrs. Neely?" he called back at me. "Oh, Mrs. Neely, yes, the good woman is all right. She had a sharp crisis; I was there, and I almost gave her up, but about nine o'clock she suddenly came through and fell asleep. And now, last night and this morning, she was on the way to complete recovery."

Nine o'clock! That was the hour. I told my mother, and she and I rejoiced. Nine o'clock was my bedtime; it was the very moment when I had prayed. We were pals, my mother and I, all the afternoon; we talked about my future, the church, and the good I would do in the world. It was great. And I thought my father was going to join in with us. He knew about my prayers; my mother had told him, no doubt, and when he came home that evening he said he had seen Mrs. Neely's doctor and that she was on the road to recovery.

"We know," my mother said. "And the crisis was passed at nine o'clock, just when Lennie was praying."

"Y-e-e-s," my father agreed, "the hour was the same, but the doctor said it was Sunday—"

"Oh, Joseph," my mother cut in, and he stopped. Nothing more was said by any of us—neither then nor afterward—about that, but the tradition grew both at home and on the farm that I had saved Mrs. Neely by my prayers. And it was a pretty tradition, a pleasant belief, which even my father respected. For I remember how once, when I was thinking about the Duke's last words, I asked my father at table what the cowboy meant by saying romance was everywhere, even at home, and my father said, "Well, but it is, isn't it?"

And somehow I knew that he meant that that was true of me and religion, or—something like that. And he was a religious man, too.

I GET A COLT TO BREAK IN

COLONEL CARTER gave me a colt. I had my pony, and my father meanwhile had bought a pair of black carriage horses and a cow, all of which I had to attend to when we had no "man." And servants were hard to get and keep in those days; the women married, and the men soon quit service to seize opportunities always opening. My hands were pretty full, and so was the stable. But Colonel Carter seemed to think that he had promised me a horse. He had not; I would have known it if he had. No matter. He thought he had, and maybe he did promise himself to give me one. That was enough. The kind of man that led immigrant trains across the continent and delivered them safe, sound, and together where he promised would keep his word. One day he drove over from Stockton, leading a two-year-old which he brought to our front door and turned over to me as mine. Such a horse!

She was a cream-colored mare with a black forelock, mane, and tail and a black stripe along the middle of her back. Tall, slender, high-spirited, I thought then—I think now that she was the most beautiful of horses. Colonel Carter had bred and reared her with me and my uses in mind. She was a careful cross of a mustang mare and a thoroughbred stallion, with the stamina of the wild horse and the speed and grace of the racer. And she had a sense of fun. As Colonel Carter got down out of his buggy and went up to her, she snorted, reared, flung her head high in the air, and, coming down beside him, tucked her nose affectionately under his arm.

"I have handled her a lot," he said. "She is kind as a kitten, but she is as sensitive as a lady. You can spoil her by one mistake. If you ever lose your temper, if you ever abuse her, she will be ruined for ever. And she is unbroken. I might have had her broken to ride for you, but I didn't want to. I want you to do it. I have taught her to lead, as you see; had to, to get her over here. But here she is, an unbroken colt; yours. You take and you break her. You're only a boy, but if you break this colt right, you'll be a man—a young man, but a man. And I'll tell you how."

Now, out west, as everybody knows, they break in a horse by riding out to him in his wild state, lassooing, throwing, and saddling him; then they let him up, frightened and shocked, with a yelling broncho-buster astride of him. The wild beast bucks, the cowboy drives his spurs into him, and off they go, jumping, kicking, rearing, falling, till by the weight of the man, the lash, and the rowels, the horse is broken—in body and spirit. This was not the way I was to break my colt.

"You must break her to ride without her ever knowing it," Colonel Carter said. "You feed and you clean her—you; not the stable man. You lead her out to water and to walk. You put her on a long rope and let her play, calling her to you and gently pulling on the rope. Then you turn her loose in the grass lot there and, when she has romped till tired, call her. If she won't come, leave her. When she wants water or food, she will run to your call, and you will pet and feed and care for her." He went on for half an hour, advising me in great detail how to proceed. I wanted to begin right away. He laughed. He let me lead her around to the stable, water her, and put her in the stable and feed her.

There I saw my pony. My father, sisters, and Colonel Carter saw me stop and look at my pony.

"What'll you do with him?" one of my sisters asked. I was bewildered for a moment. What should I do with the little red horse? I decided at once.

"You can have him," I said to my sisters.

"No," said Colonel Carter, "not yet. You can give your sisters the pony by and by, but you'll need him till you have taught the colt to carry you and a saddle—months; and you must not hurry. You must learn patience, and you will if you give the colt time to learn it, too. Patience and control. You can't control a young horse unless you can control yourself. Can you shoot?" he asked suddenly.

I couldn't. I had a gun and I had used it some, but it was a rifle, and I could not bring down with it such game as there was around Sacramento—birds and hares. Colonel Carter looked at my father, and I caught the look. So did my father. I soon had a shotgun. But at the time Colonel Carter turned to me and said:

"Can't shoot straight, eh? Do you know what that means? That means that you can't control a gun, and that means that you can't control yourself, your eye, your hands, your nerves. You are wriggling now. I tell you that a good shot is always a good man. He may be a 'bad man' too, but he is quiet, strong, steady in speech, gait, and mind. No matter, though. If you break in this colt right, if you teach her her paces, she will teach you to shoot and be quiet."

He went off downtown with my father, and I started away with my colt. I fed, I led, I cleaned her, gently, as if she were made of glass; she was playful and willing, a delight. When Colonel Carter came home with my father for supper, he questioned me.

"You should not have worked her today," he said. "She has come all the way from Stockton and must be tired. Yes, yes, she would not show fatigue; too fine for that, and too young to be wise. You have got to think for her, consider her as you would your sisters."

Sisters! I thought; I had never considered my sisters. I did not say that, but Colonel Carter laughed and nodded to my sisters. It was just as if he had read my thought. But he went on to draw on my imagination a centaur; the colt as a horse's body—me, a boy, as the head and brains of one united creature. I liked that. I would be that. I and the colt: a centaur.

After Colonel Carter was gone home I went to work on my new horse. The old one, the pony, I used only for business: to go to fires, to see my friends, run errands, and go hunting with my new shotgun. But the game that had all my attention was the breaking in of the colt, the beautiful cream-colored mare, who soon knew me—and my pockets. I carried sugar to reward her when she did right, and she discovered where I carried it; so did the pony, and when I was busy they would push their noses into my pockets, both of which were torn down a good deal of the time. But the colt learned. I taught her to run around a circle, turn and go the other way at a signal. My sisters helped me. I held the long rope and the whip (for signaling), while one of the girls led the colt; it was hard work for them, but they took it in turns. One would lead the colt round and round till I snapped the whip; then she would turn, turning the colt, till the colt did it all by herself. And she was very quick. She shook hands with each of her four feet. She let us run under her, back and forth. She was slow only to carry me. Following Colonel Carter's instructions, I began by laying my arm or a surcingle over her back. If she trembled, I drew it slowly off. When she could abide it, I tried buckling it, tighter and tighter. I laid over her, too, a blanket, folded at first, then open, and, at last, I slipped up on her myself, sat there a second, and as she trembled, slid off. My sisters held her for me, and when I could get up and sit there a moment or two, I tied her at a block, and we, my sisters and I, made a procession of mounting and dismounting. She soon got used to this and would let us slide off over her rump, but it was a long, long time before she would carry me.

That we practiced by leading her along a high curb where I could get on as she walked, ride a few steps, and then, as she felt me and crouched, slip off. She never did learn to carry a girl on her back; my sisters had to lead her while I rode. This was not purposeful. I don't know just how it happened, but I do remember the first time I rode on my colt all the way around the lot and how, when I put one of the girls up, she refused to repeat. She shuddered, shook and frightened them off.

While we were breaking in the colt a circus came to town. The ring was across the street from our house. Wonderful! I lived in that circus for a week. I saw the show but once, but I marked the horse-trainers, and in the mornings when they were not too busy I told them about my colt, showed her to them, and asked them how to train her to do circus tricks. With their hints I taught the colt to stand up on her hind legs, kneel, lie down, and balance on a small box. This last was easier than it looked. I put her first on a low big box and taught her to turn on it; then got a little smaller box upon which she repeated what she did on the big one. By and by we had her so that she would step up on a high box so small that her four feet were almost touching, and there also she would turn.

The circus man gave me one hint that was worth all the other tricks put together. "You catch her doing something of herself that looks good," he said, "and then you keep her at it." It was thus that I taught her to bow to people. The first day I rode her out on to the streets was a proud one for me and for the colt, too, apparently. She did not walk, she danced; perhaps she was excited, nervous; anyhow I liked the way she threw up her head, champed at the bit, and went dancing, prancing down the street. Everybody stopped to watch us, and so, when she began to sober down, I picked her up again with heel and rein, saying, "Here's people, Lady," and she would show off to my delight. By constant repetition I had her so trained that she would single-foot, head down, along a country road till we came to a house or a group of people. Then I'd say, "People, Lady," and up would go her head, and her feet would dance.

But the trick that set the town talking was her bowing to any one I spoke to. "Lennie Steffens' horse bows to you," people said, and she did. I never told how it was done; by accident. Dogs used to run out at us, and the colt enjoyed it; she kicked at them sometimes with both hind hoofs. I joined her in the game, and being able to look behind more conveniently than she could, I watched the dogs until they were in range, then gave the colt a signal to kick. "Kick, gal," I'd say, and tap her ribs with my heel. We used to get dogs together that way; the colt would kick them over and over and leave them yelping in the road. Well, one day when I met a girl I knew I lifted my hat, probably muttered a "Good day," and I must have touched the colt with my heel. Anyway, she dropped her head and kicked—not much; there was no dog near, so she had responded to my unexpected signal by what looked like a bow. I caught the idea and kept her at it. Whenever I wanted to bow to a girl or anybody else, instead of saying "Good day," I muttered "Kick, gal," spurred her lightly, and— the whole centaur bowed and was covered with glory and conceit.

Yes, conceit. I was full of it, and the colt was quite as bad. One day my chum Hjalmar came into town on his Black Bess, blanketed. She had had a great fistule cut out of her shoulder and had to be kept warm. I expected to see her weak and dull, but no, the good old mare was champing and dancing, like my colt.

"What is it makes her so?" I asked, and Hjalmar said he didn't know, but he thought she was proud of the blanket. A great idea.

I had a gaudy horse blanket. I put it on the colt and I could hardly hold her. We rode down the main street together, both horses and both boys, so full of vanity that everybody stopped to smile. We thought they admired, and maybe they did. But some boys on the street gave us another angle. They, too, stopped and looked, and as we passed, one of them said, "Think you're hell, don't you?"

Spoilsport!

We did, as a matter of fact; we thought we were hell. The recognition of it dashed us for a moment; not for long, and the horses paid no heed. We pranced, the black and the yellow, all the way down J Street, up K Street, and agreed that we'd do it again, often. Only, I said, we wouldn't use blankets. If the horses were proud of a blanket, they'd be proud of anything unusually conspicuous. We tried a flower next time. I fixed a big rose on my colt's bridle just under her ear and it was great—she pranced downtown with her head turned, literally, to show off her flower. We had to change the decoration from time to time, put on a ribbon, or a bell, or a feather, but, really, it was not necessary for my horse. Old Black Bess needed an incentive to act up, but all I had to do to my horse was to pick up the reins, touch her with my heel, and say, "People"; she would dance from one side of the street to the other, asking to be admired. As she was. As we were.

I would ride down to my father's store, jump off my prancing colt in the middle of the street, and run up into the shop. The colt, free, would stop short, turn, and follow me right up on the sidewalk, unless I bade her wait. If any one approached her while I was gone, she would snort, rear, and strike. No stranger could get near her. She became a frightened, frightening animal, and yet when I came into sight she would run to me, put her head down, and as I straddled her neck, she would throw up her head and pitch me into my seat, facing backward, of course. I whirled around right, and off we'd go, the vainest boy and the proudest horse in the State.

"Hey, give me a ride, will you?" some boy would ask.

"Sure," I'd say, and jump down and watch that boy try to catch and mount my colt. He couldn't. Once a cowboy wanted to try her, and he caught her; he dodged her forefeet, grabbed the reins, and in one spring was on her back. I never did that again. My colt reared, then bucked, and, as the cowboy kept his seat, she shuddered, sank to the ground, and rolled over. He slipped aside and would have risen with her, but I was alarmed and begged him not to. She got up at my touch and followed me so close that she stepped on my heel and hurt me. The cowboy saw the point.

"If I were you, kid," he said, "I'd never let anybody mount that colt. She's too good."

That, I think, was the only mistake I made in the rearing of Colonel Carter's gift-horse. My father differed from me. He discovered another error or sin, and thrashed me for it. My practice was to work hard on a trick, privately, and when it was perfect, let him see it. I would have the horse out in our vacant lot doing it as he came home to supper. One evening, as he approached the house, I was standing, whip in hand, while the colt, quite free, was stepping carefully over the bodies of a lot of girls, all my sisters and all their girl friends. (Grace Gallatin, later Mrs. Thompson-Seton, was among them.) My father did not express the admiration I expected; he was frightened and furious. "Stop that," he called, and he came running around into the lot, took the whip, and lashed me with it. I tried to explain; the girls tried to help me explain.

I had seen in the circus a horse that stepped thus over a row of prostrate clowns. It looked dangerous for the clowns, but the trainer had told me how to do it. You begin with logs, laid out a certain distance apart; the horse walks over them under your lead, and whenever he touches one you rebuke him. By and by he will learn to step with such care that he never trips. Then you substitute clowns. I had no clowns, but I did get logs, and with the girls helping, we taught the colt to step over the obstacles even at a trot. Walking, she touched nothing. All ready thus with the logs, I had my sisters lie down in the grass, and again and again the colt stepped over and among them. None was ever touched. My father would not listen to any of this; he just walloped me, and when he was tired or satisfied and I was in tears, I blubbered a short excuse: "They were only girls." And he whipped me some more.

My father was not given to whipping; he did it very seldom, but he did it hard when he did it at all. My mother was just the opposite. She did not whip me, but she often smacked me, and she had a most annoying habit of thumping me on the head with her thimbled finger. This I resented more than my father's thorough-going thrashings, and I can tell why now. I would be playing Napoleon and as I was reviewing my Old Guard, she would crack my skull with that thimble. No doubt I was in the way; it took a lot of furniture and sisters to represent properly a victorious army; and you might think as my mother did that a thimble is a small weapon. But imagine Napoleon at the height of his power, the ruler of the world on parade, getting a sharp rap on his crown from a woman's thimble. No. My father's way was more appropriate. It was hard. "I'll attend to you in the morning," he would say, and I lay awake wondering which of my crimes he had discovered. I know what it is to be sentenced to be shot at sunrise. And it hurt, in the morning, when he was not angry but very fresh and strong. But you see, he walloped me in my own person; he never humiliated Napoleon or my knighthood, as my mother did. And I learned something from his discipline, something useful.

I learned what tyranny is and the pain of being misunderstood and wronged, or, if you please, understood and set right; they are pretty much the same. He and most parents and teachers do not break in their boys as carefully as I broke in my colt. They haven't the time that I had, and they have not some other incentives I had. I saw this that day when I rubbed my sore legs. He had to explain to my indignant mother what had happened. When he had told it his way, I gave my version: how long and cautiously I had been teaching my horse to walk over logs and girls. And having shown how sure I was of myself and the colt, while my mother was boring into his silence with one of her reproachful looks, I said something that hit my father hard.

"I taught the colt that trick, I have taught her all that you see she knows, without whipping her. I have never struck her; not once. Colonel Carter said I mustn't, and I haven't."

And my mother, backing me up, gave him a rap: "There," she said, "I told you so." He walked off, looking like a thimble-rapped Napoleon.

XII

I BECOME A DRUNKARD

FROM the Sacramento valley on a clear day one can see the snow-capped peaks of the Sierras, and when the young summer wheat is stretching happily in the heat of the sun, when men and animals and boys are stewing and steaming, it is good to look up through the white-hot flames at the cool blue of the mountains and let your eyes skate over the frost. All through my childhood I thirsted for those Sierras. They were a scene for daydreams and night wishes. My mother always tried to fulfill our wishes, and my father always yielded to her pressure when time had proven our demand real and strong. We went one summer vacation to the foothills; no snow; the peaks shone and called to us still from afar. After that we went higher and higher, to Blue Cañon, to Summit Station, Lake Tahoe, and, before the railroad was put through up the other way, north to Mount Shasta. I liked the mountains. They were not what I expected. It took several summers and some growth on my part to reach the snow line, and then, to my disappointment, the old snow was "rotten," as the mountain people had told me. There was no sledding, skating, or snowballing on summer snow. But there was, as always, compensation for disappointment. There was something better than what I had looked for and not found: hunting, fishing, swimming, boating, trapping in the woods; lakes, rapids, and the flumes.

My life a-horseback in the valley had prepared me to enjoy these sports with skill, joy, and imagination. Beaver-trapping without beavers had taught me to trap chipmunks and catch them; shooting hares, meadow-larks, and ducks was practice for quail and deer. And my friends in the valley below were introductory to the mountain folk.

Horse play is good business for a boy; schooling a young horse was good schooling for me, and no doubt Colonel Carter had my education in mind when he gave me a two-year-old colt to educate. I became, as he predicted, a good shot; not so good as I pretended and was thought to be, but the training of the colt had developed in me some patience, steadiness, and a degree of self-control which has been of use to me always and served me well in the mountains.

Once, for instance, when I was up on the McCloud River with a party of fishermen I made a chum of an Indian boy about my age. He was shooting fish with a rifle when I came upon him. Standing still on a low bluff over a deep, quiet pool of the river, he watched the school of salmon trout at rest in the dark, cool depths, and whenever a big one rose to the surface, he fired—just before the fish flipped—then he slipped downstream to wade out and pick up the dead or wounded trout. A silent boy—silent as an Indian—he did not greet me; he said nothing at all. I talked. I told him I could shoot too; not fish, to be sure, but deer, bear—anything else. He heard my boastings long, making no comment till we were going back to camp. Then we saw a hawk light on the top of a high pine across the canyon, perhaps two hundred yards away. I thought he was going to shoot it. He adjusted the range of his rifle to the distance and then, without a word, he handed the gun to me.

"Now make good." He might as well have said it; I was caught, and I would expose and humiliate myself, but there was no way out. I took the rifle, aimed carelessly (what was the use?), and quickly fired. And the bird fell! Amazed myself, I am sure I did not show the least surprise. I handed back the rifle and went on talking as if nothing out of the ordinary had happened, and I never mentioned the incident and I never fired a rifle again in that region. Never. That was self-possession. It was educated intelligence. That shot, reported by the Indian boy, won me among the Indians and mountaineers a reputation which could not be bettered and might easily have been damaged. I was a crack shot; only, curiously enough, shooting bored me. I am sure that, if my colt had not drilled me in the control of myself and other animals, I would have shot at something else or referred in some way to that unlucky hawk.

All this character-building, however, had interfered somewhat with my proper school work. I went through the grammar school always near the foot of my class and finally failed of promotion to high. My father blamed the colt. He was not altogether right in this. I was graduated from college, where I had no horse, last or among the last in my class. Something else was the matter, something far more educative, I think now; but horses were enough to account for my backwardness to my parents, and that diagnosis made it hard for them to deal with me. They shared my guilt.

We had become a horsy family. When my colt was broken to ride I turned over my pony to my sisters. There were three of them, and one pony was not enough. My father bought a third saddle-horse. Meanwhile he had acquired for himself and the family in general a carriage and a pair of black trotters, which I broke to the saddle because my mother caught the horseback fever. There we were, therefore, a family of six with three saddle-horses and two carriage horses. Naturally they desired to ride into my life, meet my friends, and visit the places I had talked so much about. Reluctantly, gradually, I introduced them to my circle, beginning with the bridge-tender.

One day we all drove or rode out to the trestle where the bridge-tender-prospector, properly warned, received them well and told them all about me. "All they could stand," he said afterward. "I didn't say much about walking the trestle. I didn't say anything about swimming the river in the rapids. I spoke of the Saracens, but I did not mention the Chinese and peanuts and melons." The bridge-tender was all right, a credit to me; and the family respected me on his account. "Good man," my father said. "A good friend of yours," said my mother.

Ah Hook, whom we visited a week or so later, did not rise so well to the emergency. My father liked him, bought a lot of peanuts from him, and ordered a sackful to be delivered at the store "for the boys." But my mother sought for Ah Hook's appreciation of her son; she liked to hear me admired; and the Chink grinned and gave her his honest opinion.

"Him boy allee same heap damn fool," he said. "Him no sabee; him lucky. Tellem lies all day. Tellem me lies, tellem nother man lies: tellem himself lies too. Him boy big damn fool liar. Yes."

My mother did not care to stay long at Ah Hook's; she could not see what I saw in him. We soon closed that visit and the family never went back. Ah Hook, by his tactlessness, lost his chance to become a connection of our family. There were other disappointments. Loony Louie seemed crazy even to me when my father and mother were presented to him. He had just witnessed a slaughter of veal, and bewailing his calves, he was a crazy sight which I saw through their eyes. Some of the parents of my boy friends were not as acceptable to mine as they were to me. I think that, as a rule (for boys), it is better to keep parents apart and at home.

However, in my case, the Neelys made up for Mr. Hook, Louie, and everybody else. The family visit there was carefully planned and long remembered. We all went, three mounted and three in the carriage, and the Neelys were all dressed up in their Sunday clothes, except that Mrs. Neely wore a dainty apron over her black silk dress. The greetings over, she ran back to her kitchen, and Jim and Mr. Neely and I had the horses to take care of. These chores done, the horn blew, and in we filed, an embarrassing crowd, to a dinner, a wonderful dinner. Mrs. Neely had everything for them that I had ever had and more besides, much more. Jim was delighted; he winked at me. But we all enjoyed it, the food, I mean. I did not care for the conversation. It was all about me, and it took the form of a race between my mother and Mrs. Neely to see who could tell the most. I knew all my mother's stories; so did my sisters, who snickered at me or kicked me under the table. Mrs. Neely's recollections, too, I knew, but not in the form in which she told them that day. She seemed to remember everything I had ever done or said out there, and some of my deeds and especially some of my sayings did not sound the way I had thought they would. Rather fine acts became ridiculous. My mother would exclaim that she was surprised, and my sisters would whisper that they weren't surprised. I don't mean that Mrs. Neely gave me away, or if she did, she covered it up somehow. Things that had annoyed her when they happened became almost all right somehow. The time I fell into the pig pen, for instance, and had to be washed, I and my clothes, "every stitch" —Mrs. Neely was certainly irritated that time.

"All this unnecessary extra work just for you, and you lying clean and comfortable in my nice bed while I slave for you"— that is what she had said to me, and now when she told my mother about it, she just laughed, like Jim, as if she had liked it.

But the most embarrassing subject for me and my father, the most amusing to Jim, and the most happy for my mother and Mrs. Neely, was what they called "the efficacy of prayer." The moment it was broached my father drew Mr. Neely into a discussion of some other themes like the weather, the markets, and the future of farming. Jim listened to the ladies, as I had to, and we heard them compare notes on the hour when I prayed. My mother told her she saw me on my knees and knew it was nine o'clock because that was my bedtime, and Mrs. Neely was sure of the hour because the nurse's record showed it was only a little after nine when her crisis passed. Best proof of all, however, was the sense Mrs. Neely had of relief and that some hand had lifted a great weight from her, and from that moment she began to get well. Jim squeezed my knee under the table and smiled; I didn't know whether to express approval or—what.

When late that afternoon we hitched up and drove away with the carriage full of fresh eggs, vegetables, fruit, cakes, and everything, "a good time had been had by all."

Also arrangements had been made for the regular future delivery at our house of whatever produce Mr. Neely had ready for market. There was a big contract for hay and grain. After that the Neelys, one or other of them, used to appear about once a week at our house, and sometimes they stayed or came back for the noon meal.

The two families were friends for life, even after I was gone away to college. I was in Germany when Mrs. Neely fell ill and died. They cabled me to save her, and I tried, but I couldn't. I wasn't praying those days, but I did pray for Mrs. Neely; and she knew it. It was in vain. Her death nearly ended Mr. Neely. He began to age; he sold the farm, and I don't know what became of Jim, but Mr. Neely moved into the city. My father took charge of his small savings and found him a boarding-place where he was to pay so much a week out of his capital, which they reckoned would last a certain number of years, months, and days. The limit worried Mr. Neely, so my father wrote to me, asking me to send him a written guarantee that, after my friend's own capital was used up, I would pay his board as long as he lived. I did so, and Mr. Neely seemed to be relieved and at peace. But he died just the same when his money was ended; he assured my father, who saw him nearly every day toward the end, that he was willing to accept his board from me, but I had the privilege of paying back only a few weeks—of all the good times he had given me, he and Mrs. Neely.

Mrs. Neely never knew that I took to drink and, from the broad road to the pulpit, turned off into the narrow road to hell. An eastern family of boys came to Sacramento, the Southworths, and they fascinated me and my gang, for the very reason that we despised them and tried to hurt them. They were well dressed. "Us regular fellers," we affected to ignore clothes and, since we had to wear something, preferred such careless garb as farmers and vaqueros and cowboys wore. The Southworth boys were an affront to us; they wore eastern clothes, like those you saw in the illustrated eastern papers; and they wore them without shame, without consciousness. Boys can despise and admire, resent and covertly hate and love at the same time; they are not consistent like grown-ups. We got together to see what could be done, and we decided that, while they could wear good clothes easily, they probably could not ride a horse. We would get them on a horse that would bring them down a peg.

My mother's horse was a mad animal that was gentle with her but so wild under a boy that he would run away. We called him the Yellow Streak. I asked Ernie Southworth if he would like to ride with us some day. He said very politely that he would appreciate our courtesy; so we mounted our horses after school one day and rode to the Southworths' house, I on my colt leading Yellow Streak. We boosted Ernie up on the horse, which whirled and ran away, just as we knew it would. We had to race after the Streak with the boy dude riding high; his hat flew off, his neat coat swelled with the wind, his face went white. The Streak ran to our street, turned so fast that he nearly fell, and made straight for our stable. He was going so wildly that he could not turn into the alley; he tried to but passed by and was stopped by a post at the curb. His stop was like that of a broncho—two or three terrible jerks which pitched Ernie Southworth over the post on his hands and knees.

When we rode up, caught the Streak, and jumped down to enjoy the eastern boy's rage and wounds, he stood up and—he apologized. He didn't mean to let the horse get away like that; he was unprepared for the sudden start; he would try again and, he hoped, do better. It was no fun lynching a fellow like that. We 'fessed up to our game and took him into our gang, which straightway took to drink.

No psycho-analytic novelist could guess or even follow the psychology of our downfall. Only boys will understand the perfect logic of it. Since Ernie Southworth was game about the runaway horse, he had to become one of us, and since he dressed well and we all had to stick together, we began to care about clothes. Having become dudes, we didn't exactly follow the fashions of "the east" (which, in California, meant the eastern U.S.), but we kept just a little ahead of them by copying the styles as caricatured in the comic weeklies. We found them more striking than the tailors' fashion plates. When you are dressed up you do the things that go with dress. We went in for dancing and girls. Now the world of women and dancing and fashion is a world by itself, with its own ideals and heroes. The hero of our new world was a fellow a little older than we were, who danced, dressed, and talked well. He was a favorite among the girls because the day after the dance he could describe to the girls in their technical terms what every well-dressed girl and woman wore. We wanted to be like him, but we could not describe women's clothes; so we had to do something else that he did. And the easiest of his habits to imitate was that of going into a saloon, standing at the bar, and having rounds of drink. We danced and spooned and talked, too, but drink was the thing, as vain as herding cattle or trapping beavers, but as fascinating. Once, for example, as I staggered (a little more than I had to) away from the bar, I overheard one man say to another:

"Those boys can carry some liquor, can't they?"

That was great. But better still was the other loafer's reply: "Yes," he said, "but it's tough to see young men setting out on the down grade to hell that way."

XIII

NAPOLEON

I BECAME a drunkard as I had been a knight, a trapper, and a preacher, not for long and not exactly with my whole heart, but with a large part of my imagination. My stomach saved my heart. I hated what I drank; it made me sick. If I could have taken beer or soda or lemonade I would have liked drinking, but think of walking up to a bar, putting your foot on the rail, your elbow familiarly on the polished ebony—like a man —and then asking the barkeep for an ice-cream soda! Impossible. It wasn't done. Beer, yes, but one drank beer for thirst, and I had no thirst. I was on the road to hell, and nobody would have noticed and grieved over my melancholy fate if I had ordered anything but the shuddering, sickening concoction that was the fashion just then among "bad men": rum and gum. That was what Will Ross, our ideal, took, and the whole town was mourning the downfall of this brilliant young man; so we boys ordered rum and gum, braced ourselves, and gulped it down as if it was medicine, excepting, now and then, when no one was looking, we could spill it. I was clever at this; I was caught at it sometimes, but it was worth the risk. The man who could throw away the most could outlast the others, and the manly game was to drink one another down.

"See that fellow over there?" I heard a teamster say one day, and we looked at a young bank clerk who was a crack billiard player, too. "Well, sir," the teamster continued, "that bloke can carry more liquor than a carload of watered stock."

If only that could be said of me!

We all dreaded our fathers. It seemed to be well known that they would "raise hell" with a son who was going to hell, and that was a stage of the journey. Some fellows had been turned out of house and home, some of the hardest, ablest drinkers. I never did have any luck at home. My father never came up to expectations. When he discovered what I was "up to," he did not "go straight up in the air"; he wasn't even shocked.

One night when I came home late as usual, he walked, nightgowned, white, and silent, into my room, watched me without a word as I undressed, and saw me, also speechless, tumble into bed.

"What is this all about?" he asked then.

"Nothing," I said, as distinctly as I could.

"Oh, I know it's nothing," he answered. "It always is nothing with you, but what kind of a nothing is it? If you keep it up, it will be something, something silly, of course, but you might with practice learn to like to drink."

So he knew; he really understood all about it. How did he come to know more about it—more than I did? I was disappointed and humiliated, but also I was sleepy. He saw that, and with a "Tish"—his expression of contempt—he left me to sleep. He never referred to the subject again. He acted, however.

He announced one day that I was to go to a private school, the military academy at San Mateo, south of San Francisco. I was delighted—a change. His reasons, as I remember them, were that I had failed to be graduated from the grammar school, could not go to the high school at home without repeating the last year at the grammar school, and evidently I could not study by myself at home. I seemed to need a school where there was enough discipline to compel me to work. There was too much liberty and play in my life at home. Hence, a military school.

I was delighted. My new chum, Ernie Southworth, had long had a great advantage over us. He knew all about Napoleon. I knew something about Napoleon and Richard the Lion-hearted, the Count of Monte Cristo, and many, very many, other knights; I knew something about many similarly imitable persons, poets, cowboys, trappers, preachers. My interest was scattered, my parts as various as any mere actor's. Ernie had one steady, high ideal, a hero, Napoleon Buonaparte, and when he, on his old white horse, started telling us about the great modern conqueror, we were still, awed, inspired, but humble. For Ernie, unlike the rest of us, was not himself Napoleon; he only followed him as a marshal might, or a soldier with a marshal's baton in his knapsack—a respectful distance behind, bold, worshipful, obedient.

When, then, it developed that he, Ernie, was to go east to study dentistry, while I was to go west and be trained for a Napoleon, I recovered my happy superiority. Most of the other fellows of my gang were about to go to work or to the local high school. They envied me, and they and the girls and my family made an event of my departure, a happy one for me, therefore. "Going away" to school was a distinction and an adventure.

I was about fifteen years old, but I had not a thought of what I was to learn at the new school, except soldiering, of course. And when I got there I found that the boys, all in radiant gray uniforms, loathed these clothes and everything pertaining to the military side of the establishment. Whether it was a pose with them I could not tell; anyway, it was with me, for I had to pretend not to like the orderly discipline, which fascinated me. My secret enthusiasm counted, and I was soon promoted to be a corporal, and better still, I was made a cadet drillmaster and taught the new boys tactics all the time I was there. Meanwhile I read about Napoleon as if I were reading up on my own future.

This I can remember, and I can recall a good deal of all my private reading; I was carrying on my own education in my own boy's way. But I can remember no more of what was taught me in the classrooms of this school than I can of the other schools I went to at home. It was a pretty good school for that time, probably the best of the so-called private schools in a State where the public schools were the best. But there was no attempt made, so far as I can remember, to interest us in the subjects we studied. They were work, therefore, and our minds ran freely to our play or our own curiosities and aspirations. I was not good at the games played: football, baseball, marbles, tops, hare and hounds. Too much horseback had left my running and dodging muscles undeveloped. I used to wish I could have my colt brought down to school, so as to show the great pitchers and halfbacks that there was something that I could do—besides drill. The only distinction I won in athletics was by chance.

Playing hare and hounds one afternoon, I set out with the hares, and humiliated long enough, I was determined to stay with the leaders for once. We had gone perhaps a mile when I began to fail. My distress was alarming; I thought I would fall down and die. I saw myself being carried back dead to the school, but I picked out a great oak ahead on the road; I would go that far anyway, and to my amazement, just before I got there I broke into a sweat, my breath came easily, and I sprinted up to the leaders and finished with them with a sense that I could go on for ever. They, too, were astonished and could not explain it. I had got my second wind, and counting on it thereafter, I was chosen always for long-distance running.

But I was homesick, not for home, but for my horse and my gang, for my country life games and for my interrupted career as a drunkard. There were vacations. My colt, grown now, bore me out to all my old friends, the bridge-tender, the Neelys, and the rest. That was the best of my life. It was natural; no more poses there, except that I never could be so cruel as to tell Mrs. Neely that I had, not given up, but almost forgotten about being a minister. I talked to her about the Episcopal church services we had at school. I rather liked them, as I liked drill. I must have had a taste for ritual. But to the Neely men and to my other grown-up friends I had become what I was, a schoolboy, the only difference between me and other such boys being that I was to be a great man —somehow; and I suppose that all the other schoolboys shared in that distinction.

My father, who knew me pretty well, I think, drew from me or my teachers at San Mateo enough to seek a cure. To center my interest in the school he suggested that, besides Napoleon, I read *Tom Brown at Rugby*. That had some effect. As he expected, no doubt, I began to emulate Tom Brown. This was difficult in our school. We had no fagging system. I tried to establish one, and the older boys were for it; only the little fellows objected. They had some snobbish objection to blacking our shoes, running our errands, and otherwise becoming our servants. Force was needed, and my luck gave me the power.

The discipline of the school was partly a cadet system. The officer of the day was responsible for the enforcement of the law for his twenty-four hours. One night when I was on duty I heard a soft disturbance in one of the dormitories, and slipping in there, I caught several boys out of their beds. They were with other boys. By threatening punishment, I drew from the smaller boys confessions which revealed an ancient, highly organized system of prostitution. One boy, the son of a general, was the head of it. He had as his white slaves a large number of the little boys, whom he paid with cakes, candies, etc. He let them out to other older boys at so much money, candy, or credit per night.

This appeared to me as a chance to introduce the fagging system. I called together the senior officers in my gang. Some of them owned up that they were as guilty as their juniors, but those of us who were innocent of that crime carried through our plot. We made fags of the young criminals. It was fun. It was a sort of reign of terror, and we tyrants enjoyed our power so much that, like grown-ups, we rather abused it. We could not help letting even the teachers see the craven obedience we could exact and the menial services we required.

There was an inquiry from above. Some of the boys confessed everything, and the headmaster had me up as the head of the whole conspiracy. He was furious, but also he was frightened. I could defy him. I would not tell him anything, but he knew all about it himself, the fagging system and, too, the vice foundation thereof, and he was afraid to have any detail of either evil leak out to the parents. He must have known that such things occur in many private schools in all countries; it is said to be common in the English so-called public schools. He acted, however, as if the scandal were unheard of. I don't know all that he did about it, but he compelled me to witness the whipping he administered to the vice squad, and he forbade fagging. I felt so mean that I would have submitted to any penalty, and I escaped all punishment. My first essay into muck-raking cost me nothing.

My best-remembered punishment was for getting myself and half the school drunk, and out of that punishment came some good and some bad results—a change in me.

XIV

ALL THROUGH WITH HEROISM

THE Napoleon in me ended, as the emperor himself did, in prison. As a leader I had to find worlds to conquer; so when fagging failed I took to drink, I and my followers. My custom had been to drink only in vacations in Sacramento; in San Mateo I was sober—a sort of double life. When I came back to school for my last term I was drunk, not so drunk as I seemed. I could brace up and be sober in the presence of authority, and I could let down and play drunk for the other boys, who were so astonished, so admiring, so envious, that it occurred to me to introduce the habit into the school.

Biding my time, I made some propaganda. That was uphill work. Some other leader had heard a speech against religion; he had brought with him a lot of literature, a book of Bob Ingersoll's lectures, for example, and he soon had all the boys disputing hotly the claims of revealed religion. I hated it, kept out of it as much as I could, but it was everywhere, and I had to hear some of it. And because I did not debate the question but only listened, I was half persuaded. Indeed I think I was the only boy who had his mind opened to the questions underlying the doubts of the day. But having my own leadership to defend, I could not afford to yield to the passing mania for truth, and I stuck to my guns; I stood always for drink as the solution of all such problems till, at last, when the fever of controversy lessened, my propaganda was heard and considered. A practical question superseded the academic religious issue, to wit: Where could we get the drink to get drunk on? I said I would attend to that. It was not so easy as I thought. No tradesmen dared to sell drink in quantity to schoolboys; I met only flat refusals from the saloon men. But, like all great leaders of men, I found lieutenants to do what I could not myself do.

A fellow who was slow to join our "conspiracy against the good name of the school," when finally brought in, said that he would find the drink. I had been thinking of rum and gum; he thought of beer. A brewery wagon passed our school now and then; he stopped it one day and arranged for the delivery of a keg of beer in a certain remote field the next Saturday afternoon. We were there, twenty or thirty boys; and more wanted to come, but were forbidden by us big fellows. I remember how the smaller boys cried or were indignant at our presumption at closing to them this open road to the devil. But we told them that when they grew up we would take them in with us, and so we left them and went to meet our brewer.

He came, he opened the keg for us, and he lent us a tin can "off'n the wagon." It was a warm day; the field was far from the school; we had a thirst which was not easily slaked by our one borrowed can. We drank and drank, round on round, and when we rolled the empty keg into the hiding-place agreed upon, we were a sight and a sound. I don't know whether the sight and the sound of us did it; I heard afterward that some disgruntled small boy peached on us for revenge; anyway there was a large group of spectators out on the campus to see and to hear us come home. Among the witnesses were some teachers.

There were whippings; there were temperance lectures and sermons; there were stomach-aches; and there was no more drinking at the school in my day. We all were punished, but I, as the Napoleon, was stripped of my sword and rank as cadet officer and condemned to the guard-house in solitary confinement for twenty-two days. Some other old boy, far back in the history of the school, had been locked up for twenty-one days. I must go down on the records with the longest sentence ever suffered, before or after; hence my twenty-two days.

My punishment was a blessing to me. I read. They let me have books, not novels, but histories and solid things. Among them was an encyclopedic tome which was full of statistical information. The chapter on drink was the one I was asked to read, and I did. It showed me so that I never forgot, not only the waste and the folly, but the vanity of drinking. I got this last because I myself had been half aware of the pretentiousness of my drunkenness; it was a pose with me, and when I saw it handled as a pose in men, grown men, the romance went out of it: it went the way of politics, racing, and other illusions. I never could enjoy drinking after that; I was as ashamed of it as I was of being a sucker in the betting-ring.

There was another chapter on religions that told how many of them there had been and how men, grown men, always practiced the one that dominated their day. That fed my doubting mind, and I asked for other books, which I was carelessly allowed to have: Herbert Spencer, Darwin, and others. But the subject that hit me hardest was war. That book—I don't remember the title of it—that most improper book for boys told as a story of idiotic waste the history of all the wars in the whole story of man, and I called for paper and pencil. I had to write an oration for my graduation day, and I wrote one out of that book on the stupidity of war. But what I did not write was a conclusion, tentative but emancipating, that men, the superior grown-up adults that I had always respected, were and always had been mostly ignorant fools whom a boy, even a little fellow like me, need not look up to. I had long felt, deep down, that they did not see straight, that they could not explain things to me because they did not understand them, and now I knew that, if I was to learn anything, I had to find teachers who knew, and even at that, look out for myself.

When I came out of the guard-house, my sentence served to the last minute, I was a hero on the campus—and I might have enjoyed the awed stares of the other boys. But I had seen a light. I was on to my own posings, and also I was contemptuous of the springs of those boys' admiration. They were cub dubs; their respect was worthless. I heard it said, and I do not doubt, that I looked conceited, priggish, but I know now that I was dazed by a new interest, a fixed determination. I was going to college, and I was going there, not to make a record, not, as the headmaster said, to represent the school and make it proud of me—I was going to college to find out the truth about some of the questions that had bothered me. I was not to be put off any longer with the appearances of things. I meant to know, really, and I had no doubt that some of those professors really knew the truth.

An experience I sensed at that time clinched my conclusions and my determination. I was speedily, too speedily, restored to my rank as a captain of cadets. And the reason given, that I was needed as a drillmaster, did not deceive me; I had drilled cadets in the uniform of a private. Another "reason" set my back up again. My father had been notified of my misconduct. He did not hurry to the school; he let them punish me their way, of course. It was not till my sentence was nearly over that he visited me in prison. A memorable day. When they unlocked the pretentious barred doors, threw back the silly bolts with their prison ring, for him, he came in, and turning, dismissed my jailers.

"Feel all right?" he asked. I said I did. "Of course," he said. "Your mother was worried about your health in this cell, but I knew you would take it standing up. And I know you are not going to be a drunkard, too. Your stomach won't let you, for one thing; I've noticed that it makes you sick to drink too much. All that worries me is your posings, the bunk you have seemed always to like. I never saw you do anything for the fun of doing it; you always wanted to tell about it and see yourself and be seen doing it. That's poppycock. It does no harm in a boy, but you'll soon be no longer a boy, and there are a lot of men I know who are frauds and bunkers all their lives. I'd hate to see you go on into that sort of thing. And I don't believe you will, either. I am going to give you every chance, and you can waste or use your chances, as you will. That's up to you. But it's up to you to choose your chance. You can work or study for anything you like, but do, please do, find out what you want to do and be."

So he talked and I was prepared to take it all in just as he said and meant it. I remember thinking that he was as real as the bridge-tender, as much a gentleman as Mr. Neely, as warmly for me as Mrs. Neely, but I answered him in kind. I told him I had done some reading which revealed me to myself, a little; I had seen my vanity, especially in the matter of drink, which I really hated. But also I saw, I said, the posings and the pretensions of, for example, that school.

"They aren't thinking of me and the other boys," I said; "they are doing what they do, punishing us and degrading us, for outsiders to see, for parents to hear of and so believe in the school."

He nodded. "I'll fix that," he said, and I knew by the way he looked that he would give the school authorities an unhappy half hour. And he did. He told them, I suspected then, to restore me to my cadet rank, and afterward he told me that he made it clear to them that neither I nor the other boys were in any danger of going to hell and that it would be wiser for them to drop that pretense and treat us as foolish, but not wicked; young idiots, but not much more so than our teachers and masters.

Fine! But he made a mistake himself. When we had arrived at a perfect understanding, he and I, he broke it to me that in his first anger he had sold my colt. I was appalled. He had not sold one of my sisters; he would not have thought of that. But also he did not think that my colt to me was what a child of his was to him. I loved that horse. I loved that horse as much as he loved me. True, I had no constant use for her; she was eating her head off in our stable, waiting for my vacations. I had thought myself that, when I went away to college, I would have to send her back to Colonel Carter, who appreciated her, could use her properly, and would take care of her. And that colt was used to being loved and needed care. That thought had counted against college; my colt had stayed me from accepting an appointment to West Point. And my father had sold her.

"To whom?" I asked, when I could—when I had some control over my trembling pain and grief. What kind of man was to have the power of life and death over that fine, happy, trustful, spoiled, proud creature? I asked, and I did not want to hear; and he did not answer right away. He lowered his eyes when he told me.

"I don't know. I turned her over to a dealer."

I went rigid. He looked up at me, and I stood and looked at him till he winced and, without a word, went out, leaving the cell door open. He came back later. I was lying face down on the cot.

"Good-by," he said, and he leaned over and took my hand.

"Good-by," I managed to say somehow, and I let him shake my hand.

I never found out what became of my colt. Once from a train I saw a cream-colored horse that looked exactly like her, drawing, head down, a market wagon overloaded with vegetables and driven by a Chinaman.

XV

PREPARING FOR COLLEGE

THE year 1884-85 was a period of great adventure for me. When I came up to Berkeley for the entrance examinations at the University of California I failed in Greek, Latin, and enough other subjects to be put off for a year. My father was alarmed. I was eighteen years old, and he thought, I think, that my failure was his fault; he had chosen the wrong school for me. He had, but the right school for me and my kind did not exist. There were schools that put boys into the colleges, east and west, and at a younger age than mine. I came to know those boys well. They are the boys (and they become the men) that the schools, colleges, and the world are made for. Often I have envied them; more often I have been glad that I was not of them.

The elect were, for the most part, boys who had been brought up to do their duty. They memorized whatever their teachers told them to learn. Whether they wanted to know it, whether they understood it or no, they could remember and recite it. Their own driving motives were, so far as I could make out, not curiosity; they rarely talked about our studies, and if I spoke of the implications of something we had read or heard, they looked dazed or indifferent. Their own motives were foreign to me: to beat the other fellows, stand high, represent the honor of the school.

My parents did not bring me up. They sent me to school, they gave me teachers of music, drawing; they offered me every opportunity in their reach. But also they gave me liberty and the tools of quite another life: horses, guns, dogs, and the range of an open country. As I have shown, the people, the businesses, and the dreams of this life interested me, and I learned well whatever interested me. School subjects which happened to bear on my outside interests I studied in school and out; I read more than

III

was required, and I read for keeps, too. I know these subjects to this day, just as I remember and love still the men and women, the boys and girls, who let me be friends with them then and so revealed to me some of the depths and the limitations of human nature. On the other hand I can remember few of my teachers and little of the subjects which seemed to me irrelevant to my life.

These other subjects are interesting, and they might have been made interesting to me. No one tried to interest me in them; they were put before me as things that I had to have to get into college. The teachers of them did not appeal to my curious, active mind. The result was that I did not really work at them and so got only what stuck by dint of repetition: the barest rudiments of a school education. When I knocked at the college gates, I was prepared for a college education in some branches; my mind was hungry enough for the answers to some profound questions to have made me work and develop myself, especially on lines which I know now had no ready answers, only more and ever more questions: science, metaphysics, etc. I was not in the least curious about Greek, Latin, mathematics, and the other "knowledge" required by the stand-ardization of that day.

My father discovered and put me into the best private school in San Francisco as a special student to be crammed for Berkeley—and he retained one of the teachers there, Mr. Evelyn Nixon, to tutor me on the side. Characteristically, too, my father gave me liberty: a room to sleep and work in, with no one to watch over and care for me. I could go and come as I pleased. And I came and went. I went exploring and dreaming alone around that city as I had the country around Sacramento, and the place I liked best was the ocean shore; there I lived over the lives of the Greek heroes and the Roman generals and all the poets of all the ages, sometimes with ecstasy, but never, as in my boyhood, with myself as the hero. A change had come over me.

Evelyn Nixon formed it. He was the first teacher I ever had who interested me in what I had to learn—not in myself, but in the world outside, the world of conscious culture. He was a fanatic of poetry, especially of the classic poets. When he read or recited Greek verse the Greeks came to life; romance and language sang songs to me, and I was inspired to be, like him, not a hero nor even a poet, but a Greek scholar, and thus an instrument on which

beautiful words might play. Life filled with meaning, and purpose, and joy. It was too great and too various for me to personify
with my boyish imitations and heroism. I wrote verses, but only to
learn the technique and so feel poetry more perfectly. I wanted to
read, not to write; I wanted to know, not to do and be, great
things—Mr. Nixon expressed it.

"I'm nobody," he used to say. "I'm nothing but one of the
unknown beings Homer and Dante, Shakespeare, Caesar, and the
popes and the generals and statesmen have sung and fought and
worked for. I'm the appreciator of all good words and deeds."

A new, a noble rôle, and Evelyn Nixon was a fine example of it:
the receiver, not the giver, of beautiful inventions. He was an
Englishman; he took a double first at Oxford, I heard, and came
for his health to San Francisco. There was a group of such men,
most of them with one story. They were athletes, as well as
scholars at Oxford and Cambridge; they developed muscles and
a lung capacity which they did not need and could not keep up in
the sedentary occupations their scholarship put them into. Lung
troubles exiled them.

"Keep out of college athletics," they advised. "Don't work up
any more brawn there than you can use every day afterward."

Nixon taught me Greek, Latin, and English at school, and at
his house he opened up the beauty and the meaning of the other
subjects I had to cram up for entrance. I worked for him; I worked
more, much more, for myself. He saw this, he saw my craving for
the answers to questions, and he laughed.

"I will answer no questions of yours," he shouted. "Men know
no answers to the natural questions of a boy, of a child. We can
only underline your questions, make you mad yourself to answer
them, and add ours to whip, to lash you on to find out yourself
—one or two; and tell us! That is what youth is for: to answer the
questions maturity can't answer." And when I looked disappointed
and balked, he would roar at me like a demon.

"Go to, boy. The world is yours. Nothing is done, nothing is
known. The greatest poem isn't written, the best railroad isn't
built yet, the perfect state hasn't been thought of. Everything
remains to be done—right, everything."

This said, he said it again and again, and finally, to drive me,
he set our private hour from seven till eight o'clock Saturday

evenings, so that I could stay on into the night with his group of friends, a maddening lot of cultivated, conflicting minds. There were from four to ten of them, all Englishmen, all Oxford and Cambridge men, all exiles and all interested in any and all subjects, which they discussed with knowledge, with the precise information of scholarship, but with no common opinions on anything apparently. There were Tories among them and liberals and one red: William Owen, a grandson, I think, certainly a descendant, of Robert Owen, the first of the early English socialists. There was at least one Roman Catholic, who showed me so that I never forgot it the Christianity of that church; his favorite thesis was that the Protestant churches were Old Testament, righteous sects and knew nothing really of Christ's teachings of love and forgiveness. And there were Protestants there, all schooled in church history, and when a debate came to a clinch, they could quote their authorities with a sureness which withstood reference to the books. I remember one hot dispute of the Catholic's reference to some certain papal bull. Challenged, he quoted it verbatim in the original Latin. What they knew was amazing to me, and how they knew it, but what they did not know struck me harder still. They could not among them agree on anything but a fact. With all their knowledge they knew no essential truth.

It was conversation I was hearing, the free, passionate, witty exchanges of studied minds as polished as fine tools. They were always courteous; no two ever spoke together; there were no asides; they all talked to the question before the house, and while they were on the job of exposition any one, regardless of his side, would contribute his quota of facts, or his remembrance of some philosopher's opinion or some poet's perfect phrase for the elucidation or the beautification of the theme. When the differences rose the urbanity persisted. They drank their Californian wine with a relish, they smoked the room thick, and they pressed their views with vigor and sincerity and eloquence; but their good temper never failed them. It was conversation. I had never heard conversation before; I have heard conversation sometimes since, but rarely, and never like my remembrance of those wonderful Saturday nights in San Francisco—which were my preparation for college.

For those conversations, so brilliant, so scholarly, and so consciously unknowing, seemed to me, silent in the background, to reveal the truth that even college graduates did not know anything, really. Evidences they had, all the testimony of all the wise men in the historical world on everything, but no decisions. None. I must myself go to college to find out more, and I wanted to. It seemed as if I had to go soon. My head, busy with questions before, was filled with holes that were aching voids as hungry, as painful, as an empty stomach. And my questions were explicit; it was as if I were not only hungry; I was hungry for certain foods. My curiosity was no longer vague.

When on Sundays I would take the gatherings I had made out of the talk of the night before down to the Cliff House with me and sit there on the rocks and think, I formed my ignorance into a system. I was getting a cultivated ignorance, a survey not of the solved but of the unsolved problems in every science from astronomy to economics, from history to the next tricks in versification. I thought of them; I thought, rejoicing, that there were things to do for everybody in every science, every art, every business. Why, men did not know even how to love, not technically, not beautifully! I learned of the damage done me by having my sex feelings separated from love and poetry, and as for astronomy, government, conversation, play and work, men were just crawling on their hands and knees out of their caves.

But the best that I got out of it all was objectivity. Those men never mentioned themselves; apparently they never thought of themselves. Their interest was in the world outside of themselves. I caught that. No more play-acting for me. No more dreaming I was Napoleon or a trapper, a knight, a statesman, or the younger son of a lord. It is possible that I was outgrowing this stage of a boy's growth; the very intensity of my life in subjective imagination may have carried me through it, but whether I would have come out clearly impersonal or no by myself, I don't know. All I am sure of is that their conversations, the attitude and the interest of those picked Englishmen, helped and, I think, established in me the realization that the world was more interesting than I was. Not much to see? No, but I have met men since, statesmen, scholars, business men, workers, and poets, who have never made that discovery. It is the scientific attitude, and some scientists have it—not all; and some others, too.

When I went up for my examination this time in Berkeley I passed, not well in all subjects, but I was admitted to the University, and that fall I entered the University of California with a set of examination questions for the faculty, for the professors, to answer.

XVI

I GO TO COLLEGE

G OING to college is, to a boy, an adventure into a new world, and a very strange and complete world too. Part of his preparation for it is the stories he hears from those that have gone before; these feed his imagination, which cannot help trying to picture the college life. And the stories and the life are pretty much the same for any college. The University of California was a young, comparatively small institution when I was entered there in 1885 as a freshman. Berkeley, the beautiful, was not the developed villa community it is now; I used to shoot quail in the brush under the oaks along the edges of the college grounds. The quail and the brush are gone now, but the oaks are there and the same prospect down the hill over San Francisco Bay out through the Golden Gate between the low hills of the city and the high hills of Marin County. My class numbered about one hundred boys and girls, mostly boys, who came from all parts of the State and represented all sorts of people and occupations. There was, however, a significant uniformity of opinion and spirit among us, as there was, and still is, in other, older colleges. The American is molded to type early. And so are our college ways. We found already formed at Berkeley the typical undergraduate customs, rights, and privileged vices which we had to respect ourselves and defend against the faculty, regents, and the State government.

One evening, before I had matriculated, I was taken out by some upper classmen to teach the president a lesson. He had been the head of a private preparatory school and was trying to govern the private lives and the public morals of university "men" as he had those of his schoolboys. Fetching a long ladder, the upper classmen thrust it through a front window of Prexy's house and, to the chant of obscene songs, swung it back and forth, up and down, round and round, till everything breakable within sounded broken and the drunken indignation outside was satisfied or tired.

This turned out to be one of the last battles in the war for liberty against that president. He was allowed to resign soon thereafter and I noticed that not only the students but many of the faculty and regents rejoiced in his downfall and turned with us to face and fight the new president when, after a lot of politics, he was appointed and presented. We learned somehow a good deal about the considerations that governed our college government. They were not only academic. The government of a university was —like the State government and horse-racing and so many other things—not what I had been led to expect. And a college education wasn't either, nor the student mind.

Years later, when I was a magazine editor, I proposed a series of articles to raise and answer the question: Is there any intellectual life in our colleges? My idea sprang from my remembered disappointment at what I found at Berkeley and some experiences I was having at the time with the faculties and undergraduates of the other older colleges in the east. Berkeley, in my day, was an Athens compared with New Haven, for example, when I came to know Yale undergraduates.

My expectations of college life were raised too high by Nixon's Saturday nights. I thought, and he assumed, that at Berkeley I would be breathing in an atmosphere of thought, discussion, and some scholarship; working, reading, and studying for the answers to questions which would be threshed out in debate and conversation. There was nothing of the sort. I was primed with questions. My English friends never could agree on the answers to any of the many and various questions they disputed. They did not care; they enjoyed their talks and did not expect to settle anything. I was more earnest. I was not content to leave things all up in the air. Some of those questions were very present and personal to me, as some of those Englishmen meant them to be. William Owen was trying to convert me to the anarchistic communism in which he believed with all his sincere and beautiful being. I was considering his arguments. Another earnest man, who presented the case for the Roman Catholic Church, sent old Father Burchard and other Jesuits after me. Every conversation at Mr. Nixon's pointed some question, academic or scientific, and pointed them so sharp that they drove me to college with an intense desire to know. And as for communism or the Catholic Church, I was so torn that I could not answer myself. The Jesuits dropped me and so did Owen, in disgust, when I said I was going to wait for my answer till I had heard what the professors had to say and had learned what my university had to teach me upon the questions underlying the questions Oxford and Cambridge and Rome quarreled over and could not agree on. Berkeley would know.

There were no moot questions in Berkeley. There was work to do, knowledge and training to get, but not to answer questions. I found myself engaged, as my classmates were, in choosing courses. The choice was limited and, within the limits, had to be determined by the degree we were candidates for. My questions were philosophical, but I could not take philosophy, which fascinated me, till I had gone through a lot of higher mathematics which did not interest me at all. If I had been allowed to take philosophy, and so discovered the need and the relation of mathematics, I would have got the philosophy and I might have got the mathematics which I miss now more than I do the Hegelian metaphysics taught at Berkeley. Or, if the professor who put me off had taken the pains to show me the bearing of mathematical thought on theoretical logic, I would have undertaken the preparation intelligently. But no one ever developed for me the relation of any of my required subjects to those that attracted me; no one brought out for me the relation of anything I was studying to anything else, except, of course, to that wretched degree. Knowledge was absolute, not relative, and it was stored in compartments, categorical and independent. The relation of knowledge to life, even to student life, was ignored, and as for questions, the professors asked them, not the students; and the students, not the teachers, answered them—in examinations.

The unknown is the province of the student; it is the field for his life's adventure, and it is a wide field full of beckonings. Curiosity about it would drive a boy as well as a child to work through the known to get at the unknown. But it was not assumed that we had any curiosity or the potential love of skill, scholarship, and achievement or research. And so far as I can remember now, the professors' attitude was right for most of the students who had no intellectual curiosity. They wanted to be told not only what they had to learn, but what they had to want to learn—for the purpose of passing. That came out in the considerations which decided the choice among optional courses. Students selected subjects or teachers for a balance of easy and hard, to fit into their time and yet "get through." I was the only rebel of my kind, I think. The nearest to me in sympathy were the fellows who knew what they wanted to be: engineers, chemists, professional men, or statesmen. They grunted at some of the work required of them, studies that seemed useless to their future careers. They did not understand me very well, nor I them, because I preferred those very subjects which they called useless, highbrow, cultural. I did not tell them so; I did not realize it myself definitely; but I think now that I had had as a boy an exhausting experience of *being* something great. I did not want now to be but rather to know things.

And what I wanted to know was buried deep under all this "college stuff" which was called "shop." It had nothing to do with what really interested us in common. Having chosen our work and begun to do it as a duty, we turned to the socially important question: which fraternity to join. The upper classmen tried to force our answers. They laid aside their superiority to "rush" those of us whose antecedents were known and creditable. It was all snobbish, secret, and exclusive. I joined a fraternity out of curiosity: What were the secrets and the mystic rites? I went blindfold through the silly initiation to find that there were no secrets and no mysteries, only pretensions and bunk, which so disgusted me that I would not live at the clubhouse, preferring for a year the open doors of a boarding-house. The next great university question was as to athletics. My ex-athletes from Oxford and Cambridge, with their lung and other troubles, warned me; but it was a mistake that saved me. I went with the other freshmen to the campus to be tried out for football, baseball, running, jumping, etc. Caught by the college and class spirit, I hoped to give promise of some excellence. Baseball was impossible for me; I had been riding horses when the other boys were preparing for college on the diamond. I had learned to run at the military academy and in the first freshman tests I did one hundred yards enough under eleven seconds to be turned over to an athletic upper classman for instruction. Pointing up to Grizzly Peak, a high hill back of the college, he said: "All you need is wind and muscle. Climb that mountain every day for a year; then come back and we'll see."

I did not climb Grizzly Peak every day, but I went up so often that I was soon able to run up and back without a halt. At the end of the year I ran around the cinder track so long that my student instructor wearied of watching me, but, of course, I could not do a hundred yards much under twelve seconds. Muscle and wind I had, but all my physical reactions were so slow that I was of no social use in college athletics. I was out of the crowd as I had been as a boy.

I shone only in the military department. The commandant, a U.S. Army officer, seeing that I had had previous training, told me off to drill the awkward squad of my class, and when I had made of them the best-drilled company in college, he gave me the next freshman class to drill. In the following years I was always drill-master of the freshmen and finally commanded the whole cadet corps. Thus I led my class in the most unpopular and meaningless of undergraduate activities. I despised it myself, prizing it only for the chances it gave me to swank and, once a week, to lord it over my fellow students, who nicknamed me the "D.S."—damn stinker.

My nickname was won, not only as a disciplinarian, however; I rarely punished any one; I never abused my command. I could persuade the freshmen to drill by arguing that, since it was compulsory, they could have more fun doing it well than badly; and that it was the one exercise in which they could beat and shame the upper classmen whose carelessness was as affected as their superiority. That is to say, I engaged their enthusiasm. All other student enthusiasms, athletics, class and college politics, fashions, and traditions I laughed at and damped. I was a spoilsport. I was mean, as a horse is mean, because I was unhappy myself. I could be enthusiastic in a conversation about something we were learning, if it wasn't too cut and dried; we had such talks now and then at the clubhouse in my later years. But generally speaking we were discussing the news or some prank of our own.

One night, for example, we sallied forth to steal some chickens from Dr. Bonte, the popular treasurer of the university. I crawled into the coop and selected the chickens, wrung their necks, and passed them out with comments to the other fellows who held the bag.

"Here," I said, "is the rooster, Dr. Bonte himself; he's tough, but good enough for the freshmen. Next is a nice fat hen, old Mrs. Bonte. This one's a pullet, Miss Bonte," and so on, naming each of the Bonte girls, till we were interrupted.

There was a sound from the house, the lights flashed in the windows, and—some one was coming. The other fellows ran, and I—when I tore myself out—I ran too. Which was all right enough. But when I caught up with the other thieves I learned that they had left the sack of chickens behind! Our Sunday dinner was spoiled, we thought, but no: the next day the whole fraternity was invited to dinner at Dr. Bonte's on Sunday. We accepted with some suspicion, we went in some embarrassment, but we were well received and soon put at our ease by Dr. Bonte, who explained that some thieves had been frightened while robbing his roost. "They were not students, I take it," he said. "Students are not so easily frightened; they might have run away; but students would have taken the bag of chickens with them. I think they were niggers or Chinamen."

So seated hospitably at table we watched with deep interest the great platter of roasted chickens borne in and set down before Dr. Bonte, who rose, whetted his carving-knife, and turning first to me, said: "Well, Steffens, what will you have, a piece of this old cock, Dr. Bonte? Or is he too tough for any but a freshman? Perhaps you would prefer the old hen, Mrs. Bonte, or, say, one of the Bonte girls."

I couldn't speak. No one could; and no one laughed, least of all Dr. Bonte, who stood there, his knife and fork in the air, looking at me, at the others, and back at me. He wanted an answer; I must make my choice, but I saw a gleam of malicious humor in his eye; so I recovered and I chose the prettiest of the girls, pointing to the tenderest of the pullets. Dr. Bonte laughed, gave me my choice, and we had a jolly, ample dinner.

We talked about that, we and the students generally and the faculty—we discussed that incident long enough and hard enough to have solved it, if it had been a metaphysical problem. We might have threshed out the psychology of thieves, or gamblers, but no. We liked to steal, but we didn't care to think about it, not as stealing. And some of us gambled. We had to get money for theaters, operas, and other expenses in the city. I had only my board, lodging, and clothes paid for by my father, and others had not even that. We played cards, therefore, among ourselves, poker and whist, so that a lucky few got each month about all the money all of the other hard-ups had, and so had all the fun. We played long, late, and hard, and for money, not sport. The strain was too great.

One night my roommate, sunk low in his chair, felt a light kick on one of his extended legs; a second later there were two kicks against his other leg. Keeping still and watching the hands shown down, he soon had the signal system of two men playing partners, the better hand staying in the game. We said nothing but, watching, saw that others cheated, too. We knew well an old professional gambler from the mining-camps who was then in San Francisco. We told him all about it.

"Sure," he said, "cheating will sneak into any game that's played long enough. That's why you boys oughtn't to gamble. But if you do, play the game that's played. Cards is like horse-racing. I never bet a cent except I know, and know how, the game is crooked."

Having advised against it, he took us around to the gambling-houses and the race course and showed us many of the tricks of his trade, how to spot and profit by them—if we must play. "Now you won't need never to be suckers," he said. "And ye needn't be crooks either," he added after a pause. But we had it in for our opponents. We learned several ways to cheat; we practiced them till we were cool and sure. After that our "luck" was phenomenal. We had money, more than we needed. In my last two years at the university I had a salary as military instructor at a preparatory school in the town, and my roommate, the adopted son of a rich gold-miner, had a generous allowance. But we went on playing and cheating at cards for the excitement of it, we said, but really it was for the money. And afterward, when I was a student in Germany, I played on, fair, but hard—and for money I did not need, till one night at the Café Bauer in Berlin, sitting in a poker game that had been running all night, an American who had long been playing in hard luck, lost a large amount, of which I carried away more than my share. The next day we read in the papers that when he got home he had shot himself. I have never gambled since—at cards.

XVII

I BECOME A STUDENT

I T IS possible to get an education at a university. It has been done; not often, but the fact that a proportion, however small, of college students do get a start in interested, methodical study, proves my thesis, and the two personal experiences I have to offer illustrate it and show how to circumvent the faculty, the other students, and the whole college system of mind-fixing. My method might lose a boy his degree, but a degree is not worth so much as the capacity and the drive to learn, and the undergraduate desire for an empty baccalaureate is one of the holds the educational system has on students. Wise students some day will refuse to take degrees, as the best men (in England, for instance) give, but do not themselves accept, titles.

My method was hit on by accident and some instinct. I specialized. With several courses prescribed, I concentrated on the one or two that interested me most, and letting the others go, I worked intensively on my favorites. In my first two years, for example, I worked at English and political economy and read philosophy. At the beginning of my junior year I had several cinches in history. Now I liked history; I had neglected it partly because I rebelled at the way it was taught, as positive knowledge unrelated to politics, art, life, or anything else. The professors gave us chapters out of a few books to read, con, and be quizzed on. Blessed as I was with a "bad memory," I could not commit to it anything that I did not understand and intellectually need. The bare record of the story of man, with names, dates, and irrelative events, bored me. But I had discovered in my readings of literature, philosophy, and political economy that history had light to throw upon unhistorical questions. So I proposed in my junior and senior years to specialize in history, taking all the courses required

124

and those also that I had flunked in. With this in mind I listened attentively to the first introductory talk of Professor William Cary Jones on American constitutional history. He was a dull lecturer, but I noticed that, after telling us what pages of what books we must be prepared in, he mumbled off some other references "for those that may care to dig deeper."

When the rest of the class rushed out into the sunshine, I went up to the professor and, to his surprise, asked for this memorandum. He gave it me. Up in the library I ran through the required chapters in the two different books, and they differed on several points. Turning to the other authorities, I saw that they disagreed on the same facts and also on others. The librarian, appealed to, helped me search the book-shelves till the library closed, and then I called on Professor Jones for more references. He was astonished, invited me in, and began to approve my industry, which astonished me. I was not trying to be a good boy; I was better than that: I was a curious boy. He lent me a couple of his books, and I went off to my club to read them. They only deepened the mystery, clearing up the historical question, but leaving the answer to be dug for and written.

The historians did not know! History was not a science, but a field for research, a field for me, for any young man, to explore, to make discoveries in and write a scientific report about. I was fascinated. As I went on from chapter to chapter, day after day, finding frequently essential differences of opinion and of fact, I saw more and more work to do. In this course, American constitutional history, I hunted far enough to suspect that the Fathers of the Republic who wrote our sacred Constitution of the United States not only did not, but did not want to, establish a democratic government, and I dreamed for a while—as I used as a child to play I was Napoleon or a trapper—I promised myself to write a true history of the making of the American Constitution. I did not do it; that chapter has been done or well begun since by two men: Smith of the University of Washington and Beard (then) of Columbia (afterward forced out, perhaps for this very work). I found other events, men, and epochs waiting for students. In all my other courses, in ancient, in European, and in modern history, the disagreeing authorities carried me back to the need of a fresh search for (or of) the original documents or other clinching testimony. Of course I did well in my classes. The history professors soon knew me as a student and seldom put a question to me except when the class had flunked it. Then Professor Jones would say, "Well, Steffens, tell them about it."

Fine. But vanity wasn't my ruling passion then. What I had was a quickening sense that I was learning a method of studying history and that every chapter of it, from the beginning of the world to the end, is crying out to be rewritten. There was something for Youth to do; these superior old men had not done anything, finally.

Years afterward I came out of the graft prosecution office in San Francisco with Rudolph Spreckels, the banker and backer of the investigation. We were to go somewhere, quick, in his car, and we couldn't. The chauffeur was trying to repair something wrong. Mr. Spreckels smiled; he looked closely at the defective part, and to my silent, wondering inquiry he answered: "Always, when I see something badly done or not done at all, I see an opportunity to make a fortune. I never kick at bad work by my class: there's lots of it and we suffer from it. But our failures and neglects are chances for the young fellows coming along and looking for work."

Nothing is done. Everything in the world remains to be done or done over. "The greatest picture is not yet painted, the greatest play isn't written (not even by Shakespeare), the greatest poem is unsung. There isn't in all the world a perfect railroad, nor a good government, nor a sound law." Physics, mathematics, and especially the most advanced and exact of the sciences, are being fundamentally revised. Chemistry is just becoming a science; psychology, economics, and sociology are awaiting a Darwin, whose work in turn is awaiting an Einstein. If the rah-rah boys in our colleges could be told this, they might not all be such specialists in football, petting parties, and unearned degrees. They are not told it, however; they are told to learn what is known. This is nothing, philosophically speaking.

Somehow or other in my later years at Berkeley, two professors, Moses and Howison, representing opposite schools of thought, got into a controversy, probably about their classes. They brought together in the house of one of them a few of their picked students, with the evident intention of letting us show in conversation how much or how little we had understood of their respective teachings. I don't remember just what the subject was that they threw into the ring, but we wrestled with it till the professors could stand it no longer. Then they broke in, and while we sat silent and highly entertained, they went at each other hard and fast and long. It was after midnight when, the debate over, we went home. I asked the other fellows what they had got out of it, and their answers showed that they had seen nothing but a fine, fair fight. When I laughed, they asked me what I, the D.S., had seen that was so much more profound.

I said that I had seen two highly-trained, well-educated Masters of Arts and Doctors of Philosophy disagreeing upon every essential point of thought and knowledge. They had all there was of the sciences; and yet they could not find any knowledge upon which they could base an acceptable conclusion. They had no test of knowledge; they didn't know what is and what is not. And they have no test of right and wrong; they have no basis for even an ethics.

Well, and what of it? They asked me that, and that I did not answer. I was stunned by the discovery that it was philosophically true, in a most literal sense, that nothing is known; that it is precisely the foundation that is lacking for science; that all we call knowledge rested upon assumptions which the scientists did not all accept; and that, likewise, there is no scientific reason for saying, for example, that stealing is wrong. In brief: there was no scientific basis for an ethics. No wonder men said one thing and did another; no wonder they could settle nothing either in life or in the academies.

I could hardly believe this. Maybe these professors, whom I greatly respected, did not know it all. I read the books over again with a fresh eye, with a real interest, and I could see that, as in history, so in other branches of knowledge, everything was in the air. And I was glad of it. Rebel though I was, I had got the religion of scholarship and science; I was in awe of the authorities in the academic world. It was a release to feel my worship cool and pass. But I could not be sure. I must go elsewhere, see and hear other professors, men these California professors quoted and looked up to as their high priests. I decided to go as a student to

Europe when I was through Berkeley, and I would start with the German universities.

My father listened to my plan, and he was disappointed. He had hoped I would succeed him in his business; it was for that that he was staying in it. When I said that, whatever I might do, I would never go into business, he said, rather sadly, that he would sell out his interest and retire. And he did soon after our talk. But he wanted me to stay home and, to keep me, offered to

OUR HOUSE IN SACRAMENTO
Now the Governor's Mansion

buy an interest in a certain San Francisco daily paper. He had evidently had this in mind for some time. I had always done some writing, verse at the poetical age of puberty, then a novel which my mother alone treasured. Journalism was the business for a boy who liked to write, he thought, and he said I had often spoken of a newspaper as my ambition. No doubt I had in the intervals between my campaigns as Napoleon. But no more. I was now going to be a scientist, a philosopher. He sighed; he thought it over, and with the approval of my mother, who was for every sort of education, he gave his consent.

XVIII

BERLIN: PHILOSOPHY AND MUSIC

ERMANY meant art and music to me as well as philosophy
and science. Ever since the day I had watched as a boy the
painter, Mr. Marple, sketch his sunset over the brush of the
American River bottom and heard what he said about art, I had
wanted to understand and feel painting. I had taken lessons in
drawing while at school; at college there was no art in the cur-
riculum, but in my senior year, when I had the direction of outside lectures, I persuaded a well-known painter to come to Berkeley and tell us all about art. He had never lectured before; he
probably has never lectured since. He went up on the platform,
set up a black and white copy of Millet's "Sower," and I think
he thought that he could put into words what his hand could
say with lines and colors. He couldn't; he said a few words,
and his amazement at his own helplessness was a sight to
see.

"Art," he began, "painting—painting is— It isn't pictures, you
know. It's—well, now, take 'The Sower' there." He looked at it
and began waving his right hand. He looked at us, then at the
picture, and then appealingly back at the audience, swinging his
hand as if he were drawing a line. "That isn't a sower," he blurted,
"nor a picture. It's a—don't you see—it's a line."

And, sure enough, it was a line. It was the same line he was
drawing in the air with his eloquent hand; a big, sweeping, speaking, beautiful line. I saw it; I saw one key to the understanding
of art. Paintings were not pictures only; they were, among other
things, beautiful lines detected in nature and drawn so that all
who will can see them.

The painter thought he had said nothing, and he could not go
on. With one more wild dumb look at us and another at the Millet,

he uttered a cry of despair and came down off the platform amid the shouts of student laughter.

Walking with the humiliated man to the station, I tried to tell him that he had said something to me; and I repeated in my own words what I thought it was.

"That's it," he said. "I didn't know I had said it, but you've got it. And I'll tell you how to go on and get the rest.

"You are going abroad," he said. "You will visit the art galleries, the cathedrals—everything that is beautiful. You will be tempted to read the guidebooks and other books about the arts. Look out. They can keep you from getting art. They will tell you which are the best things, and if you believe them, you will know what is called best, the best to them, but you won't know what is best to you. You won't feel art. You may become a scholar in it, you will never be a judge of art; you'll have no taste.

"My advice is to go without a guide into the galleries, often; walk along slowly, stopping to look only at those things which interest you. I am sure you will choose the wrong things, probably pictures—pictures that a writing man can describe, and describe better than the painter has painted them. No matter. You like what you like. If they are no good as art you'll tire of them; they will end by making you sick, and you'll choose better things, and better and better till finally you like the things that are best to you. You may not have perfect taste; there is no perfect taste; but you'll have taste and it will be yours, not somebody else's, but your very own; and you may not be able to lecture on it any better than I can, but you will have a feel for the painter's art, which is a fine art."

When I arrived in Berlin in the summer of 1889, I walked the galleries in just this way. There was little else to do. The university, the opera, and the theaters being closed, I loafed about the cafés, music halls, took walks in the Thiergarten and around the city. But every forenoon I put in an hour or two walking through the galleries, without a book, looking at the pictures that stopped me, and some of what my painter had predicted came true. In those few months my taste changed; I came to dislike pictures that I had liked at first; I could see and enjoy lines, designs, and even forms, while color combinations came to have as much meaning for me as a chord of music. It was work, however; a gallery is like a library. I was trying to read all the books at once.

In the fall, I was glad of a new interest: music. Hegel and his philosophy of art had threaded the arts upon an historical chain, given them a definite and a general significance, each and all. His was an intellectual key to music. But I applied to this art also the painter's key to painting. Going to the first operas offered, I took the score, and sitting on the dimly lighted stairway back of the topmost gallery, I followed the music as music and knew it well before I allowed myself to sit in a seat and see the stage and hear the words. This method of practicing the hearing of the music alone first I kept up all winter, and my reward was a growing preference for fine concert music over all but a few favorite operas.

There were pictures in music too, and also there were lines and tones, color and composition: business and art!

The university opened when the theaters did, and I was eager and ready to start. I had a small room in the Artillerie Strasse back of the university, and there I had been exercising my college German on the landlady and her son and reading up on my courses, choosing my professors, etc. Ethics was my subject, but I was not intending to study it directly. I would hear and read the men who taught it. I must know what they knew or thought or believed, but I had learned enough of their doctrines to feel pretty sure that they were not scientific; they did not have what I sought; a basis, probably in some other science, for a science of behavior. I was to start, therefore, with pure philosophy and ethics; metaphysics would be my main *Fach*, but all I wanted of it was a lead into other sciences.

Scientists were already discovering that the old, classical categories of knowledge were a hindrance. Physicists were forced into chemistry and back through mathematics to physics. But the German universities, like Berkeley, like all universities, were organized as they still are, not for inquiry and research into the unknown but for the learning (and teaching) of the known. They are scholarly, not scientific, and if I were to take a degree I must choose my categories and stick to them. I had no thought of, I had nothing but scorn for, degrees, but when I appeared for matriculation, I had to pretend to a candidacy; so I announced myself out for a

Ph.D., with philosophy for my major subject, art history and economics for seconds.

The procedure of matriculation had one surprise for me. When I presented my precious papers at the Secretariat, the clerks took my passport, but they looked askance at my bachelor's diploma.

"What's that?" asked one of them, and I told him.

"Oh, an American Doktorat!" he said. "It's worthless here. All we require is the passport," and he scribbled off the data he needed from it, gave me a form to fill out and my receipts for fees paid, and said he would deliver later my certificate of matriculation, an enormous calfskin Latin document.

He despised my degree as much as I did his, and I was hurt, with cause. I had worked, sacrificed my interests—I had cheated for that worthless baccalaureate. My cheating had been open at Berkeley. I had said that I would not half study the subjects that did not interest me and that, since they were required for a degree, which I (thought I) had to have to continue my studies abroad, I would cram for and sneak through the examinations in them. One professor, Colonel Edwards, who heard what I had threatened to do, sent for me and asked me how I could justify such conduct. I told him. His subject was conic sections. I said I did not want to know it, couldn't make head or tail of it myself, and that he, as a teacher, had failed to show me what it was all about. "It's just one of the many things," I said, "in which I find I have to submit to force; so I'll pretend to conform, but I won't really."

Pondering a moment, he asked me if I could prove any propositions. "Yes," I said, "some seven or eight. I know them by heart."

"All right," he said. "I don't want you to cheat; I won't let you cheat. I'll give you a private examination right now. You do two out of three propositions and I'll give you a pass."

Going to the blackboard, he wrote up one. "Can you do that?" I said I could. He wrote another. "That too?"

"No," I said, and he wrote another that I did not know.

"We'll make it three out of five," he suggested, and he wrote up one more and looked at me. I laughed and nodded; I could do it, and slowly he chose the fifth, which I knew. I wrote them out in a few minutes, handed them in, and—he passed me, after a long and very serious lecture on ethics, which I told him was to be my specialty. I was going to Germany on purpose to find out if there was any moral reason for or against cheating in cards, in politics, or in conic sections—"either by the student or the professor," I added.

And it was all in vain. I had been graduated (at the bottom of my class) at this cost, and I did not have to pass at all; I did not have to be a philosophic bachelor; all I had to have to enter the German and the French universities was my American citizenship, which I was born with. And so it was after I had entered. I did not have to work; no one knew or cared whether I heard my lectures or played my time away. There was the university, with its lectures, laboratories, professors, and workers. You could take all or nothing. I was free to study what and when and as my interest dictated, and the result was that I worked hard. I read everything, heard everybody, in my courses and in others. Whenever the students spoke well of a man who had anything to say on any subject, I took some of his lectures, but I held to my own trail of research for an ethics that was not merely a rationalization of folkways and passing laws, forms, and customs; taking for pleasure only music, lots of music, and staged literature, except a few weeks of nights at the poker table in the back room of the Café Bauer.

XIX

HEIDELBERG: THERE IS NO ETHICS

Wᴵᴛʜ the Black Forest behind it and the Neckar River running through it to the Rhine, Heidelberg is a place of temptation and pleasure, and this wise old university was no spoilsport. All the lectures were on the four working days of the week, Tuesday, Wednesday, Thursday, and Friday, leaving the week-end long and clear for play. Many students go there for fun. I met an American corps student who had been fighting and drinking and idling so long there that he could hardly rally his English to talk with me.

"I must quit this, go to some other university and work," he said when we parted. I had reminded him of some old drowned purpose.

I went to Heidelberg to hear Kuno Fischer, the most eloquent if not the most apostolic of the professors of Hegel's philosophy, and I studied hard with him. Other subjects also I took, continuing my Berlin courses in art history and economics. My semester at Heidelberg was a fruitful season, but it bore flowers too. I made some friends there, and together we had all the fun that was going, in the town, on the river, in the Forest—beer-drinking, dancing, swimming and boating, walking, talking, and exploring the world and one another.

My room was up on the *Anlage*, just above the city park in a little house kept by a Viennese woman who in turn was kept by a local merchant. Her gay days were over; she was a good old mother to her two children and altogether contended with her condition of dependence upon the honor of the gentleman who had "married a lady" and was devoted to her, his proper wife. He only paid, but he paid regularly for his past sins. His old mistress did not regret hers; she loved to talk about them. She took me in as her one lodger to make a little extra money out of the front room, which her small family did not need. An expressive woman with a common story, lived and seen from her Viennese point of view, she served lively entertainment and some light upon ethics with all the meals that I took in my room. These were not many.

Kuno Fischer gave his first lecture, logic, at seven o'clock in the morning; no time for more than a hot cup of coffee at home with a piece of bread, which I finished often as I finished dressing on the way down to the university. Other students also showed signs of haste at 7:15, when, on the dot, the professor began his lecture with a smile for the breathless state of his hearers and the imperfect arrangement of collars and ties. I saw some fellows in slippers, pajamas, and overcoats, looking up with admiration at the professor, neat, composed, and logical. And eloquent; I missed taking many a note to sit and listen to Kuno Fischer's poetical prose. Few Germans can either speak or write German—well. Their language is too rich, variable, and unripe for them. Only the masters can master it, and Kuno Fischer, handsome and intelligent, was a master of German as he was of his own thinking in it. I asked him once how it came that he spoke German so well.

He had a habit which I had of going from his first lecture to the river for a swim. Sometimes we walked together down to the floating bath-house, and many a pleasant talk we had on the way. He chatted as he lectured, in short, clear, incisive sentences, and he liked it that I liked his style. It was by way of a jesting compliment that I put to him my question: "Herr Geheimrat, wie kommt es dass Sie so schön deutsch sprechen?"

"It's because I speak English," he answered in English, and, laughing, he reminded me that Goethe, asked once the same question, replied that his best German was written in the period when he was soaking in French.

After the swim I had breakfast in some café or beer hall, where I completed my notes; then more lectures till one o'clock. The noon meal was usually with some crowd of students in a restaurant, under the stiff forms of the student ritual, the gossip, the controversies, the plans for excursions or fights. Once a week I had an art history course which took us up to the castle to examine the stones and trace their periods, or off to the excavations near by, as far as Wiesbaden. Other days there were other lectures or library work or home study till along about four, when I went forth either to the Schloss or to some other café for coffee or to the river for a paddle. The boatman had several canoes, "left by the English," he said.

Just above the bridge the river is artificially narrowed and deepened, making a rapid, called the Hart Teufel, for about an eighth of a mile, and it's a struggle to paddle up it. I used to do it for exercise and then drive the little craft on up the easy, broad river to some one of the many garden restaurants along shore. After a bath out in the stream, I had an appetite which made the good cooking seem perfect, and a thirst which took beer as the Hart Teufel took water. There was always some other loose student to join for a long, slow supper and a long, highbrow conversation. When the darkness fell, there was the canoe to lie in and the river to float me effortlessly back to town. I could philosophize in the dark; if there was a moon I could romance. Pleasant days, those lonely Heidelberg days. Pleasanter still the friendly days that followed.

Once, when the art history professor had his class out for field work on some ruin or other, a tall young German came up to me, struck his heels together, saluted stiffly, and said: "My name is Johann Friedrich Krudewolf. I am a German; I take you for an American. I want to learn English. I propose to exchange with you lessons in German for lessons in English."

I closed the foolish bargain, and we shook hands on it. There was one lesson in English, one in German, and no more. I did not have to study German; I was learning it fast enough by absorption, and I think now that while he did want to learn English, he was really seeking a friend. Anyhow we became so interested in each other that the conversation, even at the first and last lesson, ran away from the purpose and, of course, ran into the language easiest for both of us to understand. Bad as my German was then, it was so much better than his school English that we always spoke German and soon forgot lessons. His specialty was art history, and I was glad of that; Hegel's history of art gave a philosophic meaning to the subject, and my new friend's interest in the details filled in beautifully my efforts to feel art both in itself and as a border of flowers along the course of our civilization.

Our excursions with the class to churches, castles, and ruins were pleasant recreations for me, so pleasant that we made study trips by ourselves for fun. We foot-toured the Black Forest three days at a time, always to see things Krudewolf wished to examine for art history reasons, but his notes told by the way and the ruined castles illustrated vividly the history of the rise of great German families from robbers to robber knights, to military and social power, to riches, position, and honors. That was the way it was done of old, and I made notes on morals as studiously as my companion did on art.

The best excursion we made, however, was for its own sake. The Neckar River was navigable up to Heilbron, and a curious kind of boat-train operated on it, the *Schlepper*. There was a cable laid in the middle of the stream. The power boat picked up this cable, pulled itself up on it, and passed it out over the stern. By this means the tuglike *Schlepper* schlepped a string of cargo boats up the Neckar to Heilbron and back down to the Rhine. Johann hired a rowboat and sent it on the *Schlepper* up to Heilbron, whither we went by train to meet it. A day and a night in funny old Heilbron, with its old, old stories, and we set out in the rowboat to row (or float) home to Heidelberg. We started early one morning, meaning to go far that day, but by ten o'clock we were passing such tempting restaurants in river gardens that we yielded, stopped and had breakfast, which we thought would do for lunch, too. But we could not pass by the resorts that called to us; we had to see some of them. We chose one for luncheon, a long luncheon, and when we embarked again, chose others here, there, everywhere for beer, coffee, or—something. We could not row; it was a waste, and—even drifting was too fast.

The Neckar, from Heilbron to Heidelberg, is one of the most beautiful stretches of country that I have ever seen—or it seemed so to me then. We stayed our first night at a village inn on the river bank, and while we dined made two important discoveries. This was a *Shaumwein* (champagne) country, with the "fizz" at seventy-five cents the bottle; and this season was a church festival at which everybody drank, danced, and made love. We danced till midnight that night and then took some peasant girls out rowing in our boat. We got away late the next morning and were stopped everywhere by pretty places for coffee or wine or meals or historical sights that Johann had to investigate. We didn't make five miles the second day. That night we danced—every night we danced, and we began to get away later and later in the mornings. We were ten days making a distance that one might have rowed in three or four, and then felt and wondered that we had done so beautiful a journey so fast. And I wonder now that I have never gone back, as I declared and have always been sure that I would "some day," to do the Neckar over again in a rowboat slowly—two or three weeks of it.

Toward the end of the semester a friend of mine, Carlos J. Hittell, came over from Munich to visit me. He was an art student from California. I had known well his brother Franklin at Berkeley; his father, Theodore H. Hittell, the historian, had had more to do with my education than many a teacher. A retired attorney, he had turned to the writing of history, especially of California. He used to work on the dining-room table after dinner while I, his children and their friends, talked as youth will, finally and positively, of all sorts of things. Once he kept me when the others left, and he went into my mind and broke all the idols he found there. He was rough.

"You can't learn if you know everything already," he said. "You can't have a free mind if it's full of superstitions." And he whanged away. I took it pretty well, and because I came back for more, he continued to destroy my images. Every time I went to the house, whether to dinner, to call on his daughter, Catherine, or to sing songs with his sons, he lay for me and drew me into talk and some reading in his good library. A great service this fine old man rendered me. And his son, Carlos, did me another.

When Carlos joined me at Heidelberg, he completed our trio, one student of art history, one of ethics and philosophy, and one of the real thing, art. We played, walking, rowing, swimming, and touring, but also we talked, and the artist, without knowing or meaning it, spoke as one having authority. Johann and I listened to the man who was doing what we were merely reading and thinking about. We saw what the artist had told me at Berkeley, that we were getting scholarship about art, not art. But, like that other artist, Carlos Hittell could not express in our medium, words, what he was doing or trying to do when he was painting. We must go and be with art students when they were at work in their studios and see if we could—not hear, but see what art is. When the semester was over, therefore, we all went to Munich to study art instead of art history. No more Heidelberg for either of us.

And no more philosophy for me. There was no ethics in it. I had gone through Hegel with Kuno Fischer, hoping to find a basis for an ethics; and the professor thought he had one. I had been reading in the original the other philosophers whom I had read also in Berkeley, and they, too, thought they had it all settled. They did not have anything settled. Like the disputing professors at Berkeley, they could not agree upon what was knowledge, nor upon what was good and what evil, nor why. The philosophers were all prophets, their philosophies beliefs, their logic a justification of their—religions. And as for their ethics, it was without foundation. The only reasons they had to give for not lying or stealing were not so reasonable as the stupidest English gentleman's: "It isn't done."

This was my reluctant, disappointed conclusion, arrived at after a waste of a couple of good years of conscientious work. I must leave the philosophers and go to the scientists for my science of ethics as I must go to the artists for art. I said good-by to the good kept woman who had kept me so comfortable. She accepted my departure as she accepted everything.

"Men come and men go," she said cheerfully.

"Always?" I asked.

"They don't always come," she laughed, "but always they go, always."

"And that's all there is of it?"

"All? Nay," she protested, pointing to her two. "For me there are always the children, thank God."

MUNICH: THERE ARE NO ARTISTS

A PLAIN old third- or fourth-class café and beer restaurant called the Blüthe was the blooming center of the art-student life of München in my day (the summer of 1890). That is where the Americans I knew and some Germans dropped in when they had nothing else to do. Some of them took their meals there at one long table, which, when cleared of an evening, became the gathering-board for others who dropped in for coffee or later for a drink after the theater. It was around that board that I first heard artists themselves tear to pieces the everlasting question: "Well, and what is art anyhow?"

And if I did not get the answer, it may be in part because at that time there were no artists in Munich, not really. There were men there whose names are now well known and whose pictures are bought and sold as the works of great painters. It's all a mistake. They told me themselves that none of them was an artist. And my German friend, Johann Friedrich Krudewolf, heard the same thing from the German masters and students he met.

We parted, Johann and I, when we arrived together in Munich. He was going to study at the university there; I was going to Leipzig. We might have played around together all summer; our purposes were the same, but I did not think to suggest that. I took a room in the house where Carlos Hittell lived, met his friends, mostly Americans, and when Johann saw that I was among my own, he said he would go off among his countrymen. He looked wistful, I remembered afterward, but he said "Goodby," and I thought he was long and sentimental about it; so I was short and, as he reminded me later, American.

Carlos Hittell wanted to work; so he took me to the Blüthe, introduced me to the crowd there, and I found a fellow who had time to waste talking about art. And he could talk art, too. He showed me through the Pinakothek to illustrate his ideas, and he spoke with inside understanding and authority of the artists represented there. These were very few. Not all of the old masters in that gallery were masters, and of the modern painters there was but one who could paint: Lenbach; and even Lenbach, as you can see, Lenbach himself gave up art for portraiture, for fame and success. I betrayed some interest in the pictures of other men of whom I had heard; he showed me them, he showed me with his cutting thumb and his curling lips and his sneering eyes that, excepting only Lenbach, the other moderns were either merchants and manufacturers or, at best, struggling, unsuccessful students of the art of painting which remains to be revived by—some one.

"Any of the Americans likely to revive the art?" I asked hopefully.

He laughed himself into a knot. He'd show me. We went calling at all the studios of all the students he knew. Fine fellows, hard at work, they stopped to pull out their canvases one by one. It was pathetic or ridiculous. They looked so hungry, some of them, for a bit of appreciation, their eyes darting from their poor pictures to my poor face. I rather liked some of the "sketches" I saw, and I certainly would have said so, had my guide not warned me.

"Look out, now," he would say, as we climbed the stairs to a studio, "this poor devil is sensitive; he thinks he can paint. And he can draw, a little. But paint? Never. You'll see. But don't— don't hurt his feelings by saying what you think."

Or he would laugh before another door: "This chap, he thinks he's a genius. He is sure he can paint. But I'll tell you how he does it. His fad is Defregger. He goes out around the villages, looking for Defregger peasants in Defregger costumes and Defregger groupings. If he finds a Defregger picture, he paints it as Defregger painted it; only—nobody but himself can see the likeness. But he never does find a Defregger in real life; neither did Defregger; of course not; so the student does what his master did: he hires models off the city streets, dresses 'em up, poses 'em, and paints them as Defregger has shown they ought to be. And he sells his things. That's the trouble with art today. Some of these house painters can sell their stuff—to Americans, generally; but they sell it. They live."

And sure enough, this student of Defregger was painting when we went into his studio a Defregger-like group of Tyrolese peasants, using a saucy little wicked street girl dressed up as a peasant Madonna. She and the painter and my friend made jokes and laughed all through the work. And when my guide left me there and I turned the conversation into serious channels, this painter went off into a worship of Defregger till he became so wrought up that he quit work to take me to the gallery to see the Defreggers. He looked at nothing else; he bade me look at nobody else, not even Lenbach.

"Lenbach! Pooh!" he said. "He can paint some, but he can't see. Bring him Bismarck or the Kaiser or some prince and tell him to paint, and he'll make you a likeness, but—that man lives here and sees nothing of the life about him; nothing. I don't believe he ever looked at a peasant, and if he did, what would he see? The character, the life, the truth and beauty of the real people? Never. No. But now look at that Defregger—"

I was in despair. I could not learn to recognize a work of art unless I could see one. I had come to Munich to watch men paint and to see and feel what the painter at work was trying to do. My guide showed me in studio after studio students and painters making, not pictures—only outsiders would call such things pictures; sometimes the man painting at it spoke of it as a picture or a painting—my guide called them sketches, and he let me see and hear that the sketchers did not put their mind on what they were doing. They all talked while they worked, told jokes, laughed, poked fun at the model, flirted with her, made love. No wonder they could not be taken seriously. No wonder they were not and never would be artists; none of them, excepting my guide. We used to go often to his studio to rest, talk, and have a drink. He drank a good deal. But he never worked when I was there, and he never talked about his own things. He merely got them out, one at a time, one for each visit. He would set the picture for the day up on the easel, adjust it carefully in the light, and leave it there. "A work of art speaks for itself," he used to say. "You look at it and just let it work in." So we sat and drank, talked of other things, meanwhile letting the picture speak for itself. I did not care at first for his pictures; they were all sketches, unfinished, but it was amazing how, as he talked about painting for the imagination of the spectator who liked himself to finish what the artist only indicated—it gave one a thirst to see more and more of a line started, until between us, the painter and I, we had made a perfect picture. If I had been buying pictures, I would have bought one or two of my guide's works. As it was I was content to adore them and follow him; and he was satisfied, too. We became fast friends, but I wasn't seeing him at work; and I wanted to see a real master at work.

One night at the Blüthe some one proposed that we all go to Venice to make some sketches. I was delighted, and several voices were willing. Others opposed it, and the conversation became a debate on the subject whether Venice was the most beautiful place in the world or the filthiest, ugliest, most lied about. And the opposition won, so far as I was concerned. At least, I came away with the impression that Venice was a beastly collection of one-time palaces, now slummy tenements set down upon a network of stinking sewers navigated by intelligent rats who lived well upon the garbage dumped into the tideless, motionless drainage of a community of dirty thieves. But the wrong side won, practically. The crowd decided to go to Venice.

They got out a big butcher's book, and as they studied it I realized that its brown paper pages carried addresses, not only for Venice, but everywhere. Whenever a Blüthe student had been off sketching he noted in that book the hotels and restaurants he discovered, with prices and characterizations which were a guide for others. I often used that book. That night those men picked out of it a short list of hotels, pensions, restaurants, and cafés, which we all used in and on the way to Venice. Carlos Hittell copied out of it other addresses for Salzburg, Vienna, Trieste, and when he and I got back to his flat he proposed that we go to Venice, not with the gang direct, but around by Vienna. And so we went, pleasantly and slowly, and I remember that the butcher-book guide put us in good, cheap places all along the line, so cheap, indeed, that we made the whole round trip, all costs included, for $1.50 a day each. I could travel in Europe, as I could study, on my allowance, which was $50 a month. This gave me a sense of liberty, such as a tramp has; the whole world was open to me.

At Venice we joined the sketchers. We found there, as I had at
Heidelberg, canoes "left by Englishmen," and we paddled all
through the canals, especially the narrow back ways. Carlos and
I had good sport at Venice, and after two or three days I began to
feel the picturesque beauty of this dirty old tumbledown world-
capital. I could see it the better, I think, for having come to it with
the hopeless expectation sketched on my mind by the art students
in Munich who did not want to go there. Their description was
realistic; it served only to prepare me for the worst and so to get
the best; one should always be forewarned of the stenches, filth,
and wreckage of Venice before his first visit.

I watched the painters paint Venice, one by one, and I saw that
they saw and were pointing out the essential beauty of Venice;
and the skill, the instinctive taste, and the knowledge they put
into their work suggested that my Munich guide could not have
been altogether right: some of them were artists of some sort;
second-rate, perhaps, or third, but they had something I had not;
they could do with colors what I, for example, could not do. I
sounded them on the point, however, and each of them agreed
with my art master as to the others. "Good fellows. I like them,
but—" I wished that my guide, the only painter in Munich, were
at Venice; after watching the others at work on their "sketches,"
I would have liked to see a real painter painting—Venice.

One day I said something like this. It was the day of our departure. The train left about noon, and after breakfast and packing,
we sat around doing nothing. Carlos Hittell suggested that we
walk to the station.

"Walk!" they shouted. "You can't walk in Venice. We'd get
lost."

Carlos said that he would lead all that would follow him to the
station without a moment's hesitation at any time. How would
he do it? He said any westerner could do it. You fix in your mind
the direction of the station and you go that way, turning to be
sure, but always keeping your mental compass clear. Several of us
offered to follow him; the rest were to attend to the baggage and
report us missing in Munich.

"All right now," said Carlos to us, pointing toward the station,
far away and out of sight. "That is our direction. Come on." And
he started off at a right angle. He darted into a back street, turned

here, there, right, left, even back, but swift as an Indian he sped along till all in a whirl after twenty minutes' walk we came out upon the bridge over to the Rialto, where two fellows quit us. There was a steamboat station there; they would stay there till the crowd came. Carlos, with the rest of us, crossed the bridge, dived into the tangle of streets on the other side, and, over another bridge, came upon the station, an hour ahead of time.

How did he do it? We discussed this on the train, and no one would accept Carlos' explanation: that he had the plainsman's sense of direction. I backed him up, telling how Carlos had shot a cork out from between my thumb and finger; which was true. He was a westerner. But that did not explain his knowledge of Venetian streets, not even to me, his co-liar. He would not tell his secret till years afterward: he had observed on the corner of a building he was sketching the sign, *"Alla Strada Ferrata."* He inquired and was told that that sign marked every turn of the way to the railroad station. He knew his Latin, if not his Italian.

My staunch support of Carlos and their irritation at his feat in path-finding so aroused the wrath of the crowd that on the train they turned upon me, no longer a guest. I came back with comments on their art and, to defend my position, quoted my Munich art guide on the general principles of art.

"I wish," I said, "that he had come to Venice and painted it."

It was awful. I can't remember what they said; they all spoke at once. The judgments that stuck in my mind were that he— "He? He isn't a painter; he's a bum." "Never works, only talks art, drinks, brags, and runs down everybody else." "One of these here beginners. Never finished anything."

It was unanimous. It was convincing. My one, last, only, lonely modern painter was—dead—to me.

XXI

LEIPZIG: MUSIC, SCIENCE, LOVE

THE day before I was leaving Munich for my winter semester at Leipzig (1890-91) I interrupted my packing to go out and drink a glass of cool beer. Turning into a café, I saw a young man sitting alone with his face down on his arms folded on the table. There was something familiar about his head, and looking again, sharply, at it, I recognized my Heidelberg student friend, Johann Friedrich Krudewolf. 1 touched his shoulder. He threw up his face angrily, and there were tears in his eyes. "Nu!" I said with a push as I withdrew my hand. "*Was heisst's,* Johann?"

His anger passed, and he, tapping his chest, answered: "The doctor says I can't stay in Munich."

"Good," I said, gladly. "We will go to Leipzig then."

His face lighted up, but he wasn't sure the doctor would approve of Leipzig either. "Don't ask him," I suggested. Johann did not know whether there was any good professor of art history in Leipzig, and I didn't. But he had in his pocket the fat little paper book which gave all the courses for all the universities. We looked up Leipzig, and Johann said, "I'll go." There was a fine course in his subject. We had our beer with our planning and separated to meet on the train the next day. And there, on the train, we planned to live and study together for a year. A year of art history for both of us, and for me a year of psychology under Wundt, the leader, if not the founder, of the school of experimental psychology. I would take all his lectures and work in his laboratory, as if for a degree, and say nothing of my purpose: to see if I could find in psychology either a basis for a science of ethics or a· trail through psychology to some other science that might lead on to a scientific ethics.

146

We were early; the mob of students had not arrived, so that we had a choice of quarters. We took two connecting rooms in the Petersteinweg. The only other roomers were a working-girl who raised a living on her wages by some traffic in the business of love and a regular old street-walker who made love a business. The landlady was a lone, but not a lonely, old widow woman who envied, loved, and quarreled for fun with the girl. Johann became *Herr im Hause;* he kept order. When the row in the back room became so loud that I went out to see and enjoy it, Johann would come flying out of his room to make the peace. They came to fear him and his just wrath. Me they laughed at or with; I was the crazy American, with the queer, foreign habits. I took a bath every day, for example.

The old woman had agreed to deliver in my room every morning a large vessel of cold water, and she was astonished that I insisted upon and used it, pouring it over me as I stood in my rubber tub. She must have reported this in the neighborhood and to the *Mädel,* as we called the girl in the back room; and I infer that her report was not credited in the market-place. Anyway one morning, as I stood stripped in my tub with the water held high above my head, my door opened, and there were the old woman, half a dozen other old women, and the *Mädel,* all staring wide-eyed, open-mouthed at me, while the landlady pointed proudly, triumphantly, exclaiming:

"*Na, und was hab' ich g'sagt? Da staht er. Se'en Sie?*" ("Well, and what did I tell you? There he stands. You see?")

Johann protested. He tried to make them respect me. Even though I was a foreigner, and an American at that—queer as I was, I was a human being and not a captive animal to be shown off. It was no use. I was exhibited, with pride to be sure, but my door might be thrown open at any crisis in my life, intellectual or physical, to prove to some market man or a customer of the *Mädel* that their boasts were true. They did have a living American in the house.

The landlady told me the story of her life, often, and all her troubles, and the girl told me several versions of hers with all her passing triumphs, rights and wrongs. Some men treated her dreadfully; some men were treated dreadfully; but all were despised and loathed, except now and then one would be all right for a short while. I liked a pretty baker girl across the street; she looked like the warm rolls she sold me, but Johann took no interest in girls, and he frowned on my flirtations.

"Ah, no," he would say, "don't fool that little baker girl; she is too trustful, too easy."

He found somewhere and brought home one day Guido Peters, an Austrian student of music, who swept us into his enthusiasm and made us also students of music. Leipzig was a music center, and Guido knew everybody and everything in that distinct and devoted world. He got all the concert programs long in advance, gave us lectures on each composer and his work, illustrated. Sitting at his piano, he would pull a piece to pieces, playing it analytically and then straight through, with comments, explanations, and criticism. The weekly event was the Gewandhaus concert on Monday nights. Guido brought home the next program Tuesday, and day by day he would work with us to make us familiar with it till on Friday we all went together to the last private rehearsal to which music students were admitted; on Saturday we heard the public rehearsal; and on Monday night, we were quite ready to appreciate the finished concert. And so with all the other good music given in Leipzig that winter: we had it over and over till we knew it inside and out; harmoniously and mathematically, sensually, scientifically, and artistically.

In return for our interest in his subject, Guido Peters took some in our subjects. He heard a lecture with us now and then, went with us to the art galleries of Dresden and Berlin. He did not care much for the science and the history of art and ethics. He preferred art for art's sake, art's and love's. For he was in love; he was in love, not with any girl in Leipzig, but with many girls at home, in Austria. He wrote love-letters to his several sweethearts whom he loved—"all," he said, "equally. I pour out my whole heart to the one I am writing to, turn to the next, and I pour out my whole heart to her." And he always wanted to read us the last two or three of those letters; and he did, till I stopped him one day.

"No," I protested, "don't read it. Play it on the piano."

He looked uncomprehending a moment, then saw the point, leaped to the piano, and he played the letters. He played them all after that, and finally, by way of an experiment in applied psychology, I got him to play a letter he was full of before he wrote it. The effect astonished him. He didn't have to write it. "Nay," he exclaimed, "I can't write it now." Of course not. When he played a love-letter he was a lover in love; he poured forth his whole heart to us, and after the orgy of it, there was nothing for him or for us to do but go down to the river, take a boat, and row slowly, softly, sentimentally up the river, the pretty little river under the trees, and, in the silence of our hearts, listen to the nightingales.

A serious matter for me, these debauches. To Johann it was merely music; to Guido himself it was art and love; that's all. The Germans are sentimental idiots when drunk like that. But we Americans are a practical race. When we are moved, we are moved to action. If we get drunk, we want to break something. I broke an engagement and married.

Guido and his music and his love for his remote girls were not alone to blame for my conduct. The coming of spring at the wrong time—right after the winter—had something to do with it; and then there were Wundt's lectures and the hard scientific spirit of the experimental laboratory. "We want facts, nothing but facts," he used to declare. The laboratory where we sought the facts and measured them by machinery was a graveyard where the old idealism walked as a dreadful ghost and philosophical thinking was a sin. One day when the good old professor was looking over us and our works, his one seeing eye fell upon William James's great book on psychology, just out. Wundt had almost blinded himself by the abuse of his eyes in experimentation; he had but one tiny spot in one retina that could see. He picked up James, fixed his one spot on the first page, and beginning at once to read, started off like a somnambulist for the door.

Then he remembered, turned, and asked my indulgence. "*Sie erlauben?*" When I "allowed," he went on reading and walking into his own room. The next morning he came back, laid the book on my table, and thanked me.

"You have read it?" I asked, astonished.

"All night long," he answered. "Word for word, every word." And his familiars told me afterward that this was literally true. He had sat down with the book when he got it from me, read it word by word, as he had to with his eye-spot, and finished it the moment he returned it to me. As he was about to leave it with me, I stopped him with a question: What about it?

"Well, and—?" I said. (*"Na, und—"*)

"It is literature, it is beautiful," he stammered, "but it is not psychology."

Against this I always like to put a story Wundt's assistant, Külpe, told us after a visit to the neighboring University of Jena to see the aged philosopher Erdmann, whose history of philosophy, in some ten volumes, we all had read and studied. They had a warm, friendly talk, the old scholar and the young scientist, all about the old philosophers and their systems. But when Külpe tried to draw him out on Wundt and the newer school, Erdmann shook his head, declaring that he could not understand the modern men.

"In my day," he explained, "we used to ask the everlasting question: 'What is man?' And you—nowadays you answer it, saying, 'He *was* an ape.'" (*"Er war ein Aff'."*)

And yet Wundt had a philosophy, and not only of facts; no, and not only of theories, either. He said that theories were only aids to experiment, which was the test. He taught and I learned from him the discipline, the caution, and the method of the experimental procedure of modern science. But Wundt, in practice, had established facts, he thought, by this method, and he built upon them conclusions which formed a system of philosophy written into several volumes. With an ethics, too; it was all complete. Well we knew it. It was under attack at the time. Some fresh, young men were challenging, with facts, with experimentally determined data, some of the very foundations of Wundt's psychology, which in turn was the basis of Wundt's philosophy. We were working, for the truth, of course, but also we were fighting, and when we got results which confirmed Wundt we were glad, and when we got results that seemed to support the enemy . . .

Some of us were looking over the laboratory records of an American student who had stood high with the Professor and, therefore, with us all. He had gone home, taken a professorship, and was holding high our colors. He became afterward one of the leading men in American science and education. His student papers were models of neatness, and as we looked we saw that they were a masterpiece of caution, wisdom, and mathematical labor. The records of his experiment showed that he got, at first, results which would have given aid and comfort to the enemy and confounded one of Wundt's most axiomatic premises. He must have suffered, that promising young student; it was his thesis for the degree of Doctor of Philosophy, which he needed for his career at home; he must have thought, as a psychologist, that Wundt might have been reluctant to crown a discovery which would require the old philosopher to recast his philosophy and rewrite the published volumes of his lifework. The budding psychologist solved the ethical problem before him by deciding to alter his results, and his papers showed how he did this, by changing the figures item by item, experiment by experiment, so as to make the curve of his averages come out for instead of against our school. After a few minutes of silent admiration of the mathematical feat performed on the papers before us, we buried sadly these remains of a great sacrifice to loyalty, to the school spirit, and to practical ethics.

Ethics! There was no foundation in (experimental) psychology for a science of ethics; not that I could find. There might be some day, when psychology itself is scientific. All I got out of my year of German psychology was a lead into biology on the one hand and into sociology on the other, a curiosity to hear and see what the French thought they knew about such matters, and best of all, a training in the experimental method. I decided to go to Paris for a year at the Sorbonne, and I began to change my subject from ethics to morals; from what ought to be done to what is done, and why. Lightly I say this now, but to me, in the spring of 1891, the conflict of ideas and emotions was a crisis that weighed heavily on me. I had lost time. I had lost myself.

There is no made road across the sciences. To pursue an inquiry from one of them through others into another is like trying to travel 'cross country in England without returning to London. The sciences are laid out within perpendicular lines. The physicists, chemists, biologists, and astronomers now are making tracks across their fields, but in my day they also were fenced in, each man to his own *Fach*. My difficulties and my sense of defeat put me in a state of mind where Johann and his art, Guido Peters and his music and his loves, the river and the nightingales and the spring, and, yes, the baker girl and the *Mädel* in the back room and the funny old landlady—with the regrets of all of them, and their laughters —all these were an inspiration to me to go and make love myself to a pretty American girl who sat just behind me at Wundt's lectures. It was unethical, but I did it; and it was good for some nineteen years.

XXII

OVER THE ALPS TO PARIS

I T IS related of Frederick C. Howe that when he had laid the
finished manuscript of his autobiography proudly before his
wife and she had read it, she looked up at him with the
humor that is all hers and said, "But, Fred, weren't you ever
married?"

"Oh, yes," he answered. "I forgot that. I'll put it in."

I can understand this. A love story is worth writing, I believe,
only when it is understood, and a man seldom understands his
own romance. I don't understand mine. It seems to me that I can
see through a government or a political situation, but human relations are beyond my comprehension. They happen to me; friendship has been the music of my life, but what does music say? And
what does love mean? We should be able to answer this question.
Love is coming of age as the human mind is, and the two should
be decently married. But my intelligence stops where love begins
and begins again where love leaves off.

And so it is, I think to observe, with males generally. They
can grasp sex; that's what they practice and talk and think they
know a bit about, but sex and love are or should be one, as women
know, who can navigate cunningly through the storm that blinds
their lovers. If there is ever to be a science of love and marriage
and if it is to be an applied science, women and such effeminate
men as poets will have to make it. Eugenics will be the woman's
art as it is her business now.

Anyhow my marriage was none of my business. When Johann,
my German chum, and I rowed up the Pleisser River in the
autumn the nightingales spoke to us and we to them, of psychology
and art history, ethics, philosophy, and music. There was no sentiment about us. Johann had no girl; mine was in America. For I

had left America with a "sort of understanding" with a girl at Berkeley. Johann could be soft about anything, and he declared that that was not because he was German. "Americans are just as weak," he said. But I set the tone of our friendship, and whatever of weakness there was in me was hidden in my letters to—"home."

When winter came, closing navigation on the river, we worked till the Christmas season approached. How I hated the German Christmas! The whole world went home, closed the door, and opened the window-shades, leaving the foreigner to wander about in the cold darkness all alone and look in longingly at the light, warmth, and merriment. I had arranged with Johann to ignore Christmas. We studied while the city went silly shopping, and even when the Day fell upon us like a fog, we stuck to our dull labors till, toward evening, I could not stand it. Calling Johann, I took him for a walk in the dusk. The streets were abandoned to us and the dirty, old snow, and to make matters worse, there were the lighted windows with their tinseled trees and the sounds of domestic happiness. I could not stand that either. We went home. I slammed into my room, leaving Johann to go on to his, next door. I sat in the dark, utterly miserable, wondering what Johann had meant by saying that Americans (and the English, too) were as sentimental as Germans, only not so honest about it. He would see, I had said, and I was showing him and his tribe, the Frau *Wirthin* and the sewing-girl and the old street-walker, who held, all of them, that such sentimentality, like love and like murder, would out. I was setting them an example.

I don't know what they had seen, but I had seen quite enough of Christmas when, about suppertime, Johann's door opened and he stood, sharp-cut black in the light that shone from behind him. He stood there a moment, and then, in the dialect he fell into only when he was moved, he said:

"*Du, geh' a mal her*," which means "Come" but says "Go once here."

I went once, and I saw on his table a pretty little candled Christmas tree, blazing away, with parcels on and under it, and, all around, the plates, bottles, foods, fruits, and candies of a Christmas dinner. It looked good to me.

"Wait," said Johann. "I'll call the others." And as he went out I said, "Wait," and I slipped back into my dark room, got out from under the bed the gifts I luckily had bought secretly for—everybody who came, the Frau *Wirthin*, the *Mädel*, and the poor old smiling wreck of the streets who danced in with Johann, bringing greetings and parcels, more food, more bottles, and the odor of a goose cooking joyously in the *Wirthin's* little kitchen.

We sang songs, ate and drank; we drank, sang, and danced. There was a distribution of presents; then we sang and danced till late into the night, when we discovered all at once that we so loved one another that we hooked arms and drank solemnly a *Brüderschaft*, the whole mixed five of us. I liked it. I swam and the others nearly drowned in the Christmas spirit, and it started something in me, as the old Frau *Wirthin* predicted.

"You'll see," she said to me. "You can't go on loving without loving."

"Why not?" the street-walker asked, surprised. "Men all love without loving. That's what I'm there for." (*"Deswegen bin ich da."*)

"Ach!" the sewing-girl interpreted, "you two use the same words to say opposite things."

Johann's eyes had become fixed on me. He was seeing in the light of the women's chatter something that seemed to alarm him.

"Nay," he protested, "you wouldn't, would you? You'll be true to her that is at home?"

"Long, perhaps," the street-walker answered, "but not forever. And it's long already, as this Christmas has shown."

She turned to the door; her Christmas was over.

"Where you going?" the *Mädel* asked her, and the street-walker replied with a look at Johann:

"I am going out to meet some true lover coming home alone from his lonely Merry Christmas."

The work hardened after the holidays. Wundt's lectures got down to cases, the laboratory hummed like a factory, and there were quizzes in pure philosophy. I was busy; so was Johann; everybody was working. I was restless, too, and Johann noticed it.

"What are you forever looking for?" he asked irritably one day.

"Looking!" I exclaimed. "I'm not looking for anything."

"Seems to me you are a hunter on the hunt," he insisted.

I did not know what he meant, but I was annoyed; so I watched myself, like a psychologist, and sure enough, something in me was searching for something or somebody outside of me. And I found her. Toward the end of the winter semester it was that I noticed an American girl at Wundt's lecture, and she saw me. She was a brown-eyed, straight-standing, rather handsome young woman with a singularly direct way of looking at one. The Professor's *famulus* said her name was Josephine Bontecou.

"Why?" he asked, smiling. "Why this sudden interest? She has sat in that same seat all through the semester, and some of us Germans have seen her before." Had they? I went to the English church to meet her. She was not known there. I went for the first time to other places where Americans and the English foregathered. She was not at any of them. Following her out of the lecture one dark evening, I accosted her in the Stadt Park. She understood; she always understood. She let me go with her to her apartment, where I met her mother, a woman I understood—the only one, I think.

Susan Bontecou had divorced her husband, a physician and surgeon of Troy, N.Y. Her daughter took her mother's side, and the two came to Europe to start new lives, Josephine as a student of psychology intending to write fiction, the mother to see the scenes of the history she knew well from her life of imaginative reading. They were a devoted couple, and that devotion which they thought to be their virtue turned out to be their tragedy. They were happy enough when I met them. They must have looked alike, but now in Leipzig, there, the mother was beginning to whiten with the years, and her once straight, strong little body was weakening. Her mind was alert, keen, and kind, like her eyes; she was really a shrewd woman of the world.

When Josephine brought me home to her that first day, we all talked pleasantly along for a while; then the daughter left me with her mother. It was always so. Josephine could not waste her time; she had work to do. It was the mother who, quietly sewing, would listen to my wonderings; she must have sensed my essential youth.

"My daughter is older than you are," she said one day, and I can remember looking into her uplifted eyes with astonishment at the irrelevance of her remark. Our conversations with Josephine all turned around one question: whether she should accept the offer of marriage she had received from a young German *Junker*, a corps student and duelist, who held out to her an estate with a castle to live in and villages of poor peasants to be grand and kind to. I was for it, the mother against it, and Josephine was in doubt; so it seemed to me, and yet here was the mother telling me that her daughter was too old for me.

"Yes?" I answered, and I meant and I must have looked, "What of it?" For the mother added, "Josephine is much older than you are."

There was no answer; I could not make out what this lovely old lady was thinking about. And so with Johann. He also was opposed to what I had not the slightest intention of doing. One night when I told him I thought that the American girl was going to marry "the *Junker*," Johann stared at me so long that I felt my face flush. He hated Josephine; he called her "dominating," and this time he took off his slipper and shook it at me.

"What do I care," I said, "if the *Junker* is ruled by his wife?"

"The *Junker!*" he exclaimed. "The *Junker* is safe," and he went off to his own room.

No one seemed to be able to understand that Josephine Bontecou and I were to have a friendship; no one; not even the nightingales. For when, in the spring, Johann and I went rowing up the river, the birds sang, not, as in the fall, of science and art, but of love and romance, of adventures and new countries and other peoples. I was going to Paris. Josephine and her mother were planning a summer vacation tour through the Alps to end in Paris at the Sorbonne. That had always been my plan, to study in Paris; it just happened to be hers too. Johann knew that, but he pretended to be surprised that I was willing to give up my German doctor's degree "for a year of—Paris." He emphasized "Paris," but I knew what he meant. And he knew, too, how I despised degrees, how psychology was only a road to ethics—a blind alley; and he did not know that Josephine had finally, finally declined the *Junker's* offer of marriage. He never even asked how this came out.

"Your German friend is jealous," Mrs. Bontecou remarked when our train pulled out and left him standing on the platform.

"But what of?" I answered her.

"Of your friendship with Josephine," she said very gently.

I don't remember a single Alp. Years afterward when I traveled in Switzerland it was all new to me; and yet Josephine and I walked it that summer. Her mother was with us, but she took trains or diligences to meet us at the places we tramped to. Josephine saw everything; she was always thorough; but I saw only Josephine, I think. Anyway I fell in love with her in Switzerland, and when we arrived in Paris we were engaged. Johann was right after all. Everybody was; as usual I alone was wrong: all wrong, but all right too.

XXIII

PARIS, LONDON—HOME

PARIS is a loose merger of many, very many, small provincial communities, each of which is self-sufficient and pleasantly or offensively clannish.

"Do you live here?" they will ask in the little local shops, and your answer makes a difference, not only in the prices, but in the service. A policeman won't arrest you if you live on his beat; the accredited street-walker won't pick your pocket; they will see you safely home. Even though you are a foreigner, you may still be a *petit Parisien*, an insider, more French than a Parisian from some other quarter; he is the stranger. Some quarters boast of inhabitants who have never been to Paris—the Paris of the foreigners and the financiers. The *grands boulevards* are a place which the *petits Parisiens* make excursions to, as they visit Versailles, on a holiday, all dressed up, in family or neighborhood sight-seeing groups.

My Paris, the *petit Paris* of my student days, was the Latin Quarter, of course; but the Latin Quarter then was a simple, idyllic, fresh-water college town. Our connection with Paris was by horse busses which made the trip pleasant on a sunny day, but long, halting—a day's work; we dressed up and took the trip only to fetch money from the bank or to call on some tourist friend from home. That and the opera were the only uses we had for the Right Bank. I remember once an enterprising party of reckless fellows ventured with their girls to Montmartre; that was something like; and they had a good time, but they didn't get back till late the next forenoon and were all tired out and wretchedly sobered by the long, long journey. No, our lives were complete in the Quarter, which was the largest of all the Parisian communities, and, we thought, the most important. It had two physical centers, Montparnasse and the Boul' Mich', and it had two lobes to its brain, the Sorbonne (with the university) and the Beaux Arts (with the other private art schools), but the art students and the university students played together, and play and work were all one to them, like truth and beauty, which we all sought merrily together, seriously by day, and at night still more seriously. For gayety and earnestness were undivided, too. Anyway we were one, we, the students and our shop-keepers, our laundresses, waiters, concierges, and our *gens-d'armes*. We had rows among ourselves, but as against the world —the successful, Philistine, spoilsport Paris—we were one big union.

Maybe it is so now. Montparnasse has won out over the Boul' Mich', but I see the same all sorts of students together and I hear them using our phrases to express our ideas. The elements are not changed: wine or women; art and science, or success and business; evolution or revolution. There's a difference, however. There are taxis and the underground; students appear on the *grands boulevards,* and the tourists at Montparnasse, a flood of spectators. There's an audience. We played to ourselves. Our life seems to me to have been simpler, more naïve, much less conscious. It was, like our art, for its own sweet sake. The shop-keepers and the cafés are more businesslike now, the students more—histrionic. I recognize it all. It is just as if the fiction about us had come true. The Latin Quarter today is what it was supposed to be in my day—and wasn't.

My student friends did not feel that they had to "keep some girl or other." Some of them fell in love with the loveliest little woman in the world, and they set out to live happily with her all their lives. They did not do it, not often, but the *ménages* I knew were as real as mine. I lived with Josephine Bontecou just as they lived with their girls. We were married, to be sure, but nobody knew that, and it made no difference to our friends or to us. We had taken rooms in a Montparnasse hotel, Josephine, her mother, and I, and Josephine went to work, her mother went sight-seeing, and I looked around. We were not going to marry till our studies were over and we were back in America. I feared my father would recall me if he heard that I had taken a wife. But after a few weeks of waiting, we stole off to London, lived there the required twenty-two days, and on the twenty-second were married on the way to the boat-train for Paris. I was seasick all that first night of my married life, wretchedly and then restfully sick: it did me good, and the next day, in Paris, I, too, went to work. We told nobody of our marriage, neither at home nor in the Quarter; so we had all the advantages of the law and all the thrills and the prestige of lawlessness.

My work was interesting to me, generally, not specifically. I took all the courses I signed up for, I heard besides every lecture that any student or any book mentioned as "good" in any way, and more besides. I was like those Paris bums who drop in to the Sorbonne lectures all day long just to sit down and be warm; I would join any stream of students going in to any room to hear the lecture on any subject. That was my plan: specifically to look everywhere for a lead to ethics, and generally, to get a sense of the French methods and spirit. I heard some able, thought-breeding men and felt the difference between them and the German professors. The French speak French almost universally as few Germans can speak German: not only clearly, but with a precision and a finish that is charming. The French believe in reason; they experiment, too, of course, and their laboratory work is clean, careful, and productive of results, but they cannot stop their minds from collaborating, as the Germans do. The French are impatient mentally. Their imagination will out, and they love to think about the conclusions they cannot help foreseeing and sometimes anticipating and even forming. Their great fault I felt to be this, their greatest virtue: they worked and thought and spoke like artists, esthetically, and with all their false faith in reason and their trained skill in logic, they used their heads to prove the truth of something that was only very beautiful; and so they would express it beautifully. In any lecture room in the Sorbonne one could find some scholarly actor, with his glass of sugar and water, reciting, even singing, a prose poem on a chemcial or a metaphysical formula. It was usually convincing, too; it was not always science, but it was literature, and when Charcot, for example, was showing on the set stage of his amphitheater what his psychiatric patients could do or suffer, it was drama.

"Go," he said when he was through with a woman patient who had done her stunts, and then as she was passing off the stage, the professor struck the table with a hammer. The cataleptic stopped, stiffened, and stood rigid with her hands half lifted and her face turned back toward us.

"*La femme de Lot,*" said Charcot, with a showman's flourish, and sure enough, there stood Lot's wife, a pillar of miraculous rigidity.

Play and work live together in France, like wit and logic, art and science, and men and women. We enjoyed life in Germany, too, but we did not amuse ourselves in the laboratory; we labored there till tired; then for recreation we went out to a beer hall or into the country and, dropping business, played hard. It was pleasant. I liked the German way. But Paris was somehow a release from some sort of repression. It was good to feel free to walk into a laboratory exactly as you would into a café and jest with the other fellows, even about the experiment, speculate upon the possible results, say seriously what might not be true—just to hear how it sounded. And it was good to go to a café and join a frivolous crowd and feel that you could talk shop. It was as if the *verboten* signs had been removed from imagination, intuition, and temperament.

Perhaps my impression of Paris is pointed by the fact that I was living there, freely and fully living, with a wife, and that my friends were mostly artists rather than university students. I had a home, and some of our friends had homes; not all lawful, but warm, happy, domestic. They were French homes; the dining-room was separate—any one of the many restaurants where we met and dined together, and thought and talked and practiced our arts.

"Who can express in the fewest lines the attitude of that waiter to that girl he is serving?"

In words or in pencil strokes on the table-cloth everybody tried it, and discussed the results, graphically, psychologically, poetically, discovering, by the way, that all the arts and the sciences, too, are pretty much all one thing. There was one man, Louis Loeb, who loved this game, and through it we became lifelong friends. He picked me up as my German friend, Johann Krudewolf, had, for a purpose. Josephine had noticed that he always joined our crowd at dinner or coffee and was intensely interested whenever the talk turned to writing or to the parallel of painting and writing. She said that he was after something from me, and one night he declared it. He asked me if I would show him, technically, the difference between prose and verse. An odd question, as he knew, and he went on to justify it, oddly.

"I've never had a college education," he said. He had been a lithographer in Cleveland, Ohio, and made enough money to come to Paris to study art; that was all right; he would be a painter. But he loved music, too, and literature; he read every night, not intelligently. He needed to know the art of writing, as he had heard me say I wanted to understand the technique of painting.

"I'll teach you," he proposed. "I'll teach you painting if you'll teach me writing."

It was like Johann's proposition to exchange German for English lessons; only Loeb got the better of his bargain as I got the better of Johann's. Loeb learned to read. I asked him that night what he was reading. He drew from his pocket a volume of Milton's poems, and I turned to "Il Penseroso" and "L'Allegro." I read out loud to him a few heavy lines of the one, then a few light lines of the other, showed him the choice of words, the difference in cadence, and other tricks of the poet's craft, illustrated in those two poems. He had no prose with him, but I talked a little of the same and other tricks of prose. That was about all. He used to bring me afterward books with marked passages which he read to me as beautiful, and he analyzed them for me. He had it. He came to his reading with taste, with the artist's sense of art, and he was interested; he wanted to know. My few hints were enough, therefore. Taking them as a key, he opened book after book all that winter, all his short life—too short; and he read with much appreciation—all the literatures he had the languages for: English, French, and German. Louis Loeb became one of the best-read men I knew, a thoughtful, cultivated man of the world, far better educated than the average college graduate; but he never ceased expressing in his demeanor and in words his belief that he had missed something; he had never been to college. I argued with him; I introduced to him college-bred dubs to show him that he had taught and trained himself better than college had educated them. In vain. Louis Loeb taught me that it is worth while going through college if only to know what is not there.

That was what I learned and was learning. The universities

of the United States, Germany, and France have a classified body of knowledge, which an obedient, unquestioning student can learn the history of and, if he is clever, can add a chapter to. But if he has a question or a need in his mind he will not readily find the answer. At any rate, all the universities had to offer me by way of ethics was the long story of what man had thought about right and wrong; I felt that I could have gone home and lectured in a college on the successive systems of ethics; I certainly could have taken a degree in my specialty and written text-books for American schools with German thoroughness and French neatness. But I did not want to do that; a career did not attract me; and I did want to discover some basis for a scientific theory of ethical conduct. I could not. The French, like the Germans, had none. The best I had got out of all my scholastic wanderings was the belief, which was probably only a hope, that when there was a science of psychology, a science of sociology, and a science of biology, when we could know how man was born, bred, moved, and to what end, then we might lay out a program for the guidance of his conduct. For example, assuming that men are an evolving species, we might say that all acts, personal and social, that made for development were good, and that all conduct and conditions that hindered growth were bad. I did take that as a loose guide for myself, but to make it scientific, biology has to prove and describe evolution, psychology has to show us human possibilities, sociology has to be made a study of the effects of environment on human psychology; and even then, men have to know the possibilities of their growth and choose among them.

Talking about this and other wide, momentous problems in Louis Loeb's studio, where he was teaching me painting by letting me see him paint, I learned little of painting, not so much as he had learned of reading, but I did learn something. I learned that I could not learn to paint except by painting. Loeb himself had not learned to write, only to read; and I could read painting, some painting. But that was, I found, not what I wanted; I had wanted of painting, not only to feel, but to know what it was to paint. And I could not, without practice. Thinking of this, I applied it to ethics. I could not have even a philosophic ethics without practice; I must first study morals. The thing for me to do, I decided, was to leave the universities, go into business or politics, and see, not what thinkers thought, but what practical men did and why.

This was no revolution. I was about through anyway; my wife was already at work on a novel which, she realized, drew none of its psychology from the courses she had so faithfully worked at, but only from her own sense of personalities and experience. We would go home. I wanted to go to London for a few months' reading in the British Museum; her mother, having lived over all the historical scenes in all the churches, palaces, prisons, and public squares of Paris and much of Europe, was eager to see London; and Josephine felt like a rest. They went to London when the year in Paris was up, while I rushed up into Germany to visit a bit with Johann, who had gone, ill, to a cure for consumptives, an out-of-the-way place which required many changes and some command of German to get to. And I noticed that I had that command. My spoken German was a broken German when I left Germany, and in Paris I had never practiced at all, had not met Germans and spoke not a word of their language; yet here I was, after a year of French and English only, rattling off German like a native. And Johann noticed it.

"But," he exclaimed when we greeted each other at the station, "where have you learned to speak German so well?"

Evidently the brain is like any other muscle. While it is being worked it may not seem to learn or develop very fast the faculty needed; it becomes overtrained, so to speak, as mine was in the two years' constant strain to speak German. Give it a rest, as athletes do their bodies, and the blood-supply and growth go on and have the time to build up what is wanted. Anyhow, after two years of exercise and one year of neglect, I could really speak German, rapidly, easily, and with pleasure.

But I, too, had a cheerful surprise. Johann looked well, as well as I had ever seen him look. His summons to me had been so exigent that I feared he must be nearing the end, but no, his tall straight figure and his strong, good face were as vigorous and expressive as of old. We walked the long way to his hotel, where he introduced me to his new friends, the other patients, and for a week I lived their rather pleasant life in the air and sunshine. One day Johann asked me how bequests for scholarships were made in American universities, what my father's name, age, and birthplace were, what my mother's maiden name was, and then whether, if anything happened to him, I would return to Germany and do something he might want done.

I didn't promise blindly. My answer, after a moment of reflection, was that when I was once in America, I would probably be at work, busy and not free lightly to leave my business to come back to Germany, but that if he would have that in mind and yet ask me to I would promise. He seemed to be satisfied, even pleased, and said no more. We had a pleasant last evening together, and I left him, feeling, as I said, that he had happy, healthy years ahead for his art history researches in Italy, as he planned.

I rejoined Josephine and her mother in London. I went to my reading in the British Museum or sight-seeing with Mrs. Bontecou, who was an informed, imaginative guide; my wife was hawking the manuscript of her novel; and we all went shopping, for, after all, our return home was the chief thing in our minds. I was having all sorts of fashionable clothes made for my start in life; morning suits, evening suits, sporting and even business suits, and hats—high, low, soft, and hard, all English, the latest things. There was even a lounge suit and a cap for the steamer. When I paced the deck of the ship that was taking me "home" to the business of practical living, I was a beautiful thing, tailored and educated, an American boy of twenty-six, dressed outside like an Englishman, and filled up inside with the culture of the American and European universities.

I was happily unaware that I was just a nice, original American boob, about to begin unlearning all my learning, and failing even at that.

PART II
SEEING NEW YORK FIRST

I BECOME A REPORTER

W HEN my ship sailed into New York Harbor, my father's agent brought down to quarantine a letter which I still remember, word-perfect, I think.

"My dear son: When you finished school you wanted to go to college. I sent you to Berkeley. When you got through there, you did not care to go into my business; so I sold out. You preferred to continue your studies in Berlin. I let you. After Berlin it was Heidelberg; after that Leipzig. And after the German universities you wanted to study at the French universities in Paris. I consented, and after a year with the French, you had to have half a year of the British Museum in London. All right. You had that too.

"By now you must know about all there is to know of the theory of life, but there's a practical side as well. It's worth knowing. I suggest that you learn it, and the way to study it, I think, is to stay in New York and hustle.

"Enclosed please find one hundred dollars, which should keep you till you can find a job and support yourself."

This letter made me feel as if the ship were sinking under me; I had to swim. I did not know how, not in those waters, but it was not fear that hit me so hard. Nor disappointment. I had no plans to be disturbed. My vague idea was to go home to California and "see" what chance there was, say, at some college, to teach or lecture on the theories of ethics while making a study of morals: the professional ethics and the actual conduct of men in business, politics, and the professions. I could get no academic position in the east, where I was not known, but I might carry on my research as an insider in business just as well as I could as an observer. My wife asked me how I was going to go about getting a job in business and how meanwhile we were to live. For the first time, I think, I realized that I was expected to support my wife and that meanwhile my wife expected my father to help us. And my father would have done it. He said afterward that if he had known that I was married, he would not have thrown me off as he did—for my good, "just to see what you could do for yourself," he said. My wife was for telling him then and there, but I could not. I declared that I would never ask my father for another cent, and I didn't. The next money transaction between us was a loan I made to him.

No, my father was putting me to a test, I said, and I would show him. And my mother-in-law, Mrs. Bontecou, backed me up. She said she would see us through with her little money. Josephine was angry, and, in brief, ours was a gloomy landing-party. I alone was cheerful, secretly; I had an idea. I would write.

At the small hotel Josephine knew, I took pencil and paper and I wrote a short story, "Sweet Punch." That was a Saturday. I did it that day and rewrote and finished it on Sunday. Louis Loeb called that night. He was illustrating for *Harper's Magazine*, and he said he would offer them my story the next day. He sold it to them for fifty dollars. I sat me down to calculate. That story was done and sold in three days. Call it a week. I could make fifty dollars a week, which multiplied by fifty-two was, say, $2500 a year. Enough to live on. But I didn't do another story that week nor the next. Too busy looking for a job, I excused; but the fact was that I couldn't do another for a month, and then the second story was rejected. It was years before I got into the magazines again.

It was weeks before I found a job. I was amazed at the difficulty. There I was, all dressed up in my beautiful morning coat with top hat, answering ads, any ads for anything, from an editorship to errand boy. Literally. The juvenile literature I had read as a boy, about lads who began at the bottom and worked up, had stuck. Here I was, what I had once grieved that I was not, a poor but willing young fellow, without parents, friends, or money, seeking a start in life, just a foothold on the first rung of the ladder: I would, like my boy heroes, attend to the rest. And I couldn't get the chance! I couldn't understand it.

The most urgent ads came from the water front, and I would

go into one of those shabby little dirty, dark shops, where they dealt in ship furnishings or produce—dressed like a dude, remember; especially careful to be in my best to make a good first impression—and showing the clipping from the paper, ask for an opening. The shop-keeper would throw himself back in his chair and stare at me and splutter, "But—but do you think you can do the work? It's hard work and—and—are you—qualified? What has been your experience?" And I answered that I had studied at Berkeley, Berlin, Heidelberg, the Sorbonne! And for some reason that seemed to end it.

Those were the days when business men were prejudiced against a college education. My father's partners had the prejudice. They warned him that his course with me would ruin me, and I think that it was they who advised him to drop me in New York and see who was right, he or they. Business men have learned since that college does not unfit average young men for anything but an intellectual career; they take them on and will tell you that the colleges are the best source in the world for cheap labor. But in my day, next to my clothes and general beautifulness, the heaviest handicap I had was my claim to a college education, and not only one college, but—five. Some employers dropped their hands and jaw and stared me silently out of their sight; others pushed me out, and others again—two I remember vividly—called in all hands to "see this college graduate that wants to clean the windows and run errands."

My father was right. As I went home to my wife and mother-in-law to describe life as I found it and business men as they found me, I had to confess that I was learning something, that life wasn't what I had expected from my reading. My money was all gone, all the one hundred and also the fifty dollars, and I was paying for myself alone. Mrs. Bontecou paid for her daughter, and soon she was paying for her son-in-law too. I became desperate. My father had given me a letter from the supervising editor of all the Southern Pacific Railroad publications, the monthly magazines, weeklies, and daily newspapers that "the Road" owned or subsidized, to an editor of the *Century Magazine*. I had not used it, because I preferred not to apply "pull." I was for getting my start in life on merit alone. Mrs. Bontecou was with me on that; Josephine was impatient and practical. She pressed me to deliver the letter of introduction, and I did. I asked Mr. Robert Underwood Johnson to give me an editorial position on the *Century*.

He read the letter, pondered, asked me questions, and sized me up. Seeing through my clothes and my story, I guess, he very cautiously asked me if I would be willing to start—just for the practice—to begin my editorial career as—a—reporter. Would I? I certainly would; I would have laid off my top hat to be a copy boy. That cleared the air for him; maybe it stripped off my English clothes. Anyway he offered to get me on either the *Tribune* or the *Evening Post*, and I went home, happy and proud, to dis-

"THE EVENING POST" WHEN I JOINED IT IN 1892

cuss with my family the choice I had between those two New York papers.

I can't recall what decided us, but I think it was only that the *Evening Post* was an evening paper; I could be home at night and so have time to do some literary work. However it was, I took a note from Mr. Johnson to Joseph B. Bishop, an editorial writer on the *Post*. Bishop frowned, but he led me out to the city room and introduced me to Henry J. Wright, the city editor, who looked helplessly at me and, I thought, resentfully at Bishop.

"I don't need any more reporters," he said to Bishop, "but," to me, "you can come in next Monday and sit down out there with the reporters, and as I get a chance, I'll try you out—on space."

I didn't know what that meant, but I didn't care. I had a job. As I described it to my wife and her mother, Josephine was not elated as her mother was, and the next Monday when I sat out there in the city room, ignored, while all the world seemed to be in a whirl, I was not elated either. The next day I saw "Larry"

Godkin, the editor who wrote the leaders I read and re-read, admiring; he passed by the city door. Bishop nodded to me once, but neither Wright nor the other reporters looked my way. Interesting fellows they seemed to be; they must know all the mysteries of a great city. They did not talk much, but I overheard enough to infer that they were familiar and bored with sport, politics, finance, and society. I was awed by the way they would, upon a few words from the city editor, dart or loaf out of the room, be gone an hour or so, come in, report briefly, and then sit down, write, turn in their copy carelessly, and lie back and read, idly read, newspapers.

One afternoon about one o'clock Mr. Wright came into the room, and seeing no one there but me, exclaimed impatiently and went out. A moment later he came back and right up to me.

"See here," he said, "there's a member of a stock brokerage firm missing. Disappeared utterly. Something wrong. Go and see his partner and find out why the man is gone, whether there's funds missing, too."

He handed me a memorandum giving the firm name and address in Wall Street. An assignment! I was to report. I darted out of the office into the elevator, and asking anybody for directions, found my way to Wall Street—Wall Street!—and the office of the lost broker. His partner rebuffed me. "No, I don't know why he skipped. No idea. No, nothing missing. How should there be?" But I wasn't going to fail on my first chance; so I persisted, asking questions, all about the missing man, his character, antecedents, habits, and when that caused only irritation, I asked about Wall Street. The broker soon was talking; we moved into his private office, sat down, and I told him the story of my life; he told me his, and I was thinking all the time how I could write something interesting about the ethics of a stock broker; I had long since been convinced that the missing broker was innocent of anything more than a drink or an escapade with a woman, when all of a sudden the partner sprang up and said:

"Well, you are the most persistent son of a gun I ever met in all my life, and you win. I'll give you what you seem so damn sure of anyhow. My —— partner has not only skipped, I don't know where; he has taken every cent there was in the office, in the banks, and—then some." He named the amount, and I, astonished by the revelation, but satisfied that I had a front-page sensation, ran back to the office, where I astonished my city editor.

"Really?" he said. "You are sure? It's libel, you know, if it's wrong. He told you himself, the partner did? Sure? Umh— Well, write it, and we'll see."

I had pencils all sharpened—sharpened every day—ready for this moment, and I went to work. It was easy enough to report the facts, but I felt I must write this big news as the news was written. That I had studied in my idle hours, the newspaper style, and that was not easy. I labored till the city editor darted out to see what I was doing; he saw; he read over my shoulder the writes and re-writes of my first paragraph, and picking up one, said, "This is enough." And away he went with it. All I had to do was to lie back in a chair and wait to read my stuff in print, a long wait, perhaps half an hour, till three o'clock, when the last edition went to press, and then twenty minutes before the paper came down. And then when it came down, the damp, smelly paper, my paragraph wasn't in it! I searched again and again, with anxiety, hope, dread. I did not care for the money; the space was too short to count, but I felt that my standing as a reporter was at stake, and so, when I was at last convinced that my "story" was left out, I got up and dragged home, defeated and in despair. I told Mrs. Bontecou about it, not my wife, and was comforted some. If I failed at journalism, the old lady argued, there still was literature.

The facts of my story appeared in the morning newspapers, but they were better, more neatly, briefly stated, than I had put them; perhaps I had failed, not as a reporter, but as a writer. And this conclusion was confirmed at the office, where the city editor said "Good morning" to me and, after all the other reporters were gone out, gave me an assignment to ask the Superintendent of Schools something. One more chance.

Braced to make the most of it, I gave that official a bad hour. He had to answer, not only the question the city editor asked, but others, many others. He found himself telling me all about the schools, education and its problems, and his policy. I had some ideas on that subject, and he got them; and he had to accept or refute them. He became so interested that, when he had to break off, I was invited to come back another day to "continue our conversation." Good. I returned to the office and wrote a column interview, beginning with the city editor's question and the answer. This time, when the paper came out it had my story, but cut down to the first question and answer, rewritten as an authoritative statement of fact. My reporting was all right; my writing was not. The next day, a Friday, I had to go out, confirm a reported suicide, and telephone the news, which another reporter took down and wrote.

That afternoon I saw reporters clipping from the cut files of the *Post*. I asked what it was for, and one of them said he was making up his bill. He cut out his own stories, stuck them together in a long strip, and measuring them with a foot-rule, reckoned up the amount of space and charged for it so much a column. I did the same, and my poor little bill of earnings for my first week of practical life was something like two dollars and ten cents. And I was not ashamed of it; I was reassured, if not proud.

Nor was that all. As I was finishing this task the city editor called me up to his desk and bade me rewrite as a separate story for the Saturday paper the interview I had had with the Superintendent of Schools during the week. He suggested the idea or theme to write it around, and I, elated, stayed there in the office till closing-time, grinding out my first long "story." And the next day I had the deep gratification of reading it at full length, the whole thing as I had written it. I measured it, secretly, and it came to four dollars plus—a fine start for my next week.

That Sunday was a bore; I could hardly wait for Monday to go on with my reporting, and talking with my wife and her mother, I developed ideas and plans. There were several promising questions to put to the Superintendent of Schools; the news suggested other men to see and talk to, and no doubt now the city editor himself would ask me to do more. When I walked into the office on Monday morning, eager and confident, I was dashed by the way I was ignored. No greetings from anybody, and as the morning wore on and the other reporters were sent off on assignments, I realized heavily that I was not to be used. I took my hat and told the city editor I would like to go out on a quest of my own. He nodded consent, and I went and had with the Superintendent of Schools a long interview which I wrote and handed in. It did not appear in the paper, and for two days I was ignored and got nothing out of my own assignments. The men I tried to see were not in or would not see me. I had the experience so common for reporters of being defeated, and in an obscure way, too. Toward the end of the week I was sent out to see a Rapid Transit Commissioner and got some news which pleased the city editor: a formal, printed statement, which was printed. That was all. My space bill was about six dollars. But on Saturday, too late to be included, appeared my interview with the Superintendent of Schools.

With this to start with again, I could live over Sunday and was ready to dive on Monday into my journalism. I had to be my own city editor, but I could be, now. I got another school story, which was printed; it was news; and another which was held, I knew now, for Saturday. I called again on the Rapid Transit Commissioner, and he gave me a brief interview which I used to tempt the other Commissioners to answer. That was news and appeared right away. So was a statement by the Mayor which I went for all by myself. Somebody had said something in print that was critical in a small way of some department, and his office being open to the public, I walked in and talked to him about it. My bill that week was something like fifteen dollars.

My system was working, and, I learned afterward, was amusing the staff and interesting the city editor, who described it as I could not have described it. It was a follow-up system, well known in journalism but unknown to me as a method. Every time I was sent to or met a man in a position to furnish news, I cultivated him as a source and went back repeatedly to him for more news or more general views on the news. If there was a news story in the papers, and not too big, I would read it through for some angle overlooked and slip out to the persons involved and ask some questions. My contribution often appeared as a part of some other reporter's story, usually at the end, but several times as the lead. And always there were school news articles from my Superintendent, who was talking policy to me weekly and letting me visit and write about schools. These articles brought letters to the editor, which showed that we were tapping a field of interest. I had a free hand here till, later, there was an education department which included the universities and private schools, and so brought in advertising. But there was the Art Museum, too, to "cover" and report; Rapid Transit with its plans, not only for transportation in the city, but for real estate, park, and street development. Every time the city editor sent me into a field for a bit of news I got what he wanted and went back for more general reports. He used me very little, however, leaving me to my own devices; and his reason came out when, after a few months, my bills were running up to fifty, sixty, and more dollars a week, and the other reporters were taking rather unfriendly notice of me.

One Friday, as I was making out my bill, William G. Sirrene, a fine southern boy who was one of the star reporters, looked over my shoulder and exclaimed, "What's that? Seventy-two dollars! Why, that's nearly three times what I'm getting on salary."

He called out to the others the amount of my bill, and when they also exclaimed, he explained: "Why, you are the best-paid man on the staff!"

I felt like exclaiming myself. It was news to me. I had no knowledge of salaries or earnings on the paper; all I knew was that I was supporting myself and my wife at last, saving a little each week, and driving on for more, and more. And I would have given it all to be a regular reporter like Sirrene or the others, and that is what I was asked to do. I think now that some of the reporters, not Sirrene, "kicked" to the city editor that I, a new man, was being paid more than they were, the veterans. Anyway he sent for me, and explaining that my bills were running too high, asked me if I would be changed from space to a salary, the best salary they paid the ordinary reporter, $35 a week.

"Then," he said, "I can use you more myself on more important news."

I not only consented, I was dazed with the implication of my triumph. All became clear in that short talk with my chief. I had not been sent off on assignments because I was making too much money on my own and I had "made good." Even my first disappointment, the failure to print my news of the defalcation of the missing broker, was to my credit. The city editor did not dare print the report, by a new and untried man, of a piece of libelous news; he had sent an old reporter down to confirm it, and the broker who had talked to me not only repeated what he told me; he had spoken well of me; but by the time the confirmation was delivered, it was too late. The paper was gone to press. I was "reliable, quick, and resourceful," the city editor said, as he made me a regular reporter.

In a word I was a success, and though I have never since had such a victory and have come to have some doubt of the success of success, I have never since failed to understand successful men; I know, as I see them, how they feel inside.

WALL STREET

GENERAL reporting in New York in my day was a series of daily adventures, interesting, sometimes thrilling, but, on the *Evening Post*, rarely perilous. A conservative three-cent evening newspaper, competing with one-cent papers, it avoided crime, scandal, and the sensational generally. Mr. Lawrence Godkin, the editor-in-chief, was a reformer. Irish in breed, English in culture, his ideals both of journalism and politics were British Liberal. He was against bad government and bad journalism, which he attributed to bad men. His cure was to throw the rascals out and elect good men, regardless of party. Called a Mugwump, he was really an aristocrat. His war in New York was against the boss, Richard Croker, Tammany Hall, and the Democratic city governments, but he fought even more bitterly Boss Platt and the State machine of the Republican party, which sometimes opposed and sometimes traded with Tammany.

The news department of the *Post* had, theoretically, nothing to do with the editorial policy. Reporters were to report the news as it happened, like machines, without prejudice, color, and without style; all alike. Humor or any sign of personality in our reports was caught, rebuked, and, in time, suppressed. As a writer, I was permanently hurt by my years on the *Post*. The editorial page and, to some extent, the book, theater, and music reviews, were the only departments which were really written. I was allowed to "do" the German theaters, and they were, next to the Yiddish, the best in the city; but I was never permitted to say anything like that. After a year or two of the German "first nights," I was used often to cover the second-best English openings under the close control of the dramatic editor, who had a policy. And in general the news reporters, supposed to have no concern with the editorial policy of the paper, were led, somehow—not directly, but by the method of trial and error, we learned to gather ammunition for the editorial writers. Mr. Godkin was no hero to me; I saw very little of him, and that little was not pleasant, but I read him. I found it helpful professionally to con his editorials every day for "tips" as to what to look for in the news and how to write it. His leaders seemed to me to be shallow; clever, forceful, ripping, but personal and not very thoughtful. No matter. Nobody can read a newspaper every day and not be influenced by it; we read "our paper" in our quiet, relaxed moments, when we might be thinking, and thus unwittingly let the editors form our minds. Godkin was mind to me all those years, and I was legs to him, one of his many pairs of running feet, ears, and eyes. There were compensations.

When I was promoted, at reduced pay, from space to general reporter, Mr. Wright, the city editor, did what he said he would do. He gave me assignments every morning, and as I in my eagerness worked, plotted, persisted in getting the news expected of me, my uses became more and more important and various. In the course of a few months I had visited all parts of the city, called on all sorts of men (and women), politicians, business men, reformers; described all sorts of events, fires, accidents, fights, strikes, meetings. It was happy work for me. New York was like a great swimming-hole into which every day I dived, here, there, anywhere, and swam around for something or somebody worth getting. And all the time I had the advantage of interviewing men who gave me some of the respect or fear they felt for "Larry" Godkin.

I came to love New York; I had a sentiment about the people, the business, the politics, and the streets of the great city which cared neither for me nor for itself. My old academic interest in scientific ethics faded; it would come up when some prominent citizen was lying to me. This experience enraged the other reporters; it only set me to thinking that reporters, like judges and prosecutors, had no moral right to the truth, because they would turn it against the truth-teller. And I had to notice that the ethics of business and the ethics of politics are such different cultures that a business man in politics will commit sins appalling to the politician, and vice versa. Morals are matters of trade or profession and form the ethics they are supposed to be formed by.

But science and philosophy, like the theaters and books, seemed tame in comparison with the men and women, the unbelievable doings and the sayings, of a live city. New York was real; and life was "different." Literature and the arts did not show it as it was. So it seemed to me, and before I was sated with it and long before I could write anything about it except in the paper, I was assigned to a department, Wall Street.

One afternoon toward the end of the winter (1892-93) Mr. Wright called me up to his desk and asked me if I would take the place of the Wall Street reporter, an Englishman, who had been called home by the death of his father. Wright said that there was trouble ahead for Wall Street, a period of depression, possibly a panic, and "we" must have a man down there, a special reporter, who would give all his time and thought to the financial news. He knew, he said, that I had had no experience of banking and business, but he had noticed that I worked and read up on any subject I was reporting. My universities had taught me to study. He thought I could learn enough to "cover" Wall Street in the emergency. Anyway, he would take a chance if I would. Would I? he asked.

I was thinking, dazed. Wall Street! I remembered that the Wall Street reporter before he sailed had advised me, if I expected to stay in journalism, to specialize in something: sport, the theaters, finance. I had seen the sense of that. But did I mean to stay in journalism? And if so, would I thrive as a financial expert, I who had always avoided business? My answer to Wright was that I would consider for a day or two and then tell him my decision.

My wife laughed at the thought of me in Wall Street, as my father would have. My wise old mother-in-law listened to all that we said, and at the end, pointed my own instincts. She always saw what I wanted; she usually advised as I desired. Mrs. Bontecou thought that, since I was only taking the place of another man who was coming back in a year or so, I might do very well for myself to have the experience of Wall Street. It would be profitable to me, if not to the paper. The next day I went to Wright with a plan. He was to give me a list of five or six of the commanding Wall Street bankers; I would call on them and see if I could make with them an emergency arrangement by which they were to take care of their favorite paper and help me to the news during the bad times. I think Wright, a Scotchman, saw what I did not: that this would be a shrewd way to enlist the expert, authoritative service of big insiders. And that is what happened; the *Post* had the inside track in that panic. Anyway the city editor approved with alacrity my suggestion; he consulted with the financial editor and handed me a list of leading bankers whom I called on, after banking hours, that afternoon. One by one I saw them, and my Wall Street experience began at once.

My approach to high finance was that of most of the world, I think; it certainly was something like that of the novelists and playwrights I knew. It was the awed approach of a boy brought up in the belief that there are heroes, really giants and great persons, good or evil, to be found in life. I had not discovered any as yet. On the contrary, my boyhood experience had been explosive of illusions, and in the universities, especially in Europe, I had looked for giants under the names of the celebrated philosophers, scientists, and scholars I went hopefully to study with. My experience with them was like one or the other of two experiences I had in Munich. The great professors either destroyed themselves, as the Munich painters flattened my awe of artists by their well-nigh universal contempt for one another, or they let me see them as I saw Henrik Ibsen. I happened to be worshiping that poet-playwright when I was in Munich, and some one who heard me talking about him told me that he was in that city and where I could see him at dinner any day. Off I hurried to Ibsen's restaurant; the god came in due course. He walked up to the little table reserved for him, let the waiter take his stick, but not his hat. That he kept, and when he sat down, he put it upside down between his knees—and stared into it. As he looked, he bowed, smirked, turned his head this way and that way, and tossed his mane. What was in that hat? I had to know. Getting up quietly, I walked over, and as I passed behind him, I looked where he was looking—at a mirror, a little hand mirror.

Vanity has come to be a virtue or at least a useful gift, to my way of thinking now, but at that time it seemed a human weakness, like professional jealousy, and the sight of these and other common faults in the geniuses of Europe helped to send me home with a theory that the great men of my day were probably the masters, not of art and philosophy, but of finance and industry; and especially those of America. My Wall Street assignment was an opportunity to see giants.

The names on my list were all famous in New York; one of them was internationally known; and their banks are great institutions. The bankers received me readily enough, much less formally than a European professor would a young man; they were all *Post* readers, as they said. But when I stated my business, when I mentioned the word "panic," they almost had one themselves. Even when I changed the word, first, to "depression," then to "a strain," they denied it. All was clear and fair ahead. They were lying; I did not mind that; it is moral and not unethical to lie to a reporter. But it is not professional, it is not politic, for a reporter to lie to a banker. So I thought, and so—I passed lightly over their formal, exclamatory corrections of my business.

For some reason, I said, my paper felt that it was very important just then to have a man in Wall Street; the regular reporter, whom they knew, was away, and "we" had no properly trained person to put in his place. I was asked to serve, and I was willing to if the commanding bankers on my list, recognizing the emergency, would agree to trust and help me, not only to get but to understand the news. In return I would promise to keep confidences, and in my reports not reflect in any way the excitement and panic of the—

A list? My editor's list of commanding bankers! They had to see that list, and that list gave them their second shock. Some of them lay back and roared with laughter at my names. Others were serious, but indignant, scornful. "Bankers!" they said in effect. "You call these bankers? And commanding bankers! Who gave you this list? Your city editor! After consulting with the financial editor? I can't believe it. I know the financial editor, and he knows who is who down here."

I recalled the artists of Munich on the other artists of Munich, and I was willing to retreat and admit that my paper's half dozen financiers were not the giants of Wall Street; not all of them. They might, the six, be chosen to cover different regions or departments of financial knowledge and news. That appeased them so much that I was disposed to chuck the whole list into the scrapbasket, but no, that wasn't necessary. Some of my list were all right. And of course, I bethought me, there was always one that belonged, and the one was always willing to acknowledge, however grudgingly, that some other one or two might be of some help to me sometimes. But one of them, by way of my first lesson, bade me get it right up into the front of my brain that in the whole of the United States there were but three bankers; and this banker went so far as to name two of the three, one in Chicago, and the other—the two others, in fact, were in New York. I understood, then, and as I went on with my experience in Wall Street, I was given to understand many times that I was talking to one of the only three bankers—really, professionally bankers— in America.

For I did go on. These men on my list agreed, all but one, to help me "cover Wall Street" during the emergency for "their paper," the *Post*, and the one who only said he would "see" began right away to see. To test me, he gave me a small but important bit of news "confidentially." The trouble with this confidence as a test was that I saw through it; I reported to the city editor what the cunning banker told me and cautioned him that the news was given us to see if we would print it. Of course, Mr. Wright did not use it, and when the banker saw that it was not in the paper the next day, he tempted me again. And again. This man tried me out for a month or more and then, gradually, became my most productive source of news. But the others also trusted me, among them they added to my list, not only bankers, but brokers, speculators, arbitrage traders, money-changers,—specialists and experts of all sorts, who, altogether, gave me a pretty good theoretical schooling in the stock and money market, as well as the daily news.

And there was news. The panic of '93 was one of the great periodic depressions in our financial history, and I used to feel that I was sailing through the storm on the bridge with the officers of the ship. They were glad to have me there. A rank outsider, who did not speculate and had nothing to lose, the panic was an adventure to me, and the falling, failing banks, railroads, and busted pools of speculators were only the action and scenery of a great drama. I could write the news without excitement—if I got it in time, and the bankers soon learned the value of letting me break a bad piece of news, like a big failure, in the cool, dull, matter-of-fact terms of the *Evening Post*, as I had promised. This was made possible by their warning me weeks ahead that such and such a railroad or industrial organization was in trouble. I could gather the facts and figures, write the story, and—many a time we had it all set in type, like the obituary of a dying man, long before the event. "The United States Cordage Company went into the hands of a receiver today," and then a column or two or more of the history of the company—all quietly written and standing in type so that when it happened, I could telephone to the office and on five minutes' notice "release" the whole long story. And such news was usually announced at the close of the stock market, in order to give the traders the night to think it over, permit the banks to support the market, and so avoid too sudden a break in prices. It was, as I say, convenient for the leading financiers to have an evening paper that would report the bad news thus; it was, by the same token, a profitable advantage to the

FINANCIAL

STOCKS CONTINUE TO DECLINE

Railway Stocks Sold Heavily- All Dr —Attack on Northern Pacific Secu rities—Foreign Exchange Rates Ad vancing.

In default of further actual bad news, such as demoralized the market yesterday, professional operators for the decline had recourse to-day to rumor. They were not altogether successful. A heavy break there was in the first hour, shared by the general list, but concentrated upon Northern Pacific stock and bonds. Not the least heavy of the week's liquidation, among houses putting themselves in shape for all emergencies, has been in these securities; and from this the story suddenly sprang forth to-day that the company's June interest coupons could not be paid. The rumor was wholly false, and was in fact officially and emphatically denied. That the Northern Pacific has fallen upon unpleasant times for the necessary adjustment of its floating debt, everybody understands. Money accommodation, in the face of a partial money panic, is no easy matter to obtain. It certainly does not reflect unfavorably on the company's general situation that its managers, as is now generally known, have been able to obtain it.

On the denial of this rumor, another demonstration was made against the market by a violent attack on Reading stock. The delay in publishing officially the new reorganization plan was made a pretext for this. It is noticeable, however, that promoters of corporate reorganizations are wisely slow in appealing to shareholders in the present financial situation. Despite a temporary pause, during the noon hour, in operations for the decline, there was little semblance anywhere of actual rally. Like that of yesterday, to-

FROM THE NEW YORK "EVENING POST" DURING THE PANIC OF 1893

evening paper to have not only the news in full, but "beats," and be bought and read as an insider speaking with authority; and neither last nor least, as I saw it, was the credit I won by my "success" in a field where I was so inexperienced and ignorant. But what I prized and most profited by was the picture I was making for myself of Wall Street, its leaders, workers, and followers, their methods, manners, customs, morals, and point of view.

This came later, however. Appreciation of what I see comes usually only after a period of digestion, and I did not understand Wall Street when I was down there. Too busy. I did not try to put in order the facts I was piling up; it was enough that I spoke the language, knew whom to call on for special information or news, and where to find the nearest telephone. The geography of the Street was my chief interest. Of the facts, only those that could be written as news stood out. If a leading financier, at the end of a dark day of disaster, sat tight denying something I was sure of till, worn out, he fell across his desk, weeping and confessing, I picked up not the hysterical man but the confession, and that I wrote without tears, statistically. When a desperate bear asked me into his office, offered to put me short of one hundred—two hundred—three hundred shares of a stock if I would publish information injurious to the company, I would leave his bribe to take, investigate, and, if true, print the news. The human side of Wall Street was only gossip which made good stories to tell in the city room after the paper went to press or to entertain people at dinner. Having no prejudice for or against finance, I had no judgment, no point of view. It was as it was, neither good nor evil, and even when toward the end of my special service there I began to speculate myself, it was partly to learn the ropes and report better. I was only a reporter reporting, and what I reported did not take form in the picture I have of high finance till I had time, while doing other work, to look back and see through what I had seen.

III

BULLS AND BEARS

W HEN I was a boy, blacksmiths and niggers who had to handle mules and kicking horses used to tell me that the safest place to be in range was close up to the bad animals' heels, and I saw them rush in, pick up a hind leg, and hang on to it, while they shod the hard-hitting hoof. I never tried it myself on a mule, but I did on Wall Street, and there's some truth in it.

The panic of 1893, like all periods of business depression, was a dismal time of radiating destruction. But it had its bright side, inside; it was good for the bears and for my education. The shorts rejoiced in the ruin; they made money, and they were happy. As a reporter on the side lines in the Stock Exchange I could see and hear and feel the wild joy of the bears on a day of tumbling prices, and it was a never-ending surprise to me, because everything I had read, heard, or imagined had pictured the dark depression, despair, and anguish of the losers. And of course there were sufferers, some of them on the floor, others in the banks and brokerage houses, most of all, however, far from the market, out in the country—the public. Among the brokers generally, whether "on the floor" or in their offices, an active market, whether prices are rising or falling, means that business is good; and that's what one felt, and that's what remains to be written—the joy of a panic.

It's like a war, a revolution, a strike—like any crisis in human affairs when men have to walk up and face the consequences of their ignorance, folly, or wickedness—the panic of '93 was a period of bad times chiefly for the innocent. The news of it, the reports printed, are "bad" because they are written by, about, and for bulls. The bears are forgotten and as friendless as the strikers are who rush gleefully forth from the factories to the cafés, or the revolutionists and army officers whose day is come. On the scene one feels the prevailing spirit of activity. It is the period of reconstruction that is gloomy and sad; it is so long, so hard, and so disappointing.

Before the panic had run its course, the regular Wall Street reporter whose place I had taken came back, and I was turned into general reporting again, politics and business, chiefly business. When the constructive work began in finance, the city editor sent me more into "the Street" to discover and report the plans making by the bankers, lawyers, and industrialists for the reorganization of bankrupt concerns and, gradually, for the organization of new corporations and new combines, even, for example, the U. S. Steel Company. These schemes began during the panic; they were compelled by the circumstances, and I heard of them, but paid no heed, while we were in that period when good news was not news. But after a year or so of failures, while the receiverships continued, good news was becoming news; not the best news, but still good, secondary news, and that was my part. I was the bull reporter, the other man was the bear. He was seeing my old conservative, more or less suffering, proper bankers who are really only money-lenders. I had to do with the private bankers who are the constructive engineering financiers.

Of these last, J. P. Morgan, Senior, was the greatest. I did not see much of him, of course; nobody did. He was in sight all the time. He sat alone in a back room with glass sides in his banking-house with his door open, and it looked as if any one could walk in upon him and ask him any question. One heard stories of the payment of large sums for an introduction to him. I could not see why the tippers with business did not come right in off the street and talk to him. They did not. My business was with his partners or associates, principally Samuel Spencer, but I noticed that these, his partners, did not go near him unless he sent for them; and then they looked alarmed and darted in like office-boys. "Nobody can answer that question except Mr. Morgan," they would tell me. Well, Mr. Morgan was there; why not go in and ask him? The answer I got was a smile or a shocked look of surprise. And once when I pressed the president of one of the Morgan banks to put to him a question we agreed deserved an answer, the banker said, "Not on your life," and when I said, "But why not?" he said. "You try it yourself and see." And I did.

I went over to J. P. Morgan and Company, walked into his office, and stood before him at his flat, clean, clear desk. I stood while he examined a sheet of figures; I stood for two or three long minutes, while the whole bank seemed to stop work to watch me, and he did not look up; he was absorbed, he was sunk, in those figures. He was so alone with himself and his mind that when he did glance up he did not see me; his eyes were looking inward. He was a mathematician, you know. One of the stories told of his life was that he was so gifted in mathematics that the University of Göttingen invited him to stay there to take a lectureship that would lead up to a career in pure mathematics. I thought, as he looked at and did not see me that day, that he was doing a sum in mental arithmetic, and when he solved it he dropped his eyes back upon his sheet of figures and I slunk out.

Somebody stopped me as I was going out through the bank and laughingly asked me what had happened.

"Nothing," I said; "he didn't even see me."

"You're lucky," was the chuckling answer. "You have to call him to wake him up. If you had said, 'Mr. Morgan,' he would have come to. And then—"

"What would have happened then?" I asked.

"Oh," the partner said, "then you would have seen—an explosion."

I believed that; it was generally believed on the Street that J. P. Morgan was a dangerous man to talk to, and no doubt that made it unnecessary for him to be guarded by door men, secretaries, and stenographers. He could protect himself. I know that I came to feel, myself, what others on Wall Street felt, a vague awe of the man.

But I went through that awful circle once. I said, "Mr. Morgan." The paper received one afternoon a typewritten statement from Morgan and Company; it was some announcement about a matter of bonds that had been news for months, and the city editor called me in to read it with him. He could not make it out. It was a long, complicated statement all in one sentence, and I could not read it either. "Take it down to Mr. Morgan and ask him to read it," Mr. Wright said, and I remember I was startled. I asked Wright if he knew what he was asking of me: to go and put a question to the old man himself. "Yes," said Wright, "but it has to be done." I picked up the statement, ran down to the bank, conning the sentence, and ready for the explosion, I walked into Morgan's office and right up to his desk. He saw me this time; he threw himself back in his chair so hard that I thought he would tip over.

"Mr. Morgan," I said as brave as I was afraid, "what does this statement mean?" and I threw the paper down before him.

"Mean!" he exclaimed. His eyes glared, his great red nose seemed to me to flash and darken, flash and darken. Then he roared. "Mean! It means what it says. I wrote it myself, and it says what I mean."

"It doesn't say anything—straight," I blazed.

He sat back there, flashing and rumbling; then he clutched the arms of his chair, and I thought he was going to leap at me. I was so scared that I defied him.

"Oh, come now, Mr. Morgan," I said, "you may know a lot about figures and finance, but I'm a reporter, and I know as much as you do about English. And that statement isn't English."

That was the way to treat him, I was told afterward. And it was in that case. He glared at me a moment more, the fire went out of his face, and he leaned forward over the bit of paper and said very meekly, "What's the matter with it?"

I said I thought it would be clearer in two sentences instead of one and I read it aloud so, with a few other verbal changes.

"Yes," he agreed, "that is better. You fix it."

I fixed it under his eyes, he nodded, and I, whisking it away, hurried back to the office. They told me in the bank afterward that "J. P." sat watching me go out of the office, then rapped for Spencer and asked what my name was, where I came from, and said, "Knows what he wants, and—and—gets it."

He never offered me a partnership, but when Samuel Spencer, the receiver of the Southern Railway, arranged for an interview with him a year or so later, Mr. Morgan remembered and talked to me—"not for publication"—about the south from a financial point of view. The talk was a dry, but convincing, bull prophecy of what has happened since down there, later, much later than the prophet expected; but it was a true prophecy.

Morgan was a bull. "He gets it coming and going," the Street used to say, "but he always says that for the long pull the bull

side is the winning side in America. The U.S.A. is a bull country."
That is to say, he made money by selling on a falling market;
but he bought too on the way down and so ended, he and his
bank and his "crowd," in possession of enough stock at sacrifice
prices to give him the control. Then he could "reorganize" the railroad and other companies he had chosen as, in the long run, good;
he could finance and direct the running of them. He made his bear
profits, got his banker's commission on the reorganization, the
banker's interest on money lent, the banker's profit on underwriting
and floating the new stocks and bonds, and, best of all, the control.
This was all common practice and common knowledge when I was
in Wall Street; it was talked about as just plain business, and as
I heard it all, it seemed to me to be only good business, profitable,
proper, and—easy. I used to wonder why men went into any other
business than Wall Street if they wanted only to make money, and
I declared to myself and to my friends that when I wanted to
make money I would not write, or report, or edit, or manage;
I would go into Wall Street. I would quit working and—make
money.

And, mind you, this was not cynicism; it was plain common
sense to me. A student of ethics, I accepted it as the world does, as
the business men generally, as bankers, brokers and indeed bishops
accepted it as, not only the custom, but moral and wise. Many a
time, I have sympathized deeply with a stock operator or a banker
who was thrown into the depths of despair because he had not
made the millions he had planned to make; he had not lost, he
merely had not made his money. I watched men working and
lying to smash a company that they were trying to get cheap, the
control of it, and I rejoiced with them when they "busted" the old
crowd, drove them out ruined, and got the business. I was offered
the presidency of one such company. I considered taking it, and
when I objected that I knew nothing of business, neither that or
any other, the answer was that I did not need to; they would tell
me what I was to do; in fact I must consult them. All I had to do,
apparently, was to draw a good salary, occupy a fine office, and
make a respectable appearance. "You'll get out of reporting and
become a man of affairs." I did not grasp what this meant at the
time. When I declined to be lifted out of journalism up off the
street into high finance with a social and financial position, I did not

despise or pity as I do now the successful men who seize such opportunities. My reason was personal: business did not attract me; money was no object; I liked reporting; I did not generalize at all. I did not understand, so I did not condemn, the practices of big business. I was not thinking in those days; life was too, too interesting, the world as it was too fascinating, to stop to question anything but politics, which was all bad, just as business was all good, to me.

James B. Dill was the first man to remind me that I was an intellectual, that I might think as well as see and write. He was a masterpiece. He was the man who put through in the State of New Jersey the laws to enable the organization of trusts and combines, to free corporations, to free them to do whatever they pleased. His was a great name in Wall Street; even the big fellows spoke of James B. Dill with awe and retained him to organize their plans into going concerns. He was the man, for example, who brought Andrew Carnegie and J. P. Morgan together for the purchase and sale of the Carnegie steel properties and so laid the basis of the United States Steel Company, the biggest transaction and the biggest trust of those days. "I put Morgan in one room, Carnegie in another," he recounted, "while I took the third room in between them with my clerks and stenographers. I knew that if they met they would blow up; so I played the part of buffer and negotiator. They could express their opinions of each other to me. I could agree with both of them, sympathize with the generosity and bigness of each one, and share his contempt for the narrow meanness of the other. I was sincere, uninsultable, and true to their agreeable purposes, the one to buy, the other to sell."

Dill was a realist with insight and humor, but hardly any one knew of his humor. He was always spoken of with awe as "James B. Dill." No familiarity with him; Mr. Morgan might be "J.P."; he was called that, but James B. Dill was always and only a name, a mystery, a wonder-worker in those terrible days when the reorganization of the débris of '93 was beginning. No one but the masters ever saw him, and we, who would no more think of approaching him than we would walk in on J.P. himself, we—I thought of him as a silent, thinking, conspiring lawyer who sat still in the big back room of a great suite of offices, with an army commander's staff of almost equally great attorneys-at-law, who all joined their learning and their wits to advise, at huge fees (which rumor named), the brains of big business. He was, in brief, the great black man who showed good Business how to circumvent bad Politics and the anti-trust legislation passed to satisfy the ignorant, envious people.

For there was, at that time, a very general popular discontent, the choral accompaniment of the hard times; and the passion of the day was the anti-trust sentiment, which was a development out of the old anti-monopoly cry of the earlier period. The *Post* was not anti-trust; it was anti-Tammany; but it was for business, except now and then when there was some exceptional scandal, too outrageous to be passed by in silence. The *Post* was sincere, of course; almost everybody was, almost everybody is, sincere. I did not know it, but I can see now that what I needed then was what the world needs all the time, to find some one who was not sincere but intelligent. I found that man in James B. Dill. Bless him.

One day some morning newspaper printed a "roast" of James B. Dill, the author of the criminal New Jersey trust laws. It showed how that State had enacted statutes under which the anti-trust laws of other States could be evaded and American public opinion defied. A sovereign State, Jersey had the right to pass any laws it pleased, and if it enabled the formation of trusts in New Jersey, New York State and the other States had to recognize the creatures of the free State of New Jersey. The article declared that it was James B. Dill who had himself invented and put over this legislation, quietly, almost secretly, in New Jersey, and then it showed in some detail what was permitted: plain financial crimes.

This clipping was handed to me, with instructions to go and see Mr. James B. Dill and get his denial or correction of these charges. So! I was to see the black man! I felt as I did when I was sent to see Mr. Morgan, as an English pressman would if he were sent to interview a minister of the Crown, as a girl feels who is to be presented to the Queen. I was flattered. I was trembling with fear, I was awfully bold, as I went, hurrying and slowing up, eagerly and then dreadfully, downtown and up into the building where the silent councilor of the trusts was hidden away in—not a great suite of offices, but a small, neat set of two or three rooms. A smiling little stenographer and typist took my card, with my name and that of my paper on it, into one of the rooms, and returning instantly, swept me in to Mr. Dill, who met me with a smiling welcome on his rosy, round, happy face.

"The *Evening Post*—at last," he chuckled, and his round little body seemed to laugh as it settled back into its big chair. "I have been wondering," he said, "why you have not called on me. I have been tempted to send for you. The abuses of the Jersey Trust laws must be exposed and stopped. Yes," he added, as he glanced at the clipping I held out to him, the story that I thought would anger and drive him to a furious contradiction, "yes, all that is true, and more, much more."

And to my amazement he opened up the criminal inside of the practices under the New Jersey legislation, a picture of such chicanery and fraud, of wild license and wrong-doing, that I could not, I dared not, take it all down; I was too confused. And Dill saw that, and he laughed; his eyes twinkled and his round little belly shook with the humor of the situation.

"You are astonished?" he said. "And well you may be. But you must write what I tell you. Don't quote me. I am the founder of this legislation, and as such you may name me, but don't say I gave you these facts; it would look odd; it might be suspicious, to make me the authority for an exposure of what I am the enabling founder of, but it is your duty to describe what is done under these laws, and if your editor shows any hesitation, you may tell him to call me up on the 'phone; I will stand back of whatever you print."

I did not write all that Dill told me; not then; I never have. I could not at the time, because, as I have said, I was too imbued with the Wall Street spirit and view of things to speak as this lawyer did of the holies of the holy. Upton Sinclair learned from him; he was a socialist. I was a Wall Street man myself, unconsciously, but literally. That's how I came finally to understand what corruption is and how it gets a man, not as the Reds and the writers think, but as the Whites and the Righteous are: rogues outside, but inside, honest men. However, that's for later. When James B. Dill told me first about Wall Street and his Jersey laws, and he saw that I would not, could not, take it in, he made merry with me, laughing and quizzing and telling me ever more and more.

"Why, didn't you ever hear how they wiped out Richmond Terminal?" he would say, and he would tell me that story. "And you didn't know that? A Wall Street reporter, and you don't know that! And this—" He told me something else that I had never heard of; and then something else. "Nor that? Never knew that? What do you know?

"I say," he said, when I rose to go after that first interview, "I must know you better. And my wife and daughter; they must know you." He invited me to his house; he took me there, and thus began a friendship that lasted as long as James B. Dill himself in the body. He had incorporated himself and his fortune under his Jersey laws as "The James B. Dill Corporation"—I think that was the title of it—he told me about it with glee, a corporation with five shares—or three, which he controlled, he laughed; one share to his wife, one for his daughter (in escrow), the rest (and the control) for him. "Avoids taxes and all sorts of troubles when I die." So "The James B. Dill Corporation" may be immortal, but my jolly little imp of a Santa Claus, my mischievous professor of financial law, my good friend James B. Dill, died, a loss, a real loss, but not till he had made me see Wall Street and Business and Politics and Law as he saw them, from the inside out; and not, of course, till he had explained to me why he, of all men, had led and inspired and provided the ammunition for the exposure of the James B. Dill laws of New Jersey.

"Why, Dr. Innocent," he said, "I was advertising my wares and the business of my State. When you and the other reporters and critics wrote as charges against us what financiers could and did actually do in Jersey, when you listed, with examples, what the trust-makers were doing under our laws, you were advertising our business—free. For financiers are dubs, as you know yourself now; don't you? They have to be told, and they have to be told plain so that they get it, and so, as I say, while I gave you the facts to roast us with, what you wrote as 'bad' struck business men all over the United States as good, and they poured in upon us to our profit to do business with us to their profit. The only drawback was that when Delaware and New York and other 'bad' political sovereigns saw what Jersey was doing and how we made money and friends out of our trust policy they copied us, and they went further than we did, or, to be exact, they tried to."

And so saying, Dill laughed and laughed and laughed; not cynically; not wickedly; but merrily, with his whole body and soul. James B. Dill was one of the "wisest," wisest and, yes, about the rightest man I ever met.

"Trusts are natural, inevitable growths out of our social and economic conditions," he said often. "You cannot stop them by force, with laws. They will sweep down like glaciers upon your police, courts, and States and wash them into flowing rivers. I am for clearing the way for them. Let them go, and if they cannot be brought into social use, why—then—then"—he would laugh— "then I would be for exploring their origin and dealing with—I mean closing up—their source."

THE POLICE

E VERY newspaper that I know anything about suffers from politics, "newspaper politics." The men on it decide on some question of policy or control or places, and everybody becomes more or less involved. Joseph Pulitzer, the founder, owner, and editor of the New York *World*, cultivated warring factions. Whether his theory was that disloyalty to one another made his heads of departments loyal to him or that rivalry developed the advantages of competition, he had a business manager who did not speak to some editors, who did not all speak to one another. Charles A. Dana had the most united staff; his competition was between his morning and evening papers, but we used to hear of quarrels and contempts even on the morning edition which was the *Sun*. Godkin may never have heard of parties on the *Evening Post*; the division was not sharp and open, but Henry J. Wright, and the publisher, J. S. Seymour, were, however quietly, against Linn, the managing editor, who represented instinctively the taste and policy of the editor-in-chief. He was for keeping all police and sensational news out of the paper, and in the main he had his way. Wright and Seymour, who wanted to build up circulation and business by printing all the news, had one great victory, and it was most profitable for me.

One afternoon when I was back on my general reporting the city editor called me up to his desk and asked me if I would like to cover police headquarters. A startling suggestion. The *Post* had never had a man in Mulberry Street, where the heads of the police and detective service had their offices. It was the source of crime news—and Mr. Wright said, quick, that I was to pay no attention to crime; I was to cover the activities of Dr. Parkhurst, whom I had already interviewed several times for the paper.

The Rev. Dr. Charles H. Parkhurst was discovering the corruption of the police and denouncing the force from his pulpit. He sounded like a prophet of old in his sermons, but personally he was a calm, smiling, earnest, but not unhumorous gentleman who frankly enjoyed his notoriety and his exposures. He knew some of the doings of the police; they were dangerous facts to allege; libelous. He had to be careful, and he was cautious, but he was persistent, methodically, thoroughly. He organized in and out of his congregation a society to investigate the police, procure evidence, and put him in a position to describe New York police methods and their relations with Tammany Hall, the liquor interests, and criminals. The *Post* was interested, of course, in anybody that came out openly against Tammany; there was some suspicion of a clergyman who "profaned his pulpit with police filth," even as against Tammany; and my first assignments to see Parkhurst were reluctant. Dr. Parkhurst talked moderately, sensibly, briefly, and, as I reported him, in tone with the paper. Following up a police news lead, as I always did, I called on him every few days; we became rather friendly, and I was soon able to warn my chief of news to come; which came—at police headquarters. Mr. Wright had seen, I think, that Dr. Parkhurst offered him a good excuse for assigning a reporter to police headquarters: to report the police side of an opening controversy; and since the clergyman and I seemed to get along well together I was the man to go.

"Not to report crimes and that sort of thing," said Wright, in effect. "You will keep in touch with Dr. Parkhurst, know what he is doing, and work in with him for the purpose of reporting his findings with the police department for a background." But I got from him somehow the idea that, if I could find a way, not a sensational, conventional, but, say, a political, a literary, way to write about robberies, murders, etc., I might try putting some crime into the *Post*.

No urging was needed to make me accept the assignment. I was eager for it. "The police" meant to me a dark, mysterious layer of the life of a great city into which I had not yet penetrated. My experience in Wall Street, especially my mocking relations with James B. Dill, had driven it into my consciousness that it was possible to think that I knew all about something and yet be an innocent ignoramus. Dill had taught me that back of my bankers and brokers and their news of Wall Street there was a world which I had not even glimpsed and which the Wall Street men themselves did not really picture as it was. Few of them ever saw it. My reports of "the American X & Y Company receivership," columns long, were not "the" story, as Dill told it afterward. I had never got and printed the truth back of the financial news. It was probably so with the police news; there was probably a still greater truth back of the petty, monstrous abuses Dr. Parkhurst was disclosing. And then there were the murders, fires, robberies, and politics. I might not write, but I could learn all about such events. I went to police headquarters as I had gone to Wall Street, as I had gone to Europe, and as I had come home to America, with the suppressed ardor of a young student and with the same throbbing anxiety that an orator feels just before he rises to speak.

But, first, I called on Dr. Parkhurst to tell him of my assignment and make with him the kind of agreement I had had with my Wall Street bankers: to work together with him and exchange news and confidences. He was interested, of course; it meant support for him by the *Evening Post,* and he spent several forenoons describing his plans, methods, and best of all, the police chiefs and their system of corruption, as he knew and could not yet prove. As it turned out, Dr. Parkhurst knew well what he knew, but he did not know the system as it was exposed later by the Lexow Committee; nobody had pictured that; and that, even that, was not all. However, after a few talks with Dr. Parkhurst I felt that I knew both the chief police officers and their worst crimes, and so, with no little dread and a solid foundation of certainty, I went one morning early to police headquarters with my card to present to the Superintendent of Police, Thomas F. Byrnes.

It was his hour for receiving citizens with complaints, his inspectors, captains, heads of departments with reports, and "the press." His small outer office was crowded with people, uniformed and in plain clothes. I was embarrassed, but I handed my card to the chief's favorite sergeant, Mangin, and as he bade me wait my turn, a tall, handsome inspector of police, whom I, of course, did not know, spoke out loud into the silence.

"A reporter from the *Evening Post,*" he said, clear and distinct like a pistol shot. "The *Post* has always despised police news, true police news, but now when we are under fire they are to have a man up here to expose and clean us all out, us rascals."

I felt as if his shots had hit me, and I sank wounded into a chair; the man was not through. Sneering and pointing at my red-hot face, he said, "We'll see how long he stays here."

The challenge braced me. I asked Sergeant Mangin, "Who is that man?"

Mangin hesitated, glanced at my foe, and then said, softly but audibly, "Inspector Williams."

I knew that name. Dr. Parkhurst had told me of the audacity and force and badness of the "clubbing inspector," so I rallied to him.

"Oh," I said, "Clubber Williams. I know about him," and to him I made my bluff. "I shall stay here till you are driven out."

There was a sense of quick excitement. Mangin darted through the swinging doors into Superintendent Byrnes' inner office, an officer came out, and I was bidden to enter—out of my turn. Mangin undoubtedly had told Byrnes what had happened. The Superintendent rose to meet and greet me, reading my name from the card in his hand, and adding, "The *Evening Post*." Indicating a chair beside his desk, he said in his most formal fashion that I was welcome at police headquarters. The force was irritated, naturally, being subjected just then to criticism from places where "the finest" might expect support.

"When you stop to think that it is we, the police, who protect your lives and property, guarding you not only from thieves and robbers, but from strikers and mobs, you can see, no doubt, that it hurts us to be denounced as Dr. Parkhurst, for example, is denouncing us—from the pulpit and in the newspapers. I hope and trust that the *Evening Post*, a Wall Street paper, an organ of good business and all decent property interests, will give us aid and comfort—"

I wanted to protest; I probably gave some sign of a wish to correct him, as I did, early; he saw that and changed his note a little.

"Yes, yes, I know," he said, "the *Evening Post* will not take sides. A fair paper, it will be just and true to the facts. Right; I know that. None better. You will seek the truth, and the truth you will report, as you find it. Right. But, my dear Mr.—Mr."—he couldn't find the card—"you cannot get the truth from Dr. Parkhurst nor from any other enemy of the police."

Again he saw me shy.

"Yes, yes, you must see Dr. Parkhurst, listen to him, but you will listen to us, too, to me. You will want the news. Well, sir, I control the news from the police department, and I can—I can give and I can withhold the news. No, no, keep your seat. I am

THE CHIEF INSPECTOR
Tom Byrnes

only endeavoring to say to you that I am going to put you on the same basis here as the old reporters who have been with us for years, most of them, and in return I ask you, in all fairness, not to print the stuff you get from the enemies of the police without submitting it to me for correction or—at any rate—comment."

It was worse, it was plainer, than I had expected it to be. I could see through this doughty chief of police; he was not the awe-inspiring figure I had imagined. For Tom Byrnes was a famous police chief; few people ever saw him; he was only a name, but there were stories told about him, of his cunning, as a detective, as a master of men, as a manhandler of criminals, and as a retriever of stolen properties—stories that filled the upper world with respect and the lower with terror. He struck me as simple, no complications at all—a man who would buy you or beat you, as you might choose, but get you he would.

Not me. So I thought, and I think he felt as I meant him to:

that I was going to be a free lance at police headquarters. His eyes narrowed into two slits as he read me. To meet his covert threat to keep news from me I said that I had no use for his ordinary police news; I was sent there only to see what I might see, hear what might be said, and print what I could prove—of politics. That was all. I was willing to tell him in advance whatever of importance I meant to report—if he would always see me promptly: I could not allow any delays in news, of course.

Byrnes looked at me, listening and drumming with his fingers on the desk. When I had finished he rose, walked to his window, and drummed on the glass with his nails till, turning suddenly, he dismissed me.

"All right," he said, and he pressed a button which summoned Mangin, who came darting in as I went out through the swinging doors into and through the silent, staring crowd in the outer office into the hall. A reporter followed me, an elderly man, who turned out to be the day man of a morning newspaper.

"You have made a bad start," he said as he joined me. "You have made an enemy of the first inspector. I hope you made a friend of the chief. You'll need him, with Williams against you."

I believed this; I was depressed, but I am sure I did not show it.

"What do I need friends for?" I said. "They would only embarrass me in what I am here to do."

He did not ask me what it was that I meant to do. Like Williams, he, everybody, seemed to know what I was there for; maybe Williams had told the crowd while I was with Byrnes. But how did Williams know? I was awed by their detective sagacity; it was frightening. I did not learn till much later that the police are professional guessers, and not good ones, except in obvious cases.

"I know your city editor, Harry Wright," the reporter was saying, "and I know that he will expect you to get some news. And I can help you, if you will work with me for a while and take my advice till you know the ropes yourself."

This did not attract, it repelled me, this proposition, and I wanted to get away from this friend. He was talking about how to find an office. The best place for a police reporter was in the buildings across the street; there one could watch police headquarters, see who came and went, and run across in a moment for any news that might turn up. But all the rooms were taken; I would better have a desk in his office and pay him for half the telephone, heat, and light rates. I hardly heard. My attention was caught by a shaggy-looking fellow coming down the street and yelling, "M-m-ma-a-x. M-m-a-x."

"Who is that?" I asked.

"Oh, that! That's Jake Riis, the *Evening Sun* man."

So! That was Jacob A. Riis, the author of *How the Other Half Lives*, and not only a famous police reporter, but a well-known character in one half of the life of New York. I liked his looks.

"But what's he bawling for?" I asked.

"For his boy, Max, who gets his news for him. There he is."

And there was Max Fischel, a little old round, happy Jewish boy, coming out of the basement door of headquarters, his hand full of pieces of paper: notes. He ran across the street to Riis, who was just coming to work, and the two—geniuses—that's what they were, both of them—went into the building opposite, where on the first floor Riis reappeared to throw up his window, through which you could see him and Max settle down to work. Every morning for two or three years I saw this scene, and it came to have a meaning to me; I was soon imitating it as nearly as I could.

Jake Riis was a Danish American who "covered" police headquarters, the Health Department, which was then in the same building, and "the East Side," which was a short name for the poor and the foreign quarters of the city. And he not only got the news; he cared about the news. He hated passionately all tyrannies, abuses, miseries, and he fought them. He was a "terror" to the officials and landlords responsible, as he saw it, for the desperate condition of the tenements where the poor lived. He had "exposed" them in articles, books, and public speeches, and with results. All the philanthropists in town knew and backed Riis, who was able then, as a reformer and a reporter, too, to force the appointment of a Tenement House Commission that he gently led and fiercely drove to an investigation and a report which—followed up by this terrible reporter—resulted in the wiping out of whole blocks of rookeries, the making of small parks, and the regulation of the tenements. He had discovered these evils as a reporter, reporting, say, a suicide, a fire, or a murder. These were the news, which all the reporters got; only Riis wrote them as stories, with heart, humor, and understanding. And having "seen" the human side of the crime or the disaster, he had taken note also of the house or the block or the street where it happened. He went back and he described that, too; he called on the officers and landlords who permitted the conditions, and "blackmailed" them into reforms.

This had been going on for years when I came to police headquarters. Riis was growing old, but he had found and trained his boy, Max, to see and to understand as Riis did; and Max could see. It seemed to me that Max was born and not made. He did the early morning work, which was the key to the day. The police, stationed all over the city, reported all happenings in their precincts to headquarters—fires, accidents, crimes, and arrests—which were posted briefly in the basement telegraph office, where the reporters could see them. The morning newspaper men watched these bulletins, weighed them, and went out to investigate those that seemed likely to have a story back of them. They stayed up till their papers went to press, at two or three o'clock in the morning. When Riis first came to police headquarters as a young man, the evening newspaper men appeared at about eight or nine o'clock and began their work by conning the accumulation of bulletins dated from three o'clock on down to eight. These they divided up among themselves, each reporter going out on one. When they returned with their several stories, they exchanged the news, wrote each one all the stories, and then could settle down for the day to a poker game, which only big news could interrupt. Riis did not play poker; he joined in no "combine"; he worked alone, sometimes giving but never asking help. He began to beat the combine, which had to quit poker and work all day, still together, to keep up with and, if possible, beat Riis. They, all veterans, had the advantage of knowing the town and the police, who did not like Riis, but he carried the war into their camp by coming to work at seven o'clock, which gave him time to take two or three of the early morning bulletins, cover and write them all, and since most of the sensational incidents of a city are reported in those late night hours, the *Evening Sun* had such a lead on police news as the *Post* had had on Wall Street. And when the beaten editors drove their police reporters to work at seven o'clock, Riis, the scab, began to come at six, then five, then four. Nobody else started that early: no editor could demand it, and Riis himself could not stand it long. But each reporter had a copy boy, a messenger, to carry his stories downtown. Riis hit upon the idea of a boy who, besides carrying copy, could "cover" the city from three till seven, eight, nine, when Riis turned up to write the news. Max, who began with the facts, soon learned to see and form and deliver to Riis the stories of the night for which the *Evening Sun* was noted. Beautiful stories they were, too, sometimes, for Riis could write.

This, then, was what I was seeing, my first morning at police headquarters: Max furnishing Riis the night's stories, all ready made. I must know Riis. Waiting out in the street till he was through writing—when I saw Max take the copy and set off for his office downtown, I crossed over and called on Riis. In a loud, cheerful, hearty voice, he greeted me.

"Glad you've come," he said. "The *Post* can help a lot up here, and you've begun well."

"Begun well!" I exclaimed. "I haven't begun yet."

Riis roared his great laugh. "Oh, yes, you have. Max says you banged Alec Williams one and disappointed the old man himself."

He meant that I had failed with Superintendent Byrnes! I was about to protest, but Riis was shouting through that open window.

"That's the way to handle them! Knock 'em down, then you can pick them up and be the good Samaritan. It's their own way with us reporters. They put the fear of God into us, then they are kind to us—if we'll let them. Not to me. They are afraid of me, not I of them, and so with you. You have started off on top. Stay there."

He bade me keep out of the combine. "Play alone," he said. "The combine will beat you for a while; so will I, of course. The whole police force will help beat you. Sure. But you'll soon learn the game and hold your own."

He said, still embarrassingly aloud, that he had seen me talking with the other reporter.

"I know what he wanted," he laughed. "He proposed that you share his office, pay him—not his office, him—half the rent costs, be his Max, and—"

"How did you know that?"

"I didn't," Riis shouted, as the reporter we were talking about walked across the street and up the stairs to headquarters. "But —— tries to get every new reporter to fag for him; and most of them do. No. Don't you do it. I can't show you around much; too busy; but Max will," and he called "M-a-a-x" out of the window; then remembered: "Oh, yes, Max is gone downtown. Come on. I'll show you around."

He broke into all the offices, police and health, walked right in upon everybody he thought I should know, laughed, made them

"CLUBBER" WILLIAMS IN HIS PRIME

all laugh, and introduced me, not by name, but as the new *Evening Post* man. When we were coming back out of the building, at the front end of the hall, we saw two policemen half forcing, half carrying, a poor, broken, bandaged East Side Jew into the office opposite that of the Superintendent of Police. There were officers and citizens all about us, but Riis grasped my arm, and pointing to the prisoner as he stumbled in through the open door, he shouted —not, I think, for me alone to hear: "There you have a daily scene in Inspector Williams' office! That's a prisoner. Maybe he's done something wrong, that miserable Russian Jew; anyway he's done something the police don't like. But they haven't only arrested him, as you see; they have beaten him up. And look—"

The door opened, showed a row of bandaged Jews sitting against the wall in the inspector's office, and at his desk, Clubber Williams.

"See the others. There's a strike on the East Side, and there are always clubbed strikers here in this office. I'll tell you what to do while you are learning our ways up here; you hang around this office every morning, watch the broken heads brought in, and as the prisoners are discharged, ask them for their stories. No paper will print them, but you yourself might as well see and hear how strikes are broken by the police."

Inspector Williams had heard. He rose from his desk, pointed at the door, shouted something, and the doorman closed the door with a bang. And Jake Riis laughed. But there was no merriment in that loud laugh of Jake Riis; there was bold rage in his face, as he left me, banging out of the building. I stayed, as he suggested, and watched the scene. Many a morning when I had nothing else to do I stood and saw the police bring in and kick out their bandaged, bloody prisoners, not only strikers and foreigners, but thieves, too, and others of the miserable, friendless, troublesome poor.

V

CLUBS, CLUBBERS, AND CLUBBED

POLICE clubbing is an art, and few policemen master it. This I learned while I was spending my first idle mornings at police headquarters, watching the victims of the stick brought in to be inspected by the inspector, Clubber Williams. Nobody else seemed to be interested. Riis went straight to his office, and calling M-m-a-x, took the boy's stories of the night and wrote them. He would not, could not, look at the bruised and bleeding strikers; it made him "mad." The other reporters, seeing me standing at the front door, fascinated by the sight, advised me that it was "nothing; happens every day during a strike." An old policeman was a little more understanding.

Coming in with papers from his precinct, he halted beside me to look at a specially wretched case: an old Jew, who plainly had been hit many times with the long night sticks: across the nose and eyes, on the side of the head, on his right hand, left arm or shoulder, and his back. He was crying and shrank from the slightest touch. It was pitiful, and I must have uttered some sign of my disapproval. For the old cop spoke.

"You're right," he said. "It's rotten work. Makes a man sick to see it."

I was relieved to find that there was some one that felt as I did, and a policeman, too; but he went on to say that what I was seeing was the bad work of young policemen. "They don't understand, they aren't taught as we were how to swing the stick. It's a formidable weapon, but there's a trick to it. One lick is always enough, if it is placed right."

So, I gathered, it was not an emotional but an esthetic criticism I was hearing, and I asked for more. "How do you place it right, this stick?"

"You a reporter?" he asked, and when I nodded yes, he said, "Well, then, you ought to know that a club, especially a night stick, is meant to knock a man unconscious. You can kill with it, you know, and you can batter a man all to pieces, like that striker just gone in there. That's not necessary. All you got to do is to tap the extremities, head or feet, so as to send a current through the spine. If you land on the peak of the head your prisoner lays down; if you hit both feet exactly right—"

The old chap stopped to laugh, and to my inquisitive surprise, he offered an explanation.

"It's the funniest sight in the world to see the effect of a proper lick with a stick on a man's two feet. You don't get the chance to try it often. In my day we old cops used to practice it, very easy, on one another, and when you could do it you'd go out and find your bum. I remember the first time I got one just right. He was asleep on his back on a park bench, his two feet stuck out clear and even. Gosh, I was glad, and careful. I sneaked up on him from behind, knelt down, spit on my hand, and aimed. I was so nervous that I dropped my raised arm twice before I felt steady and ready. Then—say, but then I let her go, I whacked level and straight, hitting the bottoms of both boots at the same instant, and, well, it happened—what they always said would happen. That bum rose, stiff like a stick; he didn't bend a knee or move an arm. I think he didn't wake up. He just rose up, running—I mean that he was running by the time he came erect, and with never a holler or a look behind, he was running hell-bent across that park and—I watched him; I walked over in the direction he disappeared and—he's running yet. Yep! I bet that when he woke up, he was surprised to find himself running; it was so unusual for him to run that it woke him, but he couldn't stop, of course. His spine—"

He stopped, seemed to see it all over again, and he laughed till he remembered his errand. Then he said seriously, "It was beautiful; nothing like this"—and walked off down the long hall to the detective bureau with his papers.

His view interested and held me for a moment; I had heard of art for art's sake, but it was not satisfying, as applied to police clubbing. I had feelings about the clubbers. I would like to have had them clubbed, and by young policemen who had never heard of the art. I can see now that I had the very emotion that those rough clubbers had. I passionately desired action, and so feeling, I dashed into the office of the Superintendent and told him about this daily procession of wounded.

"Yes, I know," said Byrnes. "They should not be brought in at the front. It looks bad, and I have given orders repeatedly that prisoners, especially damaged prisoners, be brought in at the rear. I'll see now that it's done. Thank you for calling my attention to the matter."

But why, I asked, why must prisoners be so terribly beaten up? —and I must have put some feeling into my question. Byrnes changed his style. He had two styles or manners of speech, one formal, affected, and English; the other informal and native Irish. "Oh, I get you," he said, his eyes closing down small and hard. "You want to know why we give strikers the stick! Well, I'll tell you. You go over on the East Side some night or morning; you watch the blankety-blanks picketing a shop. Just stand around and look, and say, you listen, too. And then you come back here and you tell me why you would land on 'em with a night stick if you had one in your hand."

A good idea. I asked where to go; he gave me some addresses, and the next morning early I was on hand at my first strike. I neither knew nor cared anything about labor troubles. I believed, or I would have said, that the workers should work and the bosses boss. Of socialism I had heard. We had been told all about Marx and his theories, briefly and sufficiently, in college, when we were studying the more serious, scientific economists. Again in Paris I had listened at the cafés to the artists in revolt talking about socialism and anarchism, and they seemed to regard them as theories which would give art a place in life and young artists a living—considerations which had nothing to do with ethics, my specialty, or me. When I turned up, cold and a bit late, on a dirty East Side street corner to watch a shop where the sensible workers wished to return to work and the union pickets were to try to keep them "out," I had no interest in the strike, in Labor and Capital, or any of that troublesome nonsense. I wanted to see why the police clubbed people. And I saw.

I saw, first, a small group of three policemen on the corner where the sweat-shop was. The policemen pointed it out to me, on the second floor of a tenement. They recognized me as a reporter. How? "By your clothes," said one. "Say," said another, "you washed your face when you got up, didn't you? Well." There was also a small group of East Side spectators near the cops, "out to see the fun." For the rest there seemed to be only people, Jewish men, women, and children—all in their queer, black old clothes—going about their business. But one of the officers taught me to distinguish a procession of young men and women marching slowly at wide intervals along the street and turning around the corner. These were the pickets, the cop said, "laying for scabs."

"And there," he added sharply, "there comes a scab—with his father and mother to protect him." He pointed and started toward a young man with an old Jewish couple a block away. How he knew it was a worker returning to work I could not tell until, as we approached, I saw the scared white face of the fellow and the anxious looks he and his parents cast all about them. But I observed that everybody else recognized him, as the police did; the crowd stopped to look his way, and the pickets began to concentrate upon the trio, the pickets and the police, slowly racing. Several pickets reached him first. Shouting, gesticulating, they grabbed him, and just as the three policemen and I ran up, one of the pickets yanked away the old people and another struck the scab, who dropped. My policeman's night stick whizzed through the air, hit and knocked out the picket who had struck the blow, and the other pickets ran away. There were shrieks, calls, and a whistle. The parents of the scab were lying moaning and crying upon him; the police had to peel them off to lift him to his feet. He was bleeding from a cut on the cheek, and he was bawling as I had never heard a man bawl. With his father, mother, and a policeman to escort him, he staggered to the shop, where he washed up and went to work. I stayed with my cop, who kicked up the picket; his wound was a great bump on the back of the head, and as he gathered his senses, he protested.

"What for did you—"

"Ah, shut up," the policeman answered. "Look a' here." He seized the fellow's arm, held it up for him and me to see—a brass knuckle on his right fist. "The emblem of the organization," the policeman called it with a grin.

Then I learned my first lesson in the conflict between Labor and Capital: the workers are, as Capital alleges, forced into the unions;

they do not all voluntarily seek to unite; some of them, most of them, have to be driven to it by the brass knuckle and forceful persuasion.

I did not draw this generalization then and there that morning. All that I gathered on the spot was that the police used the club against the brass knuckle; and, also, against the law. For the strikers, Labor generally, are sticklers for the law.

The prisoner was led away by my policeman, who, to my question, "Police headquarters?" answered scornfully, "Oh, no, we only take prisoners we club bad to the inspector; this one goes to court." I remained with the other policemen to wait for a case of "bad clubbing," as I told them. I saw none. They had had one earlier, they said, but why was I interested? I told them I had been watching the bad cases brought in to headquarters and that Byrnes had advised me to come over and find out for myself the explanation of such violence.

"All right," one of them said, "we'll show you." He explained that picketing was not allowed within a block of a shop, and pointing to the procession of pickets passing the very door, said, "Now you watch." He stepped in front of a big, black-bearded Jew, who stopped short, and demanded, "Vell, vat you vant?"

"I want you to cut out your picketing in front of this shop."

"Picketing!" the man exclaimed. "Vat you call it, picketing?"

"You know damned well what picketing is."

"Me? Nit. I ain't no picketer, I am law-abiding citizen peaceably going to my work. I got the right to walk in the street, maybe."

"Yea," the cop sneered, "you got th' right to walk in th' street to your work, sure, but why don't you go? I been watching you for an hour walking around and around this block."

"Me? No, sir. This is the first time I been passing here."

"Come off," the policeman hissed, angry, and he threatened with his stick.

"And besides," the picket said coolly, "it is too early yet for to be in the shop. My shop—"

"Your shop, nothing. All the shops at work have been working for an hour or two."

"Not mine, Mister. No, my shop—"

"All right," the cop broke in. "Where is your shop? Lead me to it."

The picket was startled. He had been lying, but he recovered his self-possession and accepted the challenge. "All right, ve vill go to my shop. Come on."

The policemen looked at each other, one nodded, and the other, with a wink at me, said, "Come on," and the three of us started off. I heard, as we walked around the corner down toward the East River, a debate on the law, the rights of man and especially of strikers, which was as irritating to me as later the debates in the U.S. Senate were on the constitutionality of some bill proposed—and for the same reason. The argument had nothing to do with the subject before the house. It was just a case of lawyers, disputing not the right, wisdom, or justice of the matter in hand, but precedents and decisions; and the policeman and the picket knew, disputed, and strained the law to their appointed uses. They irritated me, and they so irritated each other that I could see and understand why the policeman kept feeling of, weighing, and finally whirling nervously his long night stick, like a lion waving its tail. And just as he seemed about to haul off and belt the anarchist, as he called the picket—and, I'll confess, just when I wished he would crack him one—the picket shouted, "Here's my shop," and he broke away, dashed into a café, and as we followed, disappeared through the rear while we stood, defeated and foolish, under the eyes of the smiling, chuckling, sneering crowd in the crowded room; "a crowd of bums," the cop called them.

"They drive you crazy," the policeman said, as we walked back. "You and the public, you wonder why we fan these damned bums, crooks, and strikers with the stick. I'll tell you that if you had to deal with them and their lies and their rights you would hit 'em too."

"Well?" asked the other policeman when we got back.

"Oh," said my companion, "I let him go, the blankety-blank. He would have walked me to Harlem looking for his shop, and then it would have been closed and I would have been off post, for fair. Anything doing here?"

"No, nothing except that the boss of that shop there, he's been out here to give me a song and dance about letting his workers be beaten up in broad daylight under our very eyes. Said he was going to make a complaint to headquarters."

"The —— —— ——!"

"Why," I said, "what's the matter with the boss?"

"Oh, nothing much," my cop answered, whirling his stick in rage, "only I remember this boss when he was a union organizer. I beat him up once myself for picketing, and now he's got a shop himself he's still a-fighting the police for the law and his rights."

"Just like the workers!" I exclaimed.

"Oh, hell. They're all alike, workers and bosses, the same breed, the same rights to all th' law on their side and against all the law on th' other side."

"The law is just a club then," I remarked; "the police are a weapon to be used or denounced."

"You have said it," one cop said heartily, and the other nodded, "Sure."

I went back to headquarters, cleared up on some subjects: the psychology if not the ethics of the night stick, for example; and confused and interested in, among other subjects, strikers. Passing policemen on their posts and observing that they kept twirling their clubs, long or short, on their strings—some of them gracefully—I felt the ache they conveyed to rap some head with the handy little billy, a working-man, a boss, anybody. And realizing that it did not matter which, that these employers were ex-employees, that they were the same human beings, first on one side, then on the other—it made me want to study and, if I could persuade my editor to let me, report some East Side strikes. My experiences as a labor reporter were beginning.

DR. PARKHURST'S VICE CRUSADE

L EARNING as I was that the newspapers, literature, and public opinion did not picture men and life as they are, it was nevertheless a weekly amazement to me to read in the Monday morning newspapers descriptive reports and caricatures of the Rev. Dr. Charles H. Parkhurst that represented him as a wild man, ridiculous, sensational, unscrupulous, or plain crazy; then to call on him and find a tall, slim, smiling gentleman, quiet, determined, fearless, and humorous; and then, finally, go on down to police headquarters and hear groups of policemen, politicians, and reporters talking in earnest about this fiend. I don't know how he is remembered; Dr. Parkhurst may be not remembered at all. He carried on his vice crusade all through the nineties, charging police and political corruption and forcing the State Legislature to appoint the Lexow Committee which investigated, proved, and exposed the police and Tammany corruption, caused the election of a reform administration, and led up to the whole period of muckraking and the development of the Progressive party. Such a service is not the kind that is appreciated by public opinion and history, and whenever I speak with old New Yorkers now of Dr. Parkhurst they are puzzled to hear of him as I see him: a man of strength, who was "wise" in the slangy sense and otherwise wise. He never told or preached half of what he knew. His method was simple. He received individuals, sometimes honest victims of police outrage, sometimes disgruntled politicians, policemen, or criminals with axes to grind, and he heard their stories, which multiplied as he went on his steady way of exposure and attack. The facts and hints he collected then had to be investigated by his Society for the Prevention of Crime, with attorneys and detectives who followed up these leads, proved or disproved them, discovered others by the way, and delivered the information with the evidence to the Doctor, who used them—wisely. All he gave in a sermon or a lecture was enough to startle his hearers and to frighten the police world with the suggestion that he knew all. He didn't. As it turned out he did not know "the half of it." But he knew enough, and he understood so well what he knew that by sticking within the provable facts, by selecting those that were the most typical and significant, and using these boldly, he carried his charges every time.

"The police are paid bribe money regularly by the saloons," he would charge. "That is why they do not close them. If they care to show that I am wrong, let them enforce the law and close the saloons. They will not. They cannot. They don't dare."

That is what he would say clearly, even fiercely, of a Sunday. On Monday morning, when I called and asked him how he knew that, he would give me prices, dates, and names, and, smiling, say, "Now you ask Byrnes what he is going to do."

At police headquarters I would call on the Superintendent, who knew, of course, my routine; I soon learned to "spot" detectives watching me. Byrnes was ready for me.

"Well, and what does the reverend gentleman say this morning?"

"He says that you won't close the saloons this week either."

"I'll show you," he shouted in a rage one morning. He pressed a button, and to his Sergeant Mangin, who responded, he commanded: "Summon all the inspectors to report here at eleven o'clock. And"—to me—"you too."

At eleven o'clock all the inspectors in full uniform and all the reporters were in the chief's office. He rose from his desk and said: "Inspectors of police, I have bidden you, again and again, to enforce the law requiring the closing of saloons at certain hours, especially at night and on Sundays. Once more I command you to order your captains to obey and enforce upon others obedience to the laws."

We report the news, describing the scene, and the next morning I call on Dr. Parkhurst, who says, "Good. We'll see," and smiling he adds: "You will see—if you keep your eyes open—you will see the saloon-keepers and district leaders running to police headquarters to ask Byrnes if he means it; if he does, to protest and to threaten him. And as for me, I'll wait till Sunday to say what I see."

I saw the procession of saloon-keepers, politicians, and others, many other people, calling on Byrnes. One day Tim Sullivan, the famous East Side ward boss, came up to me, straight in his direct way, and asked me what th' hell I was trying to do.

"I?" I exclaimed. "I'm not trying to do anything but get the news."

"The hell you ain't," he protested. "You are backing up that damned preacher. Before you came to headquarters the reporters paid no attention to what the blankety-blank said. But now you interview Byrnes, ask him what he's going to do about it, and the other reporters have to report what he says too. You're making it hard for the old man; he says so himself; and you're making it hard for us, too. Why? What's th' game? What do you get out of it all?"

"News," I laughed.

"News!" he echoed. "Say, if that's all you want I'll give you news; we'll all give you news. I can tip Byrnes to put you 'way inside on th' news."

"Go ahead," I answered, jesting, and to my consternation he darted back into Byrnes' office, and coming out, reported, "I've fixed that all right. Now you be good. See?"

This had consequences which I was not "wise" enough to foresee or detect. I did not understand that I was being bribed; nothing happened immediately. Riis joined me in pressing Byrnes to heed Dr. Parkhurst or at least to answer his tirades. The other reporters merely laughed at me and my naïveté, but police officers were polite and obliging. Byrnes offered me a beat on a burglary several days later and looked mystified when I declined it, saying priggishly that the *Post* did not care for that sort of news. What interested me was that the police court cases showed and the reporters reported that the liquor laws were not enforced, as Dr. Parkhurst knew. He said so in his next Sunday sermon; he said it furiously, with scathing sarcasm and jubilant triumph.

"Now," he said amiably Monday morning, "now see what Byrnes does by way of his next bluff."

I think that at that time Dr. Parkhurst was really driving at the closing of the saloons. The appeals of wives and children to him for relief from the week-end drunkenness of their husbands and fathers were worrying the clergyman and making him hope for the enforcement of the early closing laws so as to save some of the workers' wages. My interest was in the glimpses I was catching of the Tammany government, and, by the way, of political morals. The police were protecting from the law and from public opinion the law-breakers they were appointed and paid to protect the public from. That was an apparent fact about the New York government. And by way of morals there was the faithful keeping of the alleged contract of the police with the saloon-keepers. Anyway, I went from Dr. Parkhurst, not to Byrnes, but to Riis. After a talk with him, about the situation as I saw it, he went with me to interview Byrnes.

"What about it, Inspector?" Riis asked for us both.

"What about what?" Byrnes retorted, his Irish showing in his angry eyes and hanging jaw.

"Parkhurst says you were bluffing when you had us in here last Monday to hear you instruct the inspectors to shut up the town. Anyway they didn't do it. What next?"

The chief paced the floor a few times, then halted before Riis and challenged him.

"Is the *Sun* backing Parkhurst? I know the *Post* is, but as I read the *Sun*—"

He was referring to the attacks by the *Sun* upon both Parkhurst and the *Post* for their hypocritical policy of law-enforcement, but Riis, who was not only a reporter, cut him short.

"Never you mind the *Sun*," he said. "Say what you are going to do. That's the news of the day, and the *Sun* prints the news."

"Two o'clock," said Byrnes, pointing us to the door and going to his desk.

"The" inspector, as I have said, had a funny way of affecting the dignity which he thought belonged to his position as the head of the uniformed police force; he would speak English as English as he could, using the broad "a." But under the strain of a sudden temper, he would fall back into his native Irish. This happened that day.

At two o'clock, when the inspectors filed into his office with Riis and me, the Superintendent in full uniform was pretending to write at his desk. He was very busy, too busy to see us till we had stood there silent and waiting and winking at one another for a minute or two. It seemed long before Byrnes looked up, saw us, rose solemnly, and strode slowly around in front of his inspectors, who watched him come. He never looked at Riis and me. He stood glaring at his inspectors.

"Gentlemen," he began, "did not I command you last Monday on this very spot in this same office to enforce to the letter the laws regulating the saloons in this city, and—and to close them one and all at the legally fixed hours for closing?"

No answer of course, only silence and attention, while the chief, crouching low at them and balling his fists, cried, "Well, and what I want to know now is: did youse did it?"

I snorted, couldn't help it; and Byrnes whirled upon me, and his arm lifted at the door, he yelled, "Get out of here!" I ran; Riis stood, but the angry man added, "Both of you." Then Riis came out laughing too.

How Byrnes finished his broken scene, what he said further to his inspectors, we did not learn. The inspectors avoided us, slipping back into their offices with sobered faces and mute lips. But the next Saturday night and Sunday many saloons closed. Not all. There seemed to have been some request sent out from headquarters for a voluntary compliance with the law; the liquor dealers must have decided among them which were to close and which to remain open. Anyway, for the next few weeks different saloons seemed systematically to obey and disobey the law, and there were few raids, though there were some places, the most notorious, which never did close. They had "thrown away their keys" the day they opened up for business, and it was not till Theodore Roosevelt became Commissioner that these powerful men were brought to heel.

Why were these law-breakers so strong? And why was there such an opposition to the simple, superficial reforms of Dr. Parkhurst? I used to wonder at what I was seeing, and the reporters, policemen, politicians, who explained it all to me, wondered at my stupidity. I could understand the bribery and the contributions to political parties; that accounted for the police and Tammany Hall, and that satisfied the minds of my informants. But it did not explain to me the opposition to reform that was most bitter: that of good, prominent citizens who had no apparent connection with the underworld. As Dr. Parkhurst forced such results as the voluntary closing of some saloons, he was hated more and more openly by people whom one might expect to see approving his course: bankers, business men, and even other clergymen. There was something to find out about the organization of society, as it occurred in New York, something the "wise guys" of the underworld did not know or would not tell. I asked my friends in Wall Street to justify their indignation at Parkhurst, but all they would say was that his crusade "hurt business." That was the first time I heard that expression. "How can the closing of saloons hurt business in Wall Street?" I asked James B. Dill, who knew everything. He kicked my shin, hard, and when I exclaimed, he answered my question, "Why does your mouth cry out when only your shin is hurt?" That was the answer, but I could never be satisfied with a fact or a phrase; it was a picture I needed, a diagram of the connection between the saloon business and the banks, just as I had one of the nervous system that linked up my lower and upper extremities.

VII

THE UNDERWORLD

THE inspector, Byrnes, was cultivating my friendship, and he did it by letting me in to a view of his relations with thieves and the underworld generally. It may have been Tim Sullivan's hint that I could be won with "news"; it may have been that, wishing to impress me, he talked, and talking, naturally turned to the field where he was most impressive, his detective work. Before he was promoted to be Superintendent of Police, he had been for years the inspector in charge of the detective bureau. He had enjoyed that work, evidently, and his many miraculous services to prominent people who had been robbed had made him loom in their imagination as the man of mystery and of marvelous effects. They all knew him in Wall Street; big men down there envied me the privilege of knowing personally "the inspector," as they still called him.

"You see him? Every day? And he talked to you, man to man, like that?"

Few of them had seen him. Even those he had helped out of trouble had rarely met him personally. It was his pose to remain in the background, receiving communications through others—detectives or attorneys—and working in the dark, suddenly hand out his results. You saw only the hand and the restored property. Bankers told me tales of how somebody's house had been robbed; the inspector had been told about it, and having listened in silence a moment, had said, "Enough. Your diamonds will be delivered at your house within three days." And on the third day—not on the second or the fourth, but exactly when this amazing man had promised—your diamonds were handed in by two startling men "with the compliments of the inspector." Another banker had had his pocket picked of money and valuable papers; he did not mind the money, but the papers . . . Byrnes had got back the papers, all intact.

One of the most famous of our millionaire families had consulted Byrnes about a foreign nobleman who had won the love of a daughter of the house; what could be done to get rid of the fellow? "I'll see," Byrnes had answered, and a few days later he promised that the family would see no more of the foreigner. "You might let me have enough money for him to pay his passage home and perhaps a little more." Gladly they paid whatever Byrnes thought would "do," and no more was ever seen or heard of that trouble. Byrnes was the man to deal with blackmailers. Wall Street and "Society" had suffered from the possession by unscrupulous scoundrels of personal and more or less scandalous facts against its leaders; true stories. Byrnes could deal with them. You told him "all about it"; perhaps you made one more payment, and—that ended it. Byrnes established Fulton Street as the dead line beyond which no thief could go downtown. It was understood that, in return for these services, Byrnes was tipped on stocks, let in on "good things," and otherwise helped to make money, quite properly; and no doubt the gratitude to Byrnes was an element in the ingratitude to Parkhurst. But that did not explain the connection between the saloon nerves and the big-business brains. There was something else back of all these surface signs. What was it? And how did Byrnes perform his miracles?

While I was pondering these questions he did one for me. Drawing my salary one Saturday afternoon, I went home and took my wife out for dinner. As I was about to pay the waiter, I discovered that my pay envelope with the money was gone. My pocket had been picked. I complained to Byrnes by 'phone; he asked how much was in the envelope, how the envelope was addressed, and what lines of cars I had used to go home and to dinner. When I had answered all his questions, he said, "All right. I'll have it for you Monday morning." And on Monday morning Byrnes handed me the envelope with the money just as I had received it from my paper.

"How did he do it?" I asked the other reporters. They were playing their poker in a basement office and had not much time for me, a greenhorn. I had to repeat my question several times before one of them looked up and answered briefly.

"Huh," he said. "He knew what pickpockets were working the car lines you rode and he told the detectives who were watching them to tell them that they had robbed a friend of the chief's of so much money in such and such an envelope."

"But how—"

"Ah, say, you don't know enough to cover Wall Street, to say nothing of police headquarters. Byrnes passed the word that he wanted that dip back by Monday morning, and so, of course, it came back Monday morning."

What reporters know and don't report is news—not from the newspapers' point of view, but from the sociologists' and the novelists'. It enabled me, when I learned a little of it, to write my *Shame of the Cities*. But it took time and sharp listening to get that little. Though I had nothing to do, professionally, with criminal news, I used to go out with the other reporters on cases that were useless to my paper but interesting to me. Crime, as tragedy and as a part of the police system, fascinated me. I liked to go for lunch to the old Lyons restaurant on the Bowery with Max Fischel or some other of the "wise" reporters. They would point out to me the famous pickpockets, second-story men and sneaks that met and ate there; sometimes with equally famous detectives or police officials and politicians. Crime was a business, and criminals had "position" in the world, a place that was revealing itself to me. I soon knew more about it than Riis did, who had been a police reporter for years; I knew more than Max could tell Riis, who hated and would not believe or even hear some of the "awful things" he was told. Riis was interested not at all in vice and crime, only in the stories of people and the conditions in which they lived. I remember one morning hearing Riis roaring, as he could roar, at Max, who was reporting a police raid on a resort of fairies.

"Fairies!" Riis shouted, suspicious. "What are fairies?" And when Max began to define the word Riis rose up in a rage. "Not so," he cried. "There are no such creatures in this world." He threw down his pencil and rushed out of the office. He would not report that raid, and Max had to telephone enough to his paper to protect his chief.

There were fairies; there were all sorts of perverts; and they had a recognized standing in the demi-world; they had their saloons, where they were "protected" by the police for a price. That raid Riis would not report was due to a failure of some one to come through with the regular bit of blackmail overdue. And so with prostitution, so with beggars, so with thieves, as I gradually learned, first from the reporters, then from police officers I came to know well, then from the crooks themselves who learned to trust me, and all the while from Byrnes. When he discovered that, while and because I did not write criminal news, he could interest and trust me with it, he used to call me in and tell me detective stories of which he was the hero. He was bragging, and he was inventing, too. This I knew because I had found out where he hid the detective story-books he was reading, and borrowing them when he was not looking, I read and recognized in them the source of some of his best narratives. Thus I discovered that instead of detectives' posing for and inspiring the writers of detective fiction, it was the authors who inspired the detectives. For example:

One day a young policeman who had just been appointed a plain-clothes man appeared at headquarters so exultant that I asked him what he had done. He hesitated a moment; detectives are forbidden to tell of their feats; that must be left to the inspector; but he knew that I did not report crimes, and he did want to talk; so he told me that he had "got the dope" on a certain big robbery of a rich man's house up Fifth Avenue.

"You remember the case," he began. "Jewelry and silverware taken on a grand scale, and the owner hollered. That made the old man mad; with the public in on it, he had to make a showing; so we were all instructed to do our damnedest."

The police all over the world caution citizens who are robbed to report to headquarters and never to the press. They explain that detectives can work better if the thieves are not warned by the newspapers that the police are after them. This is absurd, of course. Thieves always know when the police are looking for them after a crime. The true reason of the police for privacy is that they don't like to have the public know how many unsolved crimes are committed, and they do like to deal privately and freely with the criminals. My detective assumed that I understood this; he assumed that I knew everything. His next assumption was that I knew that detectives specialized, as criminals do, in one class of crime, and that the detective's trade consists not in pursuing but in forming friendships with criminals.

"It wasn't any of my business," he said. "My assignment, of course, is to the dips [pickpockets]; I was promoted because I had cultivated them and their girls and was known to be in with 'em. The case was either a burglary or a plain robbery, a good job, too, and the burglars and such that ought to know about it were as mystified as the chief himself. They said that they hadn't any of 'em done it. The old man put some of them through the mill till he was convinced that no crook that is allowed either to operate or to live in New York was in on it in any way. He thought, and I remember I guessed, that it was an inside job: servants. But the servants had all been kept, and the old man couldn't get a word out of them; not to the point. He said that they seemed really as mystified as anybody. A pretty case, eh?

"Well, we heard no more of it for a couple of months. I had about forgotten it and the burglar gang had dropped it, when one night I saw a dip who had been on the bum all dressed up with lots of money. He used to work the Bridge cars [the old Brooklyn Bridge surface lines] but had a row with his pal and got fired. Unable to work, he was down and out. Here he was, all of a sudden, flush and sassy. I naturally asked what t'ell. 'Got a new girl,' they told me in the barroom where the dips hang out. I thought they meant that she was a young, pretty piece that earned him a lot of money, but when she was pointed out to me one night later she turned out to be a homely foreigner; couldn't pick up a dollar a night on the streets. I smelled a rat. 'She must work,' I thinks. 'A servant perhaps. But how, then, did she get the money?' I followed her home, and what do you think? She went to that house on Fifth Avenue. Say, I had something, and I knew it. I got hold of her pickpocket and asked him if he'd like to get back on the cars. He sure would; what would it cost? I said he knew what the price would be, and he said he knew, too. He'd think it over. And the next night he paid the price to the old man himself, me being there.

"The story was simple. The butler was the boy. He was a Frenchman, a regular at home, who got in wrong with his French police. He came over here to work his old game, which was to take a job and 'get' a maid, usually a homely one who would appreciate a little love. She did the actual lifting of the stuff; he sent it to pals in Paris, giving her a fair divvy. He was square with the money; square enough. She got more money than she ever saw before. But he wasn't square on the love end. He took her to dances, and there took up with other girls; neglected her, and she got mad and took up with my dip, who picked up all her money and all her story, which Byrnes has. The arrests were made last night."

This, then, was a true detective story. Two days later Byrnes called in the reporters, and announcing the arrests, related a detective yarn which was so full of clews, thought, night reflections, and acute reasoning—it was, in brief, so perfectly modeled upon the forms of the conventional detective story, that the cynical police reporters would not write it. They reported the news, the arrests, and left the story to the court. Byrnes often asked me if I knew why my colleagues did not use all his stories; I think now that he liked to tell them to me because I seemed to swallow them. We used to discuss criminals philosophically, and he then talked straight; at least he dropped remarks which confirmed the reporters' gossip about his methods.

Tapping on his window one afternoon, he beckoned me into his office, saying: "Here, now, I've got a case that puzzles me. There's a pickpocket downstairs [in the basement, he meant, where the cells were] who has always been straight with me. He operates all the big cities that I have no arrangement with; St. Paul, Seattle, 'Frisco, Los Angeles, back via New Orleans to the middle west and the east. He never works in New York. He keeps his woman here, and when he has made a pile he comes to town, every year, to go to the theaters, gamble a little, dine here and there, and, generally, live. He calls on me to report and get permission; he promises not to do a thing here, and I always have let him have his vacation. Never has he broken faith. He has never given me any information; he's no use to me; but he has been on the level till here the other day he was caught in a crowded surface car with a fine gold watch in his hand and a crowd on his neck. Why? He knew who was working that car; he knew they would kick at his butting in on their beat; he's a 'wise guy,' and yet he made his dip and, worst of all, got caught."

"Well?" I questioned. "Why don't you ask him about it?"

"Oh, I have, several times," said Byrnes. "But he gives me a rigmarole about having lifted the watch to see if he could and meaning to put it back. I can't get it; and I kind o' like the fellow. Now I'm going to send for him and leave you alone with him to see if you can get the answer."

Two detectives brought up the prisoner, and at a sign from Byrnes, left him standing just within the door.

"That's the man," said Byrnes to me for him to hear. "He can talk to you or not, as he pleases. If he does you may get his story; I can't. When you are through, press the first button."

As Byrnes went out, the thief looked curiously at me; he looked all around the room, at the windows, the doors, the desk, and back at me. Cool and silent, he looked me up and down, as I did him. He was a tall, slender, self-contained man of about thirty, with sharp, quick eyes, a sharp, thin nose, and long, beautiful hands which hung quiet but gave one a sense of life.

"The inspector," I began, "was telling me about you." I repeated exactly what Byrnes had said. "He likes you," I added. "I can see that; he wants to trust you, and he asked me, a reporter, to see if I could get your reason for operating that car-line when you had promised not to work in New York."

He walked swiftly over past me to the window, where he turned so that he could have the light on me, not himself.

"It's simple enough," he answered in a high-pitched little voice. "I did not operate that line, only that one car for that once; and that was not a dip. I didn't mean to steal the watch; I got caught putting it back."

I did not understand, and he must have seen my mystification. He sighed and said, "Some people think money is all there is to it." And when he saw that this added nothing to my understanding, he went on rapidly: "It was this way: I was riding that crowded car to get up to my hotel. Didn't need money. But I spotted a fellow standing up in the aisle with a thief-guard on his watch and as I studied the thing I saw it was a new trick—a new one on me. I would have liked to beat it; I didn't intend to, because of Byrnes, who has been square to me, pretty square; as square as a cop can be. You're not a bull, you say?"

"No, a reporter."

"A writer. Well, then, you ought to believe me," he answered.

"I moved up close to the smart Aleck with his wonderful watch-guard only to study it, and I couldn't see it all; only the bit of it that stuck out. It was fastened somehow in the vest pocket; I wanted to see how. My hands did, I mean. That's what you ought to get that the old man can't; that my fingers asked me to let them feel out that guard and—and—they bet they could break it, get the watch—and—and they promised they would put the watch back into the pocket on to the guard."

He looked distressed, even as he told me. "I oughtn't to have done it—in my position. Risking everything. I do like to come to New York and feel safe while I loaf. And I had no pal, you see, nobody to bump the fellow and draw off his attention. I think that it was that maybe, added to the new guard, which made me want to see if I could. Anyway I let my hands go, and they went in, felt and understood the guard; they got it, opened it, and I had the watch and all. And, honest, it was the best guard I ever went up against. I held it in my hands, looking it over, and was just about to put it back when the two dips that work that line jumped on the car front and back!"

He looked his exclamation; he was frightened.

"Now," he said proudly, "I ain't afraid of no bulls, see? But dips, and New York dips with a monopoly on that line, they hate us Westerners anyhow— I had to hurry."

His quiet hands began to work, his quick eyes darted here, there, about the room. He was seeing his emergency again, and as he saw it, his hands reached out to me.

"I saw those two pick me out; I saw them look at each other, then at the fellow I was dipping, then at what I had in my hands. We can see in my business, you know. So they saw me slip back the watch and—leave it. No time to replace the guard as it was. I just dropped it, and they were on me. They came from both ends of the car, banged on to the man as they wedged me, and 'Feel for your watch,' one of 'em called to the sucker.

" 'Humph!' he said, throwing up his hands. Of course, they had me. The sucker, other passengers, and my two—two competitors, my two monopolists, they all jumped me and yelled, till the two plain-clothes men at Fourteenth Street came aboard and pinched me."

He paced nervously across the room, returned, and stopped before me.

"Do you understand?" he asked, and he very much wanted me to.

"We'll see," I answered. I pressed the button, and Byrnes came slowly back.

"Well," he said most casually. "What are we up against?"

"An artist," I said.

"What!"

"A poor helpless artist," I repeated, and I explained to the inspector that when a man is a master of his craft, he does sometimes practice his art when he should not; he cannot help it. I went into some detail, talking about the follies of painters and the weaknesses of writers, while Byrnes frowned and the pickpocket's face shone like a saint's with happiness. When Byrnes' frown cleared I knew I had put over my theory, and stopped. The thief seized my hand in both his and wrung it. Byrnes watched him a moment, then said to the prisoner, "All right. You can go. Only remember, New York is no place for artists. Get me?"

He rang the bell, the two plain-clothes men reappeared, and their chief commanded, "Turn him out."

I met that thief a few years later on a train going from Chicago to St. Louis, where I was muckraking. He came up to me in the dining-car, handed me my pocketbook, and as I recognized it and him, he said: "Never carry your wallet in your coat pocket. I know you don't care for money; an artist has his mind on other, more important matters than money—sometimes. But I find that, besides money, you carry your railroad tickets and other valuable or private papers, all in the same wad."

"Where did you lift it?" I asked.

"I saw you come to the train," he answered, "saw where you put the book when the conductor handed you back your slips, and —you really ought to know better—I thought I would teach you a lesson in the fine art of traveling. So I went to wash up when you did; I hung my coat up beside yours and at the same time transferred your pocketbook to my pocket."

I invited him to sit down and dine with me, and we had a long and to me at that time a very helpful talk about how the police do business with criminals in other cities than New York, the cities I was then working in and writing about, as he knew. That grateful thief paid me in full for what he called my "pull for him with Byrnes," who, by the way, never had any further cause to complain of his artist guest in New York.

"He used to call me in and tell me when some city was asking him to pick me up for them," the man said that night. "He tipped me, but he never gave me up. He was as square after that, almost as square, as one of us."

VIII

BOSSES: POLITICAL AND FINANCIAL

Reporting at police headquarters was like a college education in this, that one had to take several courses all together. There was the police news, police policies and politics; the Ghetto, with its synagogues, theaters, and moral struggles; the strikes; and, on the side, Wall Street. It differed from college in this, that I was interested in each of these courses and could see that they belonged together. They all contributed to the learning of life as it is lived. The difficulty was to dovetail them into my time.

My daily routine began at breakfast with the reading of the morning newspapers for a general sense of the general news, for a definite idea of financial developments to see if there was anything in my (constructive) line, and a careful sifting of the police and political reports for leads to follow up. My wife and her mother used to help in this pleasant work; they learned to notice "uncovered ends" of stories; to raise questions which remained to be answered. We were acquiring the habitual attitude of the editorial mind: to look not only for information but for the lack of needed knowledge. I rose from breakfast with questions to go out and seek answers to.

My first call was on Dr. Parkhurst, who also had read the papers and was ready with his informed comments on the news in his field, explanations of raids and other police activities, which he had from his Society. He often had new experiences to report, his and his agents'. If he had attacks to refute or fresh charges to make, if some orator, politician, police officer, or newspaper accused him and his agents of, say, cruelty in causing the arrest of street walkers, he would dictate a statement, quiet, quick, that it was not worse to drive these women off the streets than it was to take away from them, as the police did, a share of their hard-earned money. If the police had raided a gambling-house he had designated as "running full-blast" and found "nothing doing," "nobody at home"; if, in other words, the papers said that the alleged gambling-joint was closed or vacant the night of the raid, Dr. Parkhurst would smile and say, "Advise Byrnes to call again and not to have the gamblers tipped off next time."

Sometimes he would warn me of the business that was to come up that day for action by the Board or by the Superintendent of Police, give me the bearing and background of it and the probable decision. At other times he would point his remarks at Richard Croker as the guilty head of Tammany just as Byrnes was the responsible head of the system of police graft. I usually left Parkhurst with an improved picture of the invisible government of New York and fresh lines of inquiry to follow up.

Arriving at my office across Mulberry Street from police headquarters, I looked over the night reports from the precincts in the basement, and if there was anything interesting, like a big fire, a murder, or a street row, I asked Max Fischel about it. He was loyal to Riis; he would not give me a "beat," but my point of view was so different from Riis's that Max could tell me enough for me to decide whether to go out myself and get the story or let it go. It was seldom that I had to write any of the "early morning news" for the *Post*. When Riis turned up, bawled for "M-a-a-x," and sat down to write, I went through the police offices, saw and talked with Byrnes about "what that crazy Parkhurst had said or done," with the inspectors and the Health Department. Then, if there was a meeting of the bi-partisan Board of (four) Police Commissioners, I attended and reported it. On tense days when the Parkhurst attacks were pressing, the meetings of these helpless politicians were dramatic and absurd. Two of them were Republican machine men; two were Tammany officials. They had full power under the law, but actually they had nothing to do with anything but routine expenditures and details of policy. The uniformed police governed themselves in cahoots with certain politicians and associations of liquor dealers, gamblers, and other law-breakers. The poor, weak, conspicuous Commissioners were nothing but a "front" to take the punishment. My professional job was, by their acts and sayings, to show this,

and I did it gradually. Many a time I have sat with that Board
with them all glaring at me and making, as I reported, speeches
for me to hear and report, me and the other reporters. When in
desperation they met behind closed doors, we reported that they
were up to some chicanery which the public was not to know. They
held no more private meetings for a while. When they had promotions to make, we used to find out and print in advance the
names of the men the politicians and grafters had chosen for
them to name, tell the political and scandalous reasons for the
choice, and then watch and report their unhappy, humiliating
obedience to "orders." It was an amazing example of professional
political morality to me that these politicians were true to their
backers and to one another. I offered the two Republicans many
chances to serve their (theoretical) party interests and fight their
(theoretical) enemy, Democratic Tammany, by turning against
the system and joining the reform forces to put the rascals out.
They were loyal to the graft, of which, so far as I could ever discover, they got no share. They were not good men, but there was
honor among them. They suffered in silence like heroes for a
cause; a bad cause and not their fault.

When there was no board meeting or other important police
business, I reported by 'phone to the city editor, and he gave me
other work, usually in or about Wall Street. I liked to keep in
touch there. New corporations and combinations were forming,
and when a great, rich company was announced in Wall Street as
born in Jersey City and I had to run down the unknown directors
only to find out that they were obscure clerks and bookkeepers in
some bank or lawyer's office, James B. Dill would explain to me
that they were "dummy directors."

"Dummy directors?"

"Yes, don't you know that all directors are dummies? Most
presidents too. Chairmen of Boards, managers, and heads of departments are real enough, but the bosses of business are the bankers and financial operators; they have no office at all in the company, but they run it through—dummies."

"Well, but these directors are clerks, no use as a front."

"Yes, yes," Dill would laugh. "We're in a hurry now. We'll
pick out some prominent, rich—gentlemen to go on the boards
by and by when we get around to this detail. But perfectly tame

dummies with good names of able fathers are not so easy to find. Wall Street is young. England has her nobility and old families and decaying rich houses to choose her 'guinea pigs' from; we have to wait for the sons of our rich old families to grow up and be college-bred to take orders, punishment, and ask no questions."

It was police and political parallels that enabled me to see Wall Street clearly. And by and by, as my wonder about politics outgrew my Wall Street interest, the financial practice began to light up the police and political government. In brief, as my dummy police commissioners were the key to Dill's dummy directors, so his dummy directors opened up my feeling for the dummy police board, dummy aldermen, mayors, governors. I remember, for example, how one day when I was bragging to my wife that, after all, though I was only a reporter, I had had chances to be something else, something respectable, she showed me a truth.

"I was offered the presidency of that book trust," I reminded her.

"Yes," she reminded me, "dummy president."

My wife was often a help to me. I saw in a flash, when she said that, how much less "position" meant than I had thought, how unflattering the offer was that I had boasted about. Would I take orders, as the head of a company, from the banker who appointed me, a banker who knew and cared nothing about books? What did he care about, that banker boss?

"Banker boss." I recall the day when that phrase occurred to me. I was on my way back from Wall Street to my office at police headquarters, with instructions to arrange for an interview with Richard Croker. Both Dr. Parkhurst and the editor of the *Post* asked me to question him about the police graft, some of which was supposed to be passed on up to him. He had no public office; "Dick" Croker was the boss, who nominated candidates for office, both elected and appointed, and so was being denounced as the actual, responsible ruler of the city. An absurd, illegal, disgraceful arrangement, my paper and my friends said. And it was, in my opinion too. I had accepted also, unthinkingly, the reformers' proposed remedy:

"Down with the boss. Away with politics and the politicians. Elect to office good business men who would give us a business government."

As I reviewed all this that day, for the purpose of questioning Croker about his boss-ship, I asked myself suddenly what was the difference between a political boss and a banker boss. None that I could see, except that one was a political, the other a financial, boss. Both political government and business government were run on the same lines, both had unofficial, unresponsible, invisible, actual governments back of the legal, constitutional "fronts." A keen personal interest inspired me, not to telephone, but to go on up to Croker's office, where he rarely appeared, in Tammany Hall on Fourteenth Street. He was there. He had his overcoat and hat on, ready to go out, and he invited me to walk along with him.

A sweet-faced man he was, all iron gray; his hair, his hat, his neat suit of clothes were of one tone of dark gray. His eyes were kind, and at my announcement that "the *Post* wanted to know—" a winning smile spread from his lips up to his eyes.

"Yes, I know that the *Post* wants to know; the *Post* needs to know, but 'Larry' Godkin would not learn anything from 'Dick' Croker. He sends you up here to get me to say something to quote and roast."

He strolled along slowly, watching his step; then he glanced amiably around at me and said: "Isn't that so? If I said something —no matter what—wouldn't he jump on it and me? He would not be content to print it as I would say it and as you would write it, letting his readers judge, and take or forget it. He would pick it up and pound me with it. Sure, boy, you know he would. And so you know that it would be foolish for me to say a word for publication."

I did not answer, but I could see the sense of his remarks, and I think he could see that I saw. "Sure," he said, as the smile disappeared. "You see that. A man in my position has got to keep his mouth shut. Let 'em talk, let 'em roast, and no matter how hot and fast and hard they throw it into you, stand up and take it. I will not talk to you—" He stopped, faced me down, and his eyes bored into me with a steady, unsmiling stare. Suddenly he relented. The sweet smile came back into his kind old face, and he added, "As a reporter.

"But," after a short pause, "I will talk to you, man to man. On the understanding that not a word of what I say is to be printed or even repeated to your editor, I will tell you anything you want to know, always, straight, unless it is about some one else. See?"

I knew perfectly well that a reporter should not accept confidences; it is unprofessional to let his personal curiosity cross his paper's interest in "news." The New York *World* of my day had a rule forbidding a correspondent, even at Washington, even with the President, to take any statement except for publication. But I was young. I was eager to know; knowledge was my price; and Mr. Richard Croker, as I always called him, had something in

MR. RICHARD CROKER

him that appealed to something in me. I respected, I came to like, that man. Anyway, I nodded my agreement, and often as I "saw" and interviewed him after that, I kept faith with him.

"Now, then," he said that day as we crossed Union Square, "what do you want to ask me?"

"Well, about this boss-ship," I began. "Why must there be a boss, when we've got a mayor and—a council and—"

"That's why," he broke in. "It's because there's a mayor *and* a council *and* judges *and*—a hundred other men to deal with. A government is nothing but a business, and you can't do business with a lot of officials, who check and cross one another and who come and go, there this year, out the next. A business man wants to do business with one man, and one who is always there to remember and carry out the—business."

"Business? Business?" I repeated. "I thought government was all politics."

He smiled, turning to look into my face.

"Ever heard that business is business?" he teased. "Well, so is politics business, and reporting—journalism, doctoring—all professions, arts, sports—everything is business."

"But business hasn't any bosses," I said.

He stopped, serious, and as I stopped with him to face him, he protested.

"Now, now, you ain't talking for publication either, and you tell me you have been a Wall Street reporter. If that is true, then you know as well as I do that Wall Street has its bosses just like Tammany and just like the Republican machine."

My blundering answer was the confession, first, that I did know that, and second, that I did not know it till that very day. Recounting to him the thoughts I had had on my way uptown about the parallel of dummy directors and dummy police commissioners, and banker bosses and political bosses, I felt ashamed of the fact that I had not seen those things while I was in Wall Street. My humiliation was wasted. Perhaps my chatter was naïve. Anyway it seemed to please Mr. Croker. He put his arm through mine, saying, "I guess you are on the square all right."

The change of subject embarrassed me; so I blurted out another question.

"But they don't have graft in business. They don't take bribes from saloons, and they don't take away the earnings of the women of the street. How can you stand for that in politics?"

We were walking again, slowly up Broadway, and he strode along in silence for so long that I was about to repeat my question, when he answered.

"There is graft in Wall Street, of course. You don't mean what you say about that. You mean that there isn't any dirty graft, like the police graft, don't you?"

"Yes, that was what I meant."

"Police graft is dirty graft," he said as if to himself. "We have to stand for it. If we get big graft, and the cops and small fry politicians know it, we can't decently kick at their petty stuff. Can we now?" He was looking at me again as he added with sharp emphasis, "We can't be hypocrites, like the reformers who some-times seem to me not to know that they live on graft."

Again he stopped, and again he wanted to be believed. "This I tell you, boy, and don't you ever forget it: I never have touched a cent of the dirty police graft myself."

I believed it; I never forgot it. It turned out to be true. Richard Croker never said anything to me that was not true unless it was a statement for publication, and then, if it was a lie, he had a way of letting you know it. He had morality. He was true to his pro-fessional ethics. And he said things that could be used against him; that day, for example.

"But you do make money out of politics," I said as we paused to part at Madison Square.

"Like a business man in business," he answered, hard as nails, "I work for my own pocket all the time."

He faced me down with it, waiting to hear what I would answer, and when I did not answer, when he saw that I was thinking in a whirl, he turned warm and sweet again, held out his soft, small, white hand, and bade me good-by.

"Come and see me again," he invited, holding my hand. "Morn-ings are best, after breakfast, at the Club, but come whenever you like, and if I have time we'll talk it all over."

My days ended as that day did. I went home, told my little family all that I had seen and heard, and tried to find out what I thought about what I had learned. A bore? My wife may have felt it so, but her mother understood.

"Go on. Talk yourself clear," she would say. Sometimes I did, but most often I talked myself unclear. I seem to have had a conception, a diagram, of life which every new discovery wrecked or, if it held, had no place for new facts. Facts. It seems to me now that facts have had to beat their way into my head, banging on my brain like the bullets from a machine gun to get in; and it was only by being hit over and over again that I could let my old ideal and college-made picture of life be blown up and let the new, truer picture be blown in. No wonder some men cannot learn; they are subject only to a few shots, not riddled with volleys, daily, all their lives.

THE GHETTO

D EW is a shower of jewels—in the country, and as it melts in the morning sun it sweetens the air. Not in a city. Police headquarters was in a tenement neighborhood, which seemed to steam on warm nights and sweat by day. I can remember still the damp, smelly chill of the asphalt pavement that greeted me when I came to my office in the early mornings. The tenements stank, the alleys puffed forth the stenches of the night. Slatternly women hung out of the windows to breathe and to gossip or quarrel across the courts; idle men and boys hung, half dressed, over the old iron fences or sat recovering from the night on the stoops of the houses which once had been the fine homes of the old families long since moved uptown. There was a business man in a new building next door to headquarters. He was a handsome, well-dressed wholesale dealer in brass fixtures and plumbers' supplies, and he may have thought he was waiting for buyers, but he was looking for something to happen, like the other neighbors. When a Black Maria drove up and discharged a load of thieves, prostitutes, broken strikers, or gambling-implements, he joined the crowd of loafers, men, women, and children, who gathered to enjoy the sight.

I looked for him, I looked for all the bums, when I turned into Mulberry Street; they were signs of expectancy from which I could guess whether there was news to write. If they were idle I might have time to breathe. I could not be sure, however, till I saw and spoke to the patrolman who acted as doorman of police headquarters. He was always on the stoop, idle, humorous, and Irish. He could not be surprised; he was always expectant and aware. I had to ask him, "Anything doing, Pat?"

"Not yet," he would say, and nodding his wise old head up

and down the street at the reporters, bums, business man, and women at their doors and windows, "They're all out, you see."

If these were not on post, if the reporters were in their offices and the neighbors stood in groups, Pat would answer my question with "Well, as you see, they're all telling—something." And slowly, with proper dignity and police mystery, he would tell me enough to judge whether it was a story I had to write. If I was in doubt, Riis's boy, Max, would settle it.

"What's up, Max?"

"Oh, nothing for you. A slum murder." Or "a roof chase after a thief," or "a baby fell off a fire-escape," or "a gang of toughs broke fences, door-bells, windows all along East Thirty-fifth Street."

The last was a common event. It was as unimportant as similar student pranks are in a college town. Reporters wrote it up only when they had nothing else to report and had to send in something to justify a day of poker. I wrote it once—twice. I had begun to break through my instructions to stick to police politics and Parkhurst exposures and ignore criminal news. I wrote crimes now and then, and the eagerness with which my city editor received them and the cautious way he slipped them into obscure parts of the paper encouraged me to believe that he wanted me gradually to get and so report regular police news that he could broaden the narrow scope of *Evening Post* news. He had been himself a police reporter; he knew the many kinds of stories that came out at headquarters, and he thought that Mr. Godkin would not mind if it was "written right"—not sensationally. Also he knew that I could not help trying it—somehow.

I took from Max that day the exact, outrageous details of the destructive raid of a gang of toughs in East Thirty-fifth Street and I described cheerfully, almost joyously, the breakages those drunks wreaked; I wrote it as nearly as I could in the jolly spirit of the night out. Max was a born seer; he had it all, and I must have reported it with his inspiration and his smile, for it was printed, and a few days later Wright called me down to the office and said that "the editor" had been receiving a stream of indignant letters asking how a paper like the *Post* could report such an outrage against order and property without a single syllable of indignation. I was so flattered that Wright was puzzled and rather angry. I had to remind him that there were two ways to report an incident like that: to express "our" indignation or to arouse the readers' rage; and that I thought the readers' emotion was more literary and more effective than ours.

"Such outrages happen frequently," I said. "The next time one occurs I will write it as an outrage instead of a descriptive narrative, and you will see that no reader will write to us; they will all be satisfied." And I did that. I began my next story, "An outrageous series of depredations was committed by a gang of drunken young hoodlums—" and all through the narrative I sprinkled denunciation. Not a letter, no protest; Wright was convinced, and he convinced Godkin that the editor did not always know the difference between a report and an editorial and that a description is often more editorial in effect than a Godkin editorial. Best of all, "we" let me report more.

Wright's wish and my ambition was to "do" a murder. One day as I was standing beside the doorman waiting for something to happen, we saw a reporter come running out of the basement and dart across into his office. The doorman winked at me and I stepped down to the telegraph bureau. A woman had been killed in Mulberry Bend. I came out and called, "Max!" Out he ran from his office, and we hurried down to the address in Little Italy. There was a crowd standing watching some children dancing beautifully around an organ-grinder who was playing a waltz.

"There's your story," said Max, pointing at the street scene. "Mine is inside."

Max understood. I went inside with him. We saw the dead woman, the blood, the wretched tenement apartment, and we talked to the neighbors, who told us how the murderer came into the court with the organ-grinder, and while the organ played and the children danced, he had seen the woman's face at the window, recognized her, rushed up, and cut her all to pieces; the crowd gathered and were about to beat the man to death when the police came, saved and arrested him. The poker-playing reporters came tearing up, asked for names, ages, and—details. Theirs was the sensational story of the day, all blood and no dancing. Riis wrote it as a melodrama with a moral, an old cry of his: "Mulberry Bend must go." And, by the way, it went. Such was the power of Riis! There's a small park now where Mulberry Bend was.

I wrote the murder as a descriptive sketch of Italian character, beginning with the dance music, bringing the murder in among the children whose cries called the mob; the excitement, the sudden rage, the saving arrest; and ending with the peaceful after-scene of the children dancing in the street, with the mob smiling and forgetting out in the street.

I saw and heard just such a story in Naples long afterward. Lying abed in the front room of the Hotel Santa Lucia, I was listening to the singers and players entertaining the late diners at the fish restaurants on the quay. One tenor sang high and clear above the rest; a pure, sweet voice, it rose over all the scene and seemed to abash all the other music. The whole dock grew quiet to listen. A victory; and the victor profited by, he seemed to abuse, his power. I could hear, I could feel, him swagger and strut, till a baritone in a boat lifted the same aria, took it away from the tenor, who tried to carry on, but hesitated, halted. The baritone laughed, a musical, a gleeful, provoking laugh. The challenge in it roused the tenor, who sang again, the "Santa Lucia," and we listened; I mean that the whole bay turned to him to hear, and the baritone too. A few thrilling bars and the tenor slipped, a false and over-drawn high note, and the baritone mocked it, laughed, and joining the tenor, sang with him, supporting him to the end. The tenor sang another, and another, the baritone playing him, now in unison, now the second; the two made glorious music, but it was a clinch. The baritone—a fisherman putting his boat in order; I got up, looked out, and saw him—the unprofessional singer corrected, helped, and—he spoiled parts of *Pagliacci* beautifully. His was the purer voice, his the more perfect mastery of the music. He yielded only when he liked, when he had to attend to his nets, to his boat. Sometimes the tenor had it alone for a whole song. I tired, I must have slept. Shouts wakened me, the excited cries and curses of a scuffle. Leaping to the window, I saw a writhing crowd on the wide stone stairway down into the water. It was a fight; I could see blows struck, hands flashing, up and down. The police came. . . . There was silence. The diners moved on, the boatmen went back into their boats, the crowd melted. They had seen a stabbing; an arrest, an ambulance call; they had taken sides, judged, and gone about their own businesses. In the dead quiet outside I went back to bed, but before I could sleep I heard a voice pipe up, a few notes of song, which, after a moment, another voice picked up and finished. By dawn the Bay of Naples was singing again, the dock was passing a bar from one opera, and laughing, matching it with a run from another, which made harmony. At sunrise when I glanced out, the sparkling waters and the villainous Neapolitans were shining as innocently as the sun himself.

The *Post* printed a murder, a mere mean murder, as news, and there was no news in it; only life. "We" published crime after that, all sorts of sensational stuff. Why not? Nobody noticed it, as crime. I soon found out that by going with the reporters to a fire or the scene of an accident was a way to see the town and the life of the town.

A synagogue that burned down during a service introduced me to the service; I attended another synagogue, asked questions, and realized that it was a bit of the Old Testament repeated after thousands of years, unchanged. And so I described that service and other services. They fascinated me, those old practices, and the picturesque customs and laws of the old orthodox Jews from Russia and Poland. Max, an East Side Jew himself, told me about them; I read up and talked to funny old, fine rabbis about them, and about their conflicts with their Americanized children. The *Post* observed all the holy days of the Ghetto. There were advance notices of their coming, with descriptions of the preparations and explanations of their sacred, ancient, biblical meaning, and then an account of them as I saw these days and nights observed in the homes and the churches of the poor. A queer mixture of comedy, tragedy, orthodoxy, and revelation, they interested our Christian readers. The uptown Jews complained now and then. Mr. Godkin himself required me once to call personally upon a socially prominent Jewish lady who had written to the editor asking why so much space was given to the ridiculous performances of the ignorant, foreign East Side Jews and none to the uptown Hebrews. I told her. I had the satisfaction of telling her about the comparative beauty, significance, and character of the uptown and downtown Jews. I must have talked well, for she threatened and tried to have me fired, as she put it. Fortunately, the editorial writers were under pressure also from prominent Jews to back up their side of a public controversy over the blackballing of a rich Jew by an uptown social club. "We" were fair to the Jews, editorially, but personally irritated. I was not "fired"; I was sent out to interview the proprietor of a hotel which excluded Jews, and he put his case in a very few words.

"I won't have one," he said. "I have had my experience and so learned that if you let one in because he is exceptional and fine, he will bring in others who are not exceptional, etc. By and by they will occupy the whole house, when the Christians leave. And then, when the Christians don't come any more, the Jews quit you to go where the Christians have gone, and there you are with an empty or a second-class house."

It would have been absurd to discharge me since I at that time was almost a Jew. I had become as infatuated with the Ghetto as eastern boys were with the wild west, and nailed a mazuza on my office door; I went to the synagogue on all the great Jewish holy days; on Yom Kippur I spent the whole twenty-four hours fasting and going from one synagogue to another. The music moved me most, but I knew and could follow with the awful feelings of a Jew the beautiful old ceremonies of the ancient ortho- dox services. My friends laughed at me; especially the Jews among them scoffed. "You are more Jewish than us Jews," they said, and since I have traveled I realize the absurdity of the American who is more French than the French, more German than the Kaiser. But there were some respecters of my respect. When Israel Zangwill, the author of *Tales of the Ghetto*, came from London to visit New York, he heard about me from Jews and asked me to be his guide for a survey of the East Side; and he saw and he went home and wrote *The Melting Pot*.

The tales of the New York Ghetto were heart-breaking com- edies of the tragic conflict between the old and the new, the very old and the very new; in many matters, all at once: religion, class, clothes, manners, customs, language, culture. We all know the difference between youth and age, but our experience is between two generations. Among the Russian and other eastern Jewish families in New York it was an abyss of many generations; it was between parents out of the Middle Ages, sometimes out of the Old Testament days hundreds of years B.C., and the children of the streets of New York today. We saw it everywhere all the time. Responding to a reported suicide, we would pass a synagogue where a score or more of boys were sitting hatless in their old clothes, smoking cigarettes on the steps outside, and their fathers, all dressed in black, with their high hats, uncut beards, and temple curls, were going into the synagogues, tearing their hair and rending their garments. The reporters stopped to laugh; and it was comic; the old men, in their thrift, tore the lapels of their coats very carefully, a very little, but they wept tears, real tears. It was a revolution. Their sons were rebels against the law of Moses; they were lost souls, lost to God, the family, and to Israel of old. The police did not understand or sympathize. If there was a fight—and sometimes the fathers did lay hands on their sons, and the tough boys did biff their fathers in the eye; which brought out all the horrified elders of the whole neighborhood and all the sullen youth—when there was a "riot call," the police would rush in and club now the boys, now the parents, and now, in their Irish exasperation, both sides, bloodily and in vain. I used to feel that the blood did not hurt, but the tears did, the weeping and gnashing of teeth of the old Jews who were doomed and knew it. Two, three, thousand years of continuous devotion, courage, and suffering for a cause lost in a generation.

"Oh, Meester Report!" an old woman wailed one evening. "Come into my house and see my childer, my little girls." She seized and pulled me in (me and, I think, Max) up the stairs, weeping, into her clean, dark room, one room, where her three little girls were huddled at the one rear window, from which they —and we—could see a prostitute serving a customer. "*Da, se'en Sie,* there they are watching, always they watch." As the children rose at sight of us and ran away, the old woman told us how her children had always to see that beastly sight. "They count the men who come of a night," she said. "Ninety-three one night." (I shall never forget that number.) "My oldest girl says she will go into that business when she grows up; she says it's a good business, easy, and you can dress and eat and live."

"Why don't you pull down your curtain?" I asked.

"We have no curtain," she wept. "I hang up my dress across, but the childer when I sleep or go out, they crowd under it to see."

"Ask the woman to pull her blind."

"I have," she shrieked. "Oh, I have begged her on my knees, and she won't."

I went over and asked the girl to draw her curtain.

"I won't," she cried in a sudden rage. "That old woman had me raided, and the police—you know it—you know how they hound us now for Parkhurst. They drove me from where I was and I hid in here. That old woman, she sent for the police, and now I have to pay—big—to stay here."

"All right, all right," I shouted to down her mad shrieks of rage. "But her children look—"

"I don't care," the girl yelled back. "It serves her right, that old devil. I will get even. I will ruin her nasty children, as she says."

I threatened to "make" the police close her up, and down she came, all in tears.

"Don't, please don't, Mr. Reporter," she cried. "They'll run me out, the cops will, for you; I know; and I'll have a hell of a time to get found again by my customers. I'm doing well here now again; I can soon open a house maybe and get some girls and be respectable myself if—"

So we compromised. She pinned up a blanket on her window, and I promised not to have her driven out. When I came out into the street there was a patrolman at the door.

"What's the kick?" he asked.

I told him briefly all about it; he knew, nodded. "What's to be done?" he asked.

"Nothing," I answered hastily. "I have fixed it. Don't do anything. It's all all right now."

It wasn't, of course. Nothing was all right. Neither in this case, nor in prostitution generally, nor in the strikes—is there any right —or wrong; not that the police could do, nor I, nor the *Post*, nor Dr. Parkhurst. It was, it is, all a struggle between conflicting interests, between two blind opposite sides, neither of which is right or wrong.

THE LEXOW POLICE INVESTIGATION

NEW YORK in the nineties was about what Tennessee is now-adays, a provincial, moral community with a conscience, to which Dr. Parkhurst and the reformers could appeal, as they did, with fine blind faith. His mind represented our mind. He and we, the people, took a moral view of politics, government, business—everything. I do not mean that we were all good men and women. Some of us did some pretty bad things ourselves now and then, but we all meant well and so, on the whole, we felt that we were a pretty good people who wished for, voted for, and deserved a good government. We did not define "good" or "good government"; we did not have to. Everybody knew what was bad; our city government was bad. We knew that in a general way, and Dr. Parkhurst was making our vague sense of evil acutely definite by the simplest sort of moral revelation and reasoning.

He pointed out that there was a gambling-house running in the Tenderloin. Gambling is bad. No doubt about that; even gamblers admitted that gambling was wrong. There was a law against it. The law was all right; nobody doubted the righteousness of such a law. All that was necessary was to enforce that law, and we had a police force to do it. But when Dr. Parkhurst called upon the police to close the said gambling-house they would not do it, or if they made a raid, it was only to find the place all ready for them: with no business doing. Dr. Parkhurst said and we believed that the police had warned the gamblers. Why? Huh, we could guess the answer, and Dr. Parkhurst said it right out: bribery.

So it was with prostitution, which likewise is bad and against the law. There was some doubt, I remember, about the wisdom of this law. "Prostitution always has been, is everywhere, and always will be." This we heard, and it did seem cruel to hound these wretched women to distress. But Dr. Parkhurst was an able general, a clever strategist; he changed the question. Prostitution was in itself bad enough, but why should the police, who are there to enforce the law, permit these bad women to walk the streets and run their bad houses? And the answer was again: bribery.

The saloons, too. Drinking is bad. True, some of us drink; the best clubs of the best people have bars; and the saloon is the poor man's club. But the law allowed for all that. The law only regulated the liquor business; it designated reasonable opening and closing hours. If it was wrong in any particular, the remedy was to change the law. But why should the police, appointed and well paid to enforce the law, assume to amend it and protect the saloons? Bribery.

Bribery was the answer to all our questions, and bribery was wrong. Wasn't it? I never heard but one man in all those days defend bribery, and that one was an Englishman in the City Club. "If," he said to a group of us reformers, "if you are promoting a business and you encounter in the state an obstacle, you will bribe it out of your way just as you would blast a rock." I remember this because it was so "un-American" to our way of thinking. Americans did that, but even the blasters themselves did not say or think it. Our bribers in New York declared that they were "held up" by the police and the politicians; the gamblers, prostitutes, and liquor dealers were blackmailed. Whichever it was, however, whether blackmail or bribery, we were learning—Dr. Parkhurst and the investigators, I as a reporter, the people as newspaper readers—we were learning with astonishment that it was these corrupt practices that were making our good government bad.

"Well, and what are you going to do about it?"

Richard Croker asked that question. He asked it often, and I knew the spirit in which he put it to me, to us reporters. The old man, overwhelmed by the evidence produced and knowing how old and established the complicated system of bribery was, really wondered what could be done about it. He felt it was bad; our corruptest men were not cynical like that good Englishman. Croker was intellectually and morally a citizen of the civilization of New York. He had been as a youth a gang leader, the tough chief of the famous Tunnel Gang, had killed his man, and was the very type that comes up now out of the depths of our cities as bandits, or politicians, or go-getters in business. But, like a modern gunman, he had the same moral ideas as the rest of us. A bandit acknowledges our laws against robbery, and Croker never did and never could have defended bribery. When some reporter betrayed his confidence and reported his puzzled questioning it was presented and taken as a defiant challenge. But as he used to say it to me, it was an awed, a moral, question; and it served a moral purpose.

Dr. Parkhurst and the rest of us exposers and reformers were merely destructive. We were showing up the evils of our police and our Tammany politics and government. Richard Croker's exclamation, the sensation of a day, was a call upon us to do something constructive. What? We did not know. I mean that I did not find anybody with any intelligent plan for the reform of a city. There may have been, there must have been, some individuals among the million or so of people in New York who knew what to do, and it was my job as a reporter to seek them out and report them, but within the limit of my search I found not one. I could not interview radicals, of course; there were not many of them anyhow; they were only faddists: coöperators, socialists (a few), anarchists, whom nobody would listen to. The *Post* asked me to go to the meetings and the offices of the educated leaders of law and the other professions, business, and—in brief—the leaders of thought and culture in New York, and I remember jotting down a note, long since lost, to the effect that there was no more science in society than there was in the universities; there was no political science, no science of economics and no understanding of the psychology of "bribery and corruption"; no thought-out plan for municipal reform. Facts we had, but no generalizations and no capacity to generalize. I felt the need, my old need, of a picture of the government as corrupted, but nobody could help me to paint one.

Dr. Parkhurst's constructive ideas were as simple and moral as his charges, which he continued to deliver with force and effect. His analysis of his facts was that, since only bad men would take bribes and since the Tammany police and political officers not only accepted but exacted them, our government was bad because there were bad men in office. And the cure was to discharge the bad men and elect good men. That expressed our popular mind; our educated men knew no better; so that was becoming the issue. The problem was to find good men to nominate and elect. Our old habit of turning out the party in power and electing the other party, which was good enough in national elections, would not do in our exceptionally bad city of New York. Our Republicans were almost as bad as our Democrats. We knew this by experience. In past crises of this moral kind, we had let the Republican State government interfere in the city government—without any relief. We had bi-partisan boards, like our police commissioners, and they had either winked at the corrupt practices of the Democrats or divided the graft. We were now for non-partisan boards, mayors, and a "civil service reform," modeled upon the British permanent officials. Mr. Godkin and the *Post* were leaders in the civil service reform movement, as Theodore Roosevelt was. But the great idea that grew out of our disgust with the politicians of both parties was to elect as mayor not a politician but a business man who would give us a good business government.

The first step taken, however, was to demand of the State Legislature the appointment of a commission to investigate the charges of Dr. Parkhurst and the reformers against the city police. I was sent to Albany on this issue, and my first sight of that capital brought back vividly to my memory the California Legislature when I played around Sacramento with my boy chum, Charlie Marple, the page. It was the same picture. The two deliberative bodies looked alike, they sounded alike, they acted alike; and, as I worked in with the other reporters to inquire about the likelihood and the probable personnel of the police inquiry, I realized that they were organized and run alike. I heard the same honest, cynical comments. The two parties, Republican and Democratic, were both tempted to send down the investigating committee, the Republicans because there was a chance to win the city away from the Democrats, the Democrats because a controlled commission might whitewash Tammany and shut up Dr. Parkhurst. And a whitewash was what was planned and expected. But the Democrats were afraid that the inquiry might escape control and really show up what everybody in Albany seemed to know existed, and they threatened and the Republican leaders dreaded a revelation of the Republicans involved. It was "playing with fire," as the leaders of both parties said, and not only to one another; they said it to us reporters. They assumed that we knew how things were, and no doubt the other reporters did know. I did not. I was learning about the city police, of course, but I was far from taking them as a matter of course as the Albany correspondents took them. I could hardly believe what I knew of New York, and as to Albany—I was willing, I pretended, to accept all I heard, but I simply was not able to. I went home in a state of mind that is now familiar to me: trying to digest what I could neither doubt nor believe.

I believed and I reported to my paper that the Legislature would appoint an investigating commission, which would be stacked to find everything as near all right as one can expect it to be in a great city. And a commission was appointed, the famous Lexow bi-partisan committee. Whether Senator Lexow, the chairman, had instructions to go easy or hard I do not know, but the expectation of a whitewash had aroused a sneering, laughing public opinion which Dr. Parkhurst, the reformers, and the press whipped up to indignation. The committee had to do something; some show of earnestness became politically essential, and they chose as their attorney William Travers Jerome, who could not be pulled off. He was a young man of good old New York antecedents, great dash, vigor, and courage, and he knew conditions like an insider. He knew, for example, what he was up against, the pulls, the threats, the dangers he must fight through, but also he believed that if he succeeded he would have a career in law and in politics. He set out to succeed. He chose assistants, detectives, friends he could trust. He called for evidence from Dr. Parkhurst and his society, from the public, from the police and the underworld. As soon as he had a few witnesses he began his public hearings, which were the news of the day, for Jerome himself was a picturesque figure, the solemn commissioners were a study, and the witnesses and their facts and their language were curious and sensational. Back of the hearings too there were goings-on which leaked. Jerome used police methods, the practices of prosecuting attorneys. With power, not only to hear, but to indict and try, he bargained with his witnesses; he could send them to prison, he could let them go, he could compromise, according as they told the truth and gave away the system and their colleagues, which was called squealing, or preserved their "honor among thieves." So he threatened, he traded—he "fought," as I afterward saw other investi-

gators "fight the devil with fire." Evidently he had to fight both
the enemy before him and his friends behind. There were delays
—no sittings for days—and we heard rumors of "differences"
among the commissioners and their attorneys; the power of the
guilty police officers was very great. They had behind them the
most powerful politicians in both parties, whom they could
threaten, in their turn, to involve in their testimony; and the
politicians could with threats call upon statesmen and business men
high up. Once started, no one could foretell where the exposure
would stop; it was indeed like a fire. A sensation for the public,
that investigation was a worry, a tragedy, for the underworld and
indeed for the upper world. Jerome must have had to compromise.
The pressure upon him and the commission was irresistible, and
my guess was that he had to agree to keep the revelations within
the bounds of the police and their dealings with vice and small
business. Anyway he did not go beyond that limit, which was set
by the resolution under which the committee was appointed; he
may have let some individuals escape, but Jerome showed enough.

I was not at many of the hearings; my post was at police headquarters, and my job was to furnish the background and the connections and meaning of the evidence as it came out. Only on
great days did I go to sit and watch and hear with staring eyes
and staring mind. For it was news to me, as it must have been
even to the crooks themselves, to see that what we had heard was
true, to be forced to imagine what we knew, to be enabled to
generalize our facts and fill out our imperfect picture of police
corruption. The witnesses were policemen, police victims, small
business men, saloon-keepers, crooks, at first, and each one told
something you had known of others' doing or suffering. To Jerome
this early testimony was meant only to involve and so force other,
higher officials to testify; and sending for them, he would "put
them through the third degree" to compel them to "come
through." Many did. Clubber Williams, the first inspector, had to
account for his riches—he had more money, more property, than
he could have saved out of his salary. He had to admit that, but
he said that he had earned it by speculation in some "lots [of land]
in Japan." Most of the guilty witnesses dodged in some such way
as that, but so many of them admitted so much and sketched out
so many different angles of the truth that the newspaper readers,

A FLOOD OF LIGHT ON WILLIAMS.
Inspector Williams was implicated by Schmittberger's confessions in many ways. Schmitt-

berger was Williams's ward man in the "Tender-... Williams was captain of the dis-... for years when the committee ... to run in full ... and he told were allow ... precinct ... "dives" which were the re... graet under police criminals of the... blast under the worst criminals of the... Schmittberger said, and they w... cause they paid tribute to will...

THE CROWNING EXPOSURES.

SCHMITTBERGER'S STORY.

FRIGHTFUL REVELATIONS ABOUT COM-
MISSIONERS, INSPECTORS AND
CAPTAINS.

A FIELD DAY INDEED

CAPTAIN SCHMITTBERGER'S
REVELATIONS DEF...
LEXOW COMM...
...ELLS ALL ABO...
...ERLY HOUSES...
...AVOT, M...
...ONERS...

ESTABLISHED 1801.

ANOTHER CONFESS...

Story of Capt. Ma...
Schmittberger.

POLITICIANS' USE OF OFFICER

How the Force Has Been Degraded
by Pulls,

Promise of a Complete
Exposure.

The Inquiry to Be Continued Next

BY EYES ALONE IN A FAVORABLE LIGHT.

THE CAPTAIN COLLECTED MONEY AND
PAID PART OF IT TO WILLIAMS
AND M'AVOY.

PRESIDENT MARTIN MADE A WARD MAN APOLO-
GIZE TO A WOMAN WHOM HE HAD WARNED
TO CLOSE HER DISORDERLY HOUSE—SHEE-
HAN'S EFFORTS IN BEHALF OF A FRIEND
WHO WANTED TO OPEN A GAMBLING
HOUSE—POLITICAL CONTRIBUTIONS OF
THE TAMMANY MEMBERS OF
THE BOARD—MARTENS'S PAY-
MENTS FOR PROMOTION—
PRICE AS A COLLECTOR
OF BLACKMAIL IN THE
"TENDERLOIN."

N. SCHMITTBERGER ... "THE MONEY..."

The Evening Post

DECEMBER 21, 1894.

Wednesday — Senator Byrne,
Examine Supt. Byrne Anxious to

REVELATIONS ABOUT SHE...

ALL THE CITY, EXCITED.

SCHMITTBERGER'S CONFESSION ON EVERY
TONGUE.

THE DEMAND NOW IS FOR THE INDICTMENT OF
WILLIAMS, M'AVOY, MARTIN, SHEEHAN
AND THE OTHERS IMPLICATED.

Schmittberger's amazing revelations were the talk
of the town last night. In all political organizations, the
social clubs, the fashionable streets,
the theatres, the fine rum-shops and "dives" where
and avenues and side—every place in the city shock-
East and West together the one topic was the shock-
people come of the indicted police captain who had
ing confession of his superior
ing drives to exposing the connection of the Police Department
been officials with the crimes of his own escape from State
in the hope of effecting his own escape from State
Prison. Few well-posted citizens were really taken
by surprise at Schmittberger's testimony, for the
facts which were drawn from him yesterday were
already known to a number of
within, and a feeling of apprehension pervaded the
people, and ... the point efforts which have ...

SCHMITTBERGER TOLD—EVERYTHING

From the New York *Evening Post* and the New York *Tribune*, December 22, 1894 reading every line of the news, came to know what was being concealed. And as for the police themselves, they, with their knowledge and their imaginations at work to clothe all this testimony, they felt, as I knew from them directly, that "the jig was up."

"They've got us," said Captain Schmittberger one dark day at police headquarters. And a few days later he went on the witness stand and told—everything.

A tall, powerful, handsome man, Schmittberger had always been known to us at police headquarters as the collector of the Tenderloin precinct, which was the police district between Fifth and Ninth Avenues, Twenty-eighth and Forty-eighth Streets, where there was a concentration of theaters and vaudeville houses, hotels, restaurants, and saloons, the great gambling-resorts and houses of prostitution. He had been the collector of "blackmail" as a policeman, ward man, and now, as captain of the precinct, he still superintended the gathering of bribe moneys, which, by arrangement, he distributed—so much to himself and his subordinates, so much more to the inspector of that district. When he went upon the stand in full uniform he made a clean breast of all his own doings, and the king-pin in the whole system of police graft, he knew and described what other officers did in other precincts, giving names, dates, prices, rules, customs, conversations, manners. In brief, Schmittberger gave the whole system away.

After Schmittberger's "squeal," other officers "laid down," too. Byrnes resigned; other "higher-ups" confessed; and the defeat of Tammany was assured. Even the bad people, the poor and mean, who always followed their leaders and voted the Tammany ticket —as solid as the Democratic solid south—even Tammany voters voted for reform.

ROOSEVELT AND REFORM

THE man the reformers united upon for mayor was William L. Strong. He was a merchant; he knew nothing of politics, and the politicians knew nothing of him. He was an ideal candidate, therefore. He was the good business man who would throw out the rascally politicians and give us a good business administration. For him were the "honest Republicans," the fine old aristocratic Democrats, the reformers called goo-goos after their Good Government Clubs, the "decent" newspapers, and the good people generally. Richard Croker, who managed the fight against us, had his own machine, parts of the Republican machine, the saloons, gambling-houses, all vice interests, sportsmen generally, and to my curious surprise many business men—the ablest, biggest, richest business men in local business: gas, transportation, banks, and the great financiers.

"Sure," said Croker one night to me, "your reformer friends talk about business, but the business men who have business with the city government and so know about the Tammany administration—they are with us."

That was during the campaign. Croker had plenty of money from his rich backers and assurance from himself. "You won't get a look-in," he declared. He talked, he looked, he behaved in a way that convinced me, for one, that our ticket would be defeated and Tammany and the crooked police vindicated. I did not report the reform side of the fight; the political reporters covered that and indeed the whole campaign, but I used to go out of personal curiosity to reform headquarters, and the managers there tried to, but could not, radiate confidence as Croker did. They could say that we were sure to win, but they looked anxious and spoke dubiously; their willing lies did not ring true. The first time I was persuaded that we would win was after the polls closed on Election Day, when, as the counting of the ballots began, Croker received us, as his habit was on Election Day, and calmly told us, not only that Tammany was beaten, but by how large a majority.

I was so astonished, so disappointed in Croker, whom I had believed, that I hung back as the other reporters ran off—not to quote the boss; it was understood that Croker's figures were not for publication, but—to whisper the "truth" to their chiefs. Croker saw me, came over, and laid his hand on my shoulder.

"You look flabbergasted," he said. "Why? You knew all along that it was a reform wave, didn't you?"

"How should I know that?" I protested.

"A political reporter, like a politician, has to know politics," he smiled. "The betting showed; the gamblers have our figures. But one trip of inquiry into any Tammany ward would have told you that Tammany voters were going to vote against us this year, and one ward is all wards in a city. Our people could not stand the rotten police corruption. They'll be back at the next election; they can't stand reform either. But this year they—as you see—" and, giving me a gentle shove, he added, smiling kindly, "as you ought to have known, boy."

The other reporters did, they said. "What do you do, read the papers or work for them?" one of them asked me, when I had sounded him.

Police headquarters was the proper background for my humiliation the day after the election. Everybody there was humble, too, and I sympathized with them. But they did not sympathize with me. Byrnes had nothing to say; Clubber Williams, hate in his eyes, stood with some papers in his hand to watch me come into the hall.

"Well, are you satisfied now?" he sneered at me.

"Not yet," I answered boldly, but I did not feel bold. I felt ashamed. Would I never see through the appearance of things to the facts? Never get past the lie to the truth? Victory was defeat for me. Dr. Parkhurst was calmly pleased. His attention, however, was fixed on the next step, the appointments to the police board. The fight was not over, he said; Mayor Strong was making "deals." Everybody was pulling and hauling upon him to do this or not do that, to name this man and not to name the other; the police board he had to appoint was the bone of contention among the groups who thought and said that they had "made him mayor." A business man, he did not know the ethics or the ways of politics. He gave promises that could not be kept because they were contradictory. I saw enough of it to realize that reform politics was still politics, only worse; reformers were not so smooth as the professional politicians, and it seemed to me they were not so honest—which was a very confusing theory to me. I remember having a talk with Jake Riis about it. His mind was single and simple. He declared that God was running it.

"Theodore Roosevelt is the man for president of the police board, and God will attend to his appointment. That's all I want to know. I don't care who the other commissioners are. T.R. is enough."

My academic interest in the difference between reformers and politicians did not interest him; my suggestion that maybe the ethics of politics and the ethics of business were different and that, therefore, a man like Croker was better in politics than a merchant like Strong, whereas a business man in business would be better than Croker—that bored Riis. He let me express my thoughts, but after all, I could think aloud more clearly with my mother-in-law than with Riis and other reporters. She was neither religious nor cynical. But Riis was right, in a way.

Roosevelt was appointed police commissioner. We got the news from our offices one day; Riis came shouting it out in the street, and within an hour up walked T.R. and three other gentlemen: Robert Dent Grant, the son of General Grant; Avery D. Andrews, an ex-army officer, and Andrew D. Parker. I said that they walked. I mean that they came on foot; and three of them did walk, but T.R. ran. He came ahead down the street; he yelled, "Hello, Jake," to Riis, and running up the stairs to the front door of police headquarters, he waved us reporters to follow. We did. With the police officials standing around watching, the new board went up to the second story, where the old commissioners were waiting in their offices. T.R. seized Riis, who introduced me, and still running, he asked questions: "Where are our offices? Where is the board room? What do we do first?" Out of the half-heard answers he gathered the way to the board room, where the old commissioners waited, like three of the new commissioners, stiff, formal, and dignified. Not T.R. He introduced himself, his colleagues, with hand-shakes and then called a meeting of the new board; had himself elected president—this had been prearranged —and then adjourned to pull Riis and me with him into his office.

"Now, then, what'll we do?"

It was all breathless and sudden, but Riis and I were soon describing the situation to him, telling him which higher officers to consult, which to ignore and punish; what the forms were, the customs, rules, methods. It was just as if we three were the police board, T.R., Riis, and I, and as we got T.R. calmed down we made him promise to go a bit slow, to consult with his colleagues also. Then we went out into the hall, and there stood the three other commissioners together, waiting for us to go so that they could see T.R.

They did not like it a bit, as Parker told me afterward. "Thinks he's the whole board," he said; and the subsequent split of the commission was started right then and there. We warned T.R., and he tried to make it up to his colleagues. He consulted them when he thought of it, but Grant and Andrews did not know anything about the police, and Parker, a New Yorker, familiar with the conditions, had it in for T.R., who, he said, was stepping up on the police job as a ladder to something higher.

"Of course," Riis answered, when I told him Parker's opinion. "Teddy is bound for the presidency."

My theory of T.R. was that he merely forgot the courtesies due the board. He had been asked to take the police job, he had been urged to clean out the department, and considering it with his friends, had been thinking of it as his job, his alone, forgetting that it was a board; and so, when the others were appointed, he kept forgetting them. He was so intent upon the task that he did not think of his associates or anything else.

"Except the presidency," Riis would roar, and he was so happy in his certainty that God and T.R. were working toward that end that I challenged him one day.

"Let's ask him," I said.

Riis sprang up, and with a "come on" to me, dashed across the street up to T.R.'s office. And bursting in, Riis did ask him to settle our dispute. Was he working toward the presidency? The effect was frightening.

T.R. leaped to his feet, ran around his desk, and fists clenched,

OUR BOYS.

JACOB.

ONE of the nicest little boys we know is Jacob. He is very fond of another little boy named Teddy, and likes nothing better than to be with him. Teddy is a scrapper, and breaks loose every once in a while, whereas Jacob is very mild. But they get along beautifully

Jacob does not care much for toys, but likes to play with Teddy's silk hat Also any other thing that Teddy has that has been consecrated by use.

Jacob writes nice compositions and makes them into books. Once he wrote a piece about himself and then he wrote a piece about Teddy. The first was called an autobiography and the second a campaign document. Jacob is a very frank little boy and tells all he knows and feels, which sometimes makes you sorry for him. But, then again, you can't help but like him, because he loves Teddy so. Not because Teddy ought to be loved like this, but just because Jacob loves him.

Life

T.R. HAD FEW FRIENDS AS DEVOTED AS JAKE RIIS

teeth bared, he seemed about to strike or throttle Riis, who cowered away, amazed.

"Don't you dare ask me that," T.R. yelled at Riis. "Don't you put such ideas into my head. No friend of mine would ever say a thing like that, you—you—"

Riis's shocked face or T.R.'s recollection that he had few friends as devoted as Jake Riis halted him. He backed away, came up again to Riis, and put his arm over his shoulder. Then he beckoned me close and in an awed tone of voice explained.

"Never, never, you must never either of you ever remind a man at work on a political job that he may be president. It almost always kills him politically. He loses his nerve; he can't do his work; he gives up the very traits that are making him a possibility. I, for instance, I am going to do great things here, hard things that require all the courage, ability, work that I am capable of, and I can do them if I think of them alone. But if I get to thinking of what it might lead to—"

He stopped, held us off, and looked into our faces with his face screwed up into a knot, as with lowered voice he said slowly: "I must be wanting to be president. Every young man does. But I won't let myself think of it; I must not, because if I do, I will begin to work for it, I'll be careful, calculating, cautious in word and act, and so—I'll beat myself. See?"

Again he looked at us as if we were enemies; then he threw us away from him and went back to his desk.

"Go on away, now," he said, "and don't you ever mention the— don't you ever mention that to me again."

As Riis and I were going, crestfallen, thoughtful, down the stairs, I said, "Well, you win, Riis."

"I do not," he answered, hot; so loyal was Jake Riis; but he was honest, too. He hurried on ahead, and we never mentioned the matter again even to each other.

The first thing the new police board did was to order the police to enforce the law, and when they did not obey, the second step was taken: the removal of the bad police officers. Byrnes had retired voluntarily, unprompted, and the day of his going is memorable to me. There were rumors of his retirement, and many business men and politicians called quietly, saw him, and as quietly slipped away. "What will happen to us now I dread to think," said a banker, who really looked frightened. I believe there were people who felt that all that stood between them and crime was this mysterious master of the police force. But thieves came too, and they were more frightened than the honest men. They did not call on Byrnes; they simply walked along the streets around police headquarters, and one man sat on the steps going up to the high stoop of the building. He sat with his head in his hands, his elbows on his knees, and seemed to heed nothing. I asked Tom the door-man who he was.

"Oh, just an old dip that the old man was good to sometimes. Thinks the world is coming to an end."

The crooks and the business men, and for that matter many of the police and police reporters (including myself), did not under-stand that it was not Byrnes but a well-nigh universal system that they were living and working under, a system of compromise and privilege for crooks and detectives that "the inspector" inherited and left intact. When Superintendent Byrnes retired that day and walked without good-by to any of us out of his office forever, men stopped and stood to watch him go, silent, respectful, sad, and the next day the world went on as usual.

Roosevelt had to decide whether to let the other higher officers retire on a pension or be tried. Some of the commissioners and public opinion were for punishment. "Discipline," they said; "re-venge," they meant. Riis and I were against trials. With Riis, the veteran police reporter, it was sentiment, I think. He was fond even of some of the worst men. My attitude was instinctive: against punishment; but it was not clear and straight. There were excep-tions. I wanted satisfaction from the clubber, Williams, and I told T.R. I wanted to be present when he fired him, and why. My argu-ment, however, was that trials were long, the law technical and unsure, and T.R., who was swift, stood in the main for retirement. And he was strengthened by his experience. As he began to send for officers and tell them they must go; either reluctantly resign, retire, or be put on trial, "pull" interfered, and not political pull alone.

"Hey, there," he yelled to me from his window one day, "come up here." I ran upstairs to his outer office, which was filled with all sorts of respectable people, evidently business men, lawyers, doctors, women, and two priests. Waving his hand around the circle of them, he squeezed through his teeth aloud: "I just want you to see the kind of people that are coming here to intercede for proven crooks. Come on, come into my office and listen to the reasons they give for letting bribers, clubbers, and crime-protectors stay on the police force and go on grafting on the public."

Of course he spoiled the sport for that day and that crowd. I sat with him awhile, but the callers who had heard what he said could not make their pleas very well. They were too embarrassed. But on other days when I saw a "string of pulls" calling on him, I went up and listened. They were amusing; they did not know what they were talking about. Most of them merely liked personally some officer who had asked them to intercede to keep him on the force. What I got out of it was that so-called "political influence" is really a common, human plea which politicians use best. The average good citizen tried to tell T.R. that the man he was pulling for was a good officer lied about. Since the officers T.R. was firing were all men fully exposed by the Lexow Committee—the worst of them—the good citizens' appeals only angered him. But when a politician came breezing in and said: "Sure, Mr. President, Captain Bill's a crook; most of 'em are crooks; most of all of us is so crooked we get cramps in our beds at night, but, hell, why pick on Bill? He knows you're straight, and if you ask him to go straight he will. Sure he will. I know Bill since he was a kid. All I ask you is to call him up, look into his face, and tell him what to do. You'll see: he'll do it."

That sort of song and dance would tempt us; and I mean us.

"What'll we do?" T.R. would say after a plea like that from some regular Tammany leader, and I could not help laughing. I knew just how the commissioner felt. I wanted to see Captain Bill and ask him to stay and help reform, as T.R. did; and sometimes we did send for Bill, and, well, sometimes T.R. kept a proved crook for a crooked politician. The reporters observed and reported it, too.

Looking back at it now, I can see it better than I could then. I can see that the police assumed that T.R., being a reformer, might respond to a clergyman's appeal or "a word" from a business man or any other "good man" and be affronted by the plea of a politician, especially a Tammany opponent of reform. They did not know what false and offensive reasonings good people make. It was long before they learned that—for some reason, which they never did discover—the reform commission was, like the old board, subject to political pull. When they did learn it the character of the callers at police headquarters changed. Politicians came after that, prominent leaders of all parties—and failed often; they gave political reasons for mercy. The police never learned what it was that "got" T.R.

"What gets me," said an old police sergeant (the wisest rank on the police force), "what I can't unpuzzle is why he'll listen to Tim Sullivan and throw down the reform Mayor himself and laugh a Platt Republican leader out of his office; and then turn right around and tell Charlie Murphy [a Tammany leader] to go sing his song to the high marines in the harbor, and do a favor for Lem Quigg [a Platt machine leader] up the river."

Nor could I solve the riddle, any more than T.R. could. He thought he was carrying out the reform policy of "throwing out" the crooks and enforcing the law. He was having a hard time of it. He could not make the policemen on their beats close up the saloons at the closing hour. He told them to. He issued formal orders, he made personal appeals, and nothing happened. Talking it over, we guessed that the rank and file would not obey the board because the higher officers, like Inspector Williams, who gave T.R.'s instructions to their men, did so with a wink. By way of experiment I suggested that he force Williams out and then see what happened in his district. He agreed. He knew what had been disclosed of Williams's share in the blackmail fund; everybody remembered the rich inspector's "lots in Japan." I told about my experiences with this man and his brutal clubbings of East Side strikers.

"I said I'd be here at police headquarters till he was fired," I concluded.

"Did you?" T.R. asked. "Well, you will. You'll be right here in this room."

A few days later T.R. threw up his second-story window, leaned out, and yelled his famous cowboy call, "Hi yi yi." He often summoned Riis and me thus. When we poked our heads out of my window across the street this time, he called me alone.

"Not you, Jake. Steffens, come up here."

I hurried over up to his office, and there in the hall stood Williams, who glared as usual at me with eyes that looked like clubs. I passed on in to T.R., who bade me sit down on a certain chair at the back of the room. Then he summoned Williams and fired him; that is to say, he forced him to retire. It was done almost without words. Williams had been warned; the papers were all ready. He "signed there," rose, turned and looked at me, and disappeared.

He did, this one clubber; he went, but not the clubs. Skulls are still cracked—literally—in New York. My triumph was personal, mean, and incomplete.

T.R.'s was a little better. With Williams out and an acting inspector in command of that district, a young, inexperienced patrolman "took a chance," as he said. One night this young cop walked into Pat Callighan's saloon, laid his hand on Pat, and told him he was under arrest. Now Pat was a man of strength as well as power, and his gang was all there. He fought, the gang fought, there was a boozy, bloody battle, but the young cop with his night stick laid out enough men to hold off the rest. He arrested Pat Callighan. I saw this in the morning papers, and when T.R. arrived at his office I showed him his chance.

"Promote that cop," I said, "and you will show all the young policemen that you mean business. Pat Callighan is a sacred person in the underworld, a symbol. The key to his saloon was thrown in the river when he opened, and his door has never been locked since. If a patrolman dare arrest Pat and can get away with it, then all saloons can be closed."

T.R. did it. This young policeman was too newly appointed to be eligible for promotion, and there was strong opposition in the name of the law, but T.R. had announced that he would make a roundsman of this, the first policeman to believe him, and the board consented.

And sure enough, other policemen of all ranks began to obey the orders of the board. Some saloons and some gamblers were raided—not many; not all laws were enforced. T.R. went about at night with Riis as his guide to see the police at work. He had some bizarre experiences. He caught men off post, talking together; he caught them in all sorts of misconduct and had funny, picturesque adventures, which Riis described to all of us (so fair was he as a reporter) and which we all wrote to the amusement of newspaper readers. But what T.R. was really doing—the idea of Riis in proposing it—was to talk personally with the individual policemen and ask them to believe in him, in the law, which they were to enforce. T.R. knew, he said, the power they were up against, the tremendous, enduring power of organized evil, but he promised he would take care of them.

"It worked—a little," he used to say. "I told them that we

would back up and not only defend but promote those that served on our side, and I threatened we would pursue and punish those that served on the other side."

This he said, and while he was saying it, he was planning to "fire" Schmittberger, the captain, the key to the old system.

XII

SCHMITTBERGER: AN HONEST
POLICEMAN

THE next summer after the Lexow investigation and Tammany defeat, I lived as a commuter at Riverside-on-Hudson. Those were bicycle days, and one morning as my wife and I were wheeling we met and passed Captain Schmittberger, the police Samson who had pulled down the whole structure of police graft and still lived. He had been sent to Goatville, as the cops called a remote country precinct like this where there was "nothing doing." He did not greet me. I saw him look, recognize me, and turn away. He had not forgotten that all through the investigation I had sung one monotonous song, day in and day out. "Get Schmittberger." If he would squeal he would deliver everybody and everything. Therefore, "Get Schmittberger."

"What a handsome man he is on his fine horse!" my wife said, and indeed he was a handsome big fellow, whether afoot or ahorseback. His beauty had made him what he was, won him his appointment to the police force, won him favors and promotions —his beauty and his honesty.

We saw him often after that. No matter how far we rode or into what lanes and by-ways we explored, we met Schmittberger always out somewhere on his mounted patrol, and I reported to Roosevelt and Parker that Schmittberger seemed to be always on the job. T.R. made no answer. Parker, a great walker, said he knew it. "Every time I go up that way," he mused, "I meet the captain; he is all over the shop, and there isn't a thing doing up there, not a saloon open, not a law broken."

One night a big river launch that belonged to a man who lived in our boarding-house was robbed at its moorings. I reported to police headquarters in the morning, and that evening Schmittberger rode up, tied his horse, and looked over the launch. When he came back I was sitting in a hammock near by, and I asked him what he could do about it.

"Not much," he answered mechanically as he remounted. "I've sent down an old ward man of mine to find out what they know about the gangs that are working the waters, but, you know, we can't do what we used to do. No connections any more. I don't believe any of us knows now who the river thieves are."

"Do you regret the old days, Captain?" I asked.

"I do not," he replied quick and straight from deep inside. "I wouldn't go through what I have gone through for—for a million times what there was in it for me. Never again. Not on your life."

There was something in the ring of this that tempted me to go on; not what he said, but his vehemence struck me as genuine.

"Get down, Captain," I said. "Let's have a talk."

He hesitated, gave me a look of surprise, inquiry—I could not quite read it, but he got down, tied his horse, and dropping into a big wicker chair, lighted a huge cigar.

"You don't believe me," he began. "And it is tough. We had bought that big house we live in, the Missus and me, and I had been paying off the mortgage till there was only a few thousands left. I'd 'a' paid it in a year more. Now it will never be cleared."

There was something conclusive about that "never," as if his mind was made up to no more graft.

"Can't save enough on your salary alone to settle it, slowly, sometime?"

"Salary!" he exclaimed. The police were well paid; a captain's pay was pretty good. But he said it wasn't good enough to cover more than living-expenses and interest in such a big house as he had chosen. Couldn't he sell that house and buy a simpler one?

"The Missus likes this one," he said, with finality again. "It's our home."

It was my turn to hesitate, but I decided to drive in the probe and see.

"But, Captain, we get it pretty straight that some of the cops are taking it again, a little, here and there, carefully—"

"Not me," he declared with a lifting in horror of his two hands. "Never again, never again." He even looked frightened, and as I stared back at him wondering, he sat up, and astonished, he said: "Say, you don't know what I've been through. You never had your kids sit silent at dinner, nudge one another on, and so pass the buck to the big boy you always kind of—wanted the respect of, and then had him swallow a lump and blurt out, 'I say, Pop, is it true this stuff they are saying? It's all lies, ain't it!'"

He couldn't go on, and I didn't want him to. I had forgotten, when I wrote my hounding facts and suspicions, that there were families back of these crooks, and children at home who sat silent, wondering at table whether their fathers were what the newspapers said.

"The other kids ask them at school," the captain blubbered, "and so they ask you." And when he got no help from me, no belief, he explained. "And you ask me if I'll do it again!"

"How did you ever get into it, Captain?" I asked to ease him. He told me.

He was a German boy, born, if I remember aright, in Hoboken, and apprenticed to a pastry cook in New York. Tall, rosy, frank, he must have been a pleasant sight in his white cap and jacket. "Customers liked me," he said; so he was sent out to deliver his fresh cookies at houses and restaurants near by. One day a couple of Tammany leaders admired him to his face, joked him on his height and good looks. "Like to see you in a police uniform," one of them jested, and Max, the German pastry cook, was so pleased, so surprised and eager, that the two "good fellows" agreed there and then to get him on the force.

"Won't cost you a cent either," one of them said. Max did not know then that there was a fixed price for an appointment on the force, a fee paid for pull. He had to study for an examination; he could hardly believe that he would ever be called, but he prepared under a man who made it his business to cram Tammany candidates, and to his joy and amazement, he was called, passed, and appointed. He was put through an unusually long, severe initiation at the hands of the older policemen in his station barracks. His account of it showed that they regarded him as an innocent, liked him, but were amused at his simplicity. He took it good-naturedly and so became popular with the men, and he was so naïve and obedient that his officers preferred him, especially for decorative posts, street corners where he showed off well.

"There was no traffic squad in those days," he explained, "but I was set up in the middle of Broadway and Thirty-fourth Street, where I got to know lots of people, who used to say, 'Hello, Max.' They laughed, but they were for me. They used to put in good words for me with my captain. Gosh, but I did like being a policeman. Do yet."

His night beat was on a side street where there were many houses of prostitution. He had no instructions, and he knew nothing of any laws against such places. He did nothing; he saw nothing for a policeman to do. On the next post, farther west, where the colored quarter began, there was always activity, and Schmittberger used to hang around that end of his beat to watch and envy the old policeman there his tussles with the niggers, who drank, sang songs, danced, and cut one another up with razors. One evening as he was pacing his own quiet tour a colored girl ran down the steps and with a "Here, officer," pressed a ten-dollar bill into his hand and darted back into the house. Not understanding it, Schmittberger went on down to the old cop, showed him the money, and described how he got it.

"Sure," said the veteran, "that's what the Cap put you on that fat job for: to make a little on the side." And he explained how, though the ward man collected the regular pay monthly from houses of prostitution, the patrolman on all such streets "got his" now and then.

"So the captain knows about it?"

"Sure thing. He knows everything like that, knows what every post in the precinct is worth, and his putting you where you are shows he likes you and wants to feed you up."

"But why?" Schmittberger asked, who did not understand what the money was for, and he laughed when he told how the old cop misunderstood his question.

"What for!" he exclaimed. "Oh, it's because you're so thin. He wants to fatten you up."

"But," Schmittberger related, "I had plenty to eat, so I turned in the money to the captain. That is, I started to. I laid it down on his desk and was beginning to tell him about it when he jumped down my throat. What did I take him for? And where did I get my nerve? I was scared; I thought the old cop had put up a joke on me to get me in bad with the captain, till all of a sudden he cooled down and said that he didn't take chicken-feed. I and the likes of me might take it and keep it."

A look of bewilderment—the original expression that he showed the captain, I guess—recurred on Schmittberger's face as he drew for me the conclusion he evidently drew then: "It was the tip, the size of it, that made him mad."

His captain seemed to have drawn a conclusion, too. He used Schmittberger more and more, and the story showed me—I'm not sure that Schmittberger saw it even as he told it—that he was being tried out in all sorts of delicate services: to carry money, to collect money, to do detective work. It was plain to me that that old captain was convincing himself that he had an honest, extraordinarily innocent policeman whom he could trust.

"He had me cultivate the fly-by-night-hawks; you know [I didn't], the drivers of old hacks, so old they're ashamed to come out by day. The drivers patrol the Tenderloin, pick up rich drunks coming out of the houses of prostitution, and drive 'em home by way of Central Park. There a pal jumps out, opens the door, and if the drunk is 'dead,' yanks him out and robs him. That's bad, because the sucker, left there on the ground, catches cold. But it wasn't done in our precinct: 'None of our business,' the captain said. And those fly hackmen were awfully useful to us. They knew all the crooks, gamblers, and girls in the world; they were called in on all sorts of phony business, all the way from making a get-away for somebody to driving a dead body to the river after a murder. They knew all the gossip of the ward, white, black, and yellow.

"Well, I got to know all these drivers, and pretty soon they were reporting to me. If the old man wanted the stuff back from a robbery, whether it was in one of our houses or in the Park, all I had to do was to take a walk down along their stand of an evening before they got busy and tell them. They'd deliver the next day. If they didn't I harried them; you know, kept them moving. 'Can't stand here,' I'd say. Or we'd put a couple of men on bicycles out to watch them pick up a fare and then shadow them till they took him home. They had to stool-pigeon for us, but usually they did it willing, and we, on our part, didn't bother them if we could help it."

This was the ABC of detective work, getting into relationships with a kind of criminal which enabled the police to feel sure that, in an emergency, if they must, they could solve a mystery, catch a criminal, or restore stolen property. When Schmittberger had "the night-hawks on his string," his captain switched him to niggers, beginning with the panel-houses. These are houses of prostitution in which there are sliding panels in the walls of a room. When a man goes into the room with a woman, he puts his clothes on a chair, the only chair there, which is close to the panel, and the pimp or some other woman can reach in and pick the pockets. White women practice the panel game; it is permitted in some high-priced houses that keep the stealings within reason; i.e., take some, but not so much of a man's money that he comes complaining to the police. Schmittberger's first and chief business was with the colored houses. A white man seldom squeals when he is robbed in them; he doesn't want even the police to know he has crossed the color line. The colored folk grow careless, therefore; their pimps slip the panel and they can hardly restrain their temptation to take everything they find, from hundred-dollar bills to carfare and stamps. Schmittberger had to restrain them by making the acquaintance of both the women and their lovers, watching to see who was spending too much money, and organizing a system of squealing on one another. He soon knew all about all their relations, methods, peculiarities, and controlled them as well as the colored temperament can be governed by friendship and fear.

In my later days at police headquarters, Schmittberger was beloved by the colored people, but in the beginning he was so feared that mothers used to quiet their children by threatening that "Cap'n Max'll come and ketch you." I asked him once to take me to a notorious colored dance dive. "Better go alone," he said; "I'll spoil it." Upon my insistence he went, and sure enough, when he appeared there was first a hush, then a rush; negroes dived out of windows, doors, and down the stairs and up and down fire-escapes. "You see, every nigger that has been doing anything wrong has skipped. They think I know everything." Only innocent negroes remaining, the crowd was small, and since even an innocent nigger has a conscience, there was no spring in their dancing, no joy in their songs, no abandon in their drinking. They came up and petted and flattered the captain, but there was no fun in it for me. We left, and Schmittberger held me at the corner to watch the guilty blacks sneak back up to the dive. "They'll soon be happy again," he said.

After Schmittberger had been assigned to various sorts of special detective work and so obviously trained for the job, he was made a ward man. He told it with surprise. "All of a sudden, without any warning," he said, "the old Cap called me in and told me to 'shed that uniform, Max; you're going to be my ward man.'" Schmittberger shyly repeated to me the high praises the captain bestowed upon him by way of expressing his faith in his honesty. "I've watched you, young feller, tried you out, and I believe you will make straight collections and deliver the goods on the level." Schmittberger paused, embarrassed, then he boasted like a boy. "I did," he said, and I believed him.

The collections he was to make for his captain were the regular monthly payments by gamblers, prostitutes, saloons—all law-breakers—for the privilege of breaking the law, rightly called police protection. He had to go to the barrooms, gambling-houses, and houses of prostitution, take and sometimes force the payment, which amounted to some twenty plus thousand dollars a month, bring the money to the police station, count it with the captain, who split it—so much for the Superintendent, so much for the in-spector, so much for himself, and a small percentage for the ward men, of whom there were two. Other ranks and men, who got none of this regular graft, were allowed to pick up tips and "goods" as they could. Sergeants at the desk received tips from prisoners, shared in the business of feeding them, and enjoyed other priv-ileges; they earned "good money" on bail bonds. Patrolmen on "good posts" received tips, as Schmittberger did when he was a young cop. This chicken-feed mounted up in a "fat precinct" like the Tenderloin, but was beneath the dignity of a self-respecting captain. The big business was the regular graft that Schmittberger handled for years, all in the day's work, without losing either his honesty or, it seemed to me, all his innocence. I often afterward reviewed this part of his experience; it bore upon my old interest in moral and ethical psychology. My note was that the process of corruption had begun so quietly with that first tip and proceeded so gradually in an environment where it was all a matter of course that this man never realized what he was doing till the Lexow

Committee's exposure, with the public (and private) horror and the press comment on it, exposed him to himself.

"I didn't know how it looked," he said that evening by the river. "I never saw it as you saw it till I saw the other Lexow witnesses telling things. And then I had to ask the Missus if I'd look like that if I squealed. 'Ah, no,' she answered. 'You couldn't look like that.' I wasn't like them, she said, and then when I did holler I looked the worst of all."

It was true. His testimony was the completest, most appalling of all; his confession summed up the whole rotten business, and yet as he spoke of it to me he looked like a nice big boy caught stealing apples. He seemed to want me to tell him he wasn't so bad after all. When I didn't, he gave it up.

"I guess I was, but, do you know, I don't feel bad; not inside."

My wife came out to join us. I introduced him to the "Missus," as he called her.

"Can you catch the robbers that damaged the boat?" she asked him, to make conversation.

"I'm afraid not," he answered; "we're on the level now, as I've just been explaining."

She didn't know what he meant and was so puzzled that she did not try to make more conversation. The captain rose, untied and mounted his horse. He ran his hand down into the animal's mane, turned his bent head to face my wife, and said, "I wish you'd help me make your husband believe that I'm on the square —now."

"I will," she responded completely. "You come again, and we'll work together on him."

He rode off without a good-by or a look back.

"Why didn't you say something?" she reproached me.

I told her what I meant to do. "Oh, that's better," she said. "But what did he mean by saying he couldn't catch the thieves that so damaged that boat because he was honest now?"

XIII

SAVING SCHMITTBERGER

I T WAS understandable that public opinion should have expected to see Captain Schmittberger, the confessed collector of the police graft system, punished or at least discharged. The belief in the existence of good men and bad men and that the guilty should suffer is deeply implanted in all men, and the star Lexow witness was a villain in two ways, in two worlds. The good were against him for his grafting, the underworld for squealing. Both counts counted with me. But I thought I saw a chance to make an experiment in morals.

Cannot an honest man do dishonest things and remain honest?

Isn't a strong man, however bad, socially better than a weak man, however good?

Schmittberger had been strong as a crook. He was bold in the collection of blackmail, honest in the distribution of the graft. His public confession was complete, detailed, and picturesque, and as I have shown, his private story indicated that he had not realized what he was doing. He was still honest, a good man doing bad things. He struck me as a type that would serve as well on the reform as on the graft side if he were given a chance. I wanted him tried out on that theory, the theory that society can safely use some men whom we foolishly punished and outlawed. I did not say all this to those whom I appealed to. To Dr. Parkhurst I argued that we, the reformers, could not afford to penalize a policeman for coming over to our side, exposing organized evil and, in brief, for confessing his sins and reforming. The clergyman hesitated, shook his head, but partly for me, I think, and partly for my moral argument, he consented to back me up. This was his state of mind till the fight over Schmittberger began. Then he, a fighter, fought, and also a strong man, he fought to the end, which came years later when we had Schmittberger made chief of police.

Roosevelt was harder to win. He listened to my rather full report of the interview with the captain till I wound up with the suggestion that he keep and use the man. "No, no, no," he revolted. He was deep in his struggle with the police, however, trying to command or persuade them to believe in him and in reform. They would not. Here and there a young policeman made an arrest, and T.R. praised publicly and promoted such men as examples. This policy had some effect. The police gradually were convinced that T.R. personally was on the level.

"But, hell, what does he know about the police business or politics?" they would say to Riis and me. "And he and reform won't last. Look at 'em, getting all mixed up, fighting among themselves. Reform and T.R. will soon be over and out, and Tammany will be back. Then what do we get, us cops that have played the reform game? We'll get nothin' in the neck."

Many an analyzing talk we, the kitchen police board, T.R., Riis, and I, had over this problem; so when I spoke for Schmittberger I presented his as a case in point. If he would move the captain down from Goatville to a bad, fat, grafty precinct, Schmittberger would clean it up, make the police under him enforce the law, and best of all, the board would show that it knew and would favor the police officers on "our side." "The police and Tammany and the vice men and women know that Schmittberger is against them now and for us," I said. "That's why they want him out. But as Dr. Parkhurst asks, why do we want him out?"

He yielded at last. "Go to Parker," he said. "I am not cunning enough to deal with that sort of—espionage. Parker loves it. Let him try out your honest crook. I'll abide by his decision." The sneer was a spark from the waxing conflict between the president of the board and Commissioner Parker and for my interest in Parker, a new type to me. I had met in literature, in history and court memoirs, but never before in life, the man that liked to sit back and pull wires just to see the puppets jump. That was Parker. He was a Democrat, and T.R. was a Republican; but Parker won Grant, the second Republican, to his heel, and T.R. got Andrews, the second Democrat. The split, which finally broke up the board and spoiled the work, was not along party lines, and it had nothing to do with policy. They called each other names: "politicians," "fakers," even "crooks," but I listened to both sides all the time, and my conviction is that the trouble was due solely to the character of the two leaders, T.R. and Parker. T.R. liked to lead cavalry charges with a whoop out in the open, Parker to direct his troops mysteriously from the rear unseen. He hated the way T.R. took command of the police from the first day and kept saying "I" and "my policy." So did the other commissioners, and Parker enjoyed turning up at a meeting one day with Grant to block some proposition of the president. He tried to get Andrews, too, but the young West Pointer did not like the crafty conspirator; he did not approve of T.R.'s cowboy style either, but he stared Parker down and joined and stood by the president. Also he warned him to look out for Grant; too late. Grant was with Parker, and T.R. could not win him back. His efforts delighted Parker, who described them to me.

"T.R. jumped on Grant," he smiled wickedly. "The personification of obstinacy, the son of his father naturally turned into an army mule. T.R. can never get him now."

"But what are you doing it for?" I asked.

"Oh, just for ducks," he answered, "just to see the big bomb splutter, the boss leader of men blow up."

"How did you get Grant?"

"I didn't have him, except on one very reasonable proposition, till T.R. nailed him to me, as I counted upon his doing. My theory was that when Grant voted once, unexpectedly, with me, T.R. would land on him, as he did. And Grant—well, Grant has one trait at least of his father's genius. He will fight it out on this line if it takes all summer, and if he falters T.R. will kick him back to me."

T.R. tried in every way, morally, politically, and socially, to take Grant from Parker, but always spoiled his successes by some burst of impatience which caused Grant to balk, smile, and vote with Parker. Grant was always good-natured. I compared him once to the daily report of the Chicago hog market: "dull but firm."

"Mrs. Grant did not like that," he drawled to me the next morning, "but I did. It was hard on the hogs, but I don't care for hogs except as pork."

Parker knew all about T.R.'s efforts to get Grant. "They had a dinner in the swell set last night," he would say. "All the wives are against me, you know, all for T.R. Mrs. Grant, too. I have nobody to help me hold Grant but T.R. The Mayor is to talk to Grant today again, at 11:45."

Parker knew everything, exactly. When I told him about Schmittberger, that he was doing his duty as a policeman, he knew it. "He's on patrol all the time," he said. "There isn't a place open in his precinct. Not much there, but what there is is obeying the law."

I told him I had urged T.R. to use him, but—to spur Parker on, I said, "He won't. I wish you would try him out."

He looked at me, smiling. "You know how to get me, don't you? Well, we'll see."

A few days later Schmittberger was transferred to the precinct next below his, and within a week Parker said that the "new broom had swept away" two poolrooms that were running there. Very soon after that the commissioner had a severer test for "my" captain. He had the evidence on some wire-tappers in the Hundredth Street precinct. These were criminals who picked off the wires the results of horse races, held up the news till their confederates could put down some bets and then, in a few minutes, win on certainties. Parker's plan was to have the wire-tappers arrested, show them that he could convict them, and then offer to let them go if they would buy with marked money from Schmittberger the privilege of working in that precinct. When all was ready Schmittberger was transferred to that command, and a few days later Parker sent for me.

"Remember those wire-tappers that were going to bribe Schmittberger? Well, they're in the hospital. They tell me that they had hardly got started talking business when the captain leaped on them, knocked them down, and kicked them bodily out of the police station across the sidewalk into the street."

"And Schmittberger, what does he say?"

"Not a word. He hasn't reported the case. He called an ambulance and forgot it. I think that, if you'll warn him to wear gloves on his fists, we can use him to clean up all the bad precincts in town. He seems to be down on bribers, and after this gets around the underworld he is not likely to be tempted very much."

T.R. was dee-lighted with this story. "Atta boy," he shouted. He did not ask me to caution "my captain."

Thereafter Schmittberger was called "the broom," and not only the Roosevelt board, all police commissioners used him as a sweep. "Well, send Schmittberger," they would say when things got too bad anywhere, and he certainly did clean up. He was indeed terrible. He knew the crooks, knew the crooked game, and cared nothing for the technicalities of the law. Like all converts, he was worse than the accustomed righteous.

"To hell with the Constitution," he shouted once at some Reds who cited that sacred instrument as a guaranty of their rights. He was still a policeman, in this and in other ways. I saw him attacked by a mob of strikers at the Fourth Avenue car barns. He was alone for a few minutes; he stood head high above the waves of fists that broke on him, and when some policemen arrived they could not get in to him.

"Throw me a billy," he called to them, and a club was tossed hurtling over his head. He caught it in the air, brought it down on a head, and so, cracking skulls all the way, he waded out of the mess over the fallen strikers, turned with the squad that had come out, and cleared the street. He was an artist with a police club, "tapping 'em" always on the top of the skull so that they closed up like a knife. He was a trained, an expert, policeman; he could plan a parade, a march, or a traffic arrangement better than any man of his day; he understood how to creep in behind the draft at a fire and make a rescue.

His reliability, once established, was a comfort to the reform board, but his ferocity when in action, especially in strikes, troubled me, and I undertook to tame it. He had learned of my part in his restoration to favor and was so grateful that he would take any advice from me. To cure him of his police hate of strikers I had him shifted to an East Side precinct where he had never served.

"What'll I do over there?" he asked me. He had come to my house to find out why I had him sent there. "Niggers I know, but Jews—?"

I reminded him that the poor, immigrant East Side Jews were a new and friendless people who never got a square deal. They were difficult, quarreling among themselves, aggressive, acquisitive, and sharp in their dealings with other people; and they were insistent upon their rights. No matter. They had to fight, not only for their life, but for a living wage. He might be patient, considerate, and fair with them, giving them plenty of leeway for their peculiarities, no matter how offensive they were.

"When they come to you," I said, "listen to them and try to settle their quarrels without a fight or an arrest."

"I'll do it," he said, and he did it. He allotted his first morning hours to his friendly court, hearing not only of ecclesiastical, financial, and art disputes, but taking complaints of husbands against wives, wives against husbands, parents against children, children against parents, employers against workers, and workers against bosses. Letting both sides argue themselves tired, he decided cases unofficially and with such common sense that the arrests in that precinct lessened perceptibly. He cautioned his men against the use of the night stick and learned himself to spare heads. "My fists are good enough," he said. With these he cleared the vice resorts, to the tearful joy of the old Jewish families who were relieved thus of one menace to their boys and girls. He became a non-partisan in strikes, seeing what I had seen: that employers were as grasping and unreasonable as the men. He tolerated the Reds, letting the socialists and anarchists hold meetings, demonstrations, and parades, and he came to be so respected by those agitators that one socialist parade cheered him when he appeared with a squad of policemen to lead and protect the marchers.

My ex-collector of bribes was a success. He could learn; he had learned as much from us reformers as he had from the old grafters. I was proud of him, Dr. Parkhurst was astonished and pleased, Parker called him "my broom," and Roosevelt called him "my big stick." There were other "reformed cops," not many, but enough to put most of the gamblers out of business, keep prostitutes within bounds, and enforce, a little, the laws regulating saloons. The police commissioners were changing the environment and the spirit of the police gradually, and they might have succeeded as well as later boards if they had not quarreled among themselves. Divided two against two, they became deadlocked and could go only as far as T.R. could drive by himself. The board would not always support him, but it could not keep him from breaking through and giving orders and examples on his own.

"I'll do that," he would say; "I'll do it first and fight it out with Parker afterward."

The public and the press watched and were disgusted; the politicians waited and laughed; the police sneered. The tide of political approval that had elected the reform administration was ebbing, and Mayor Strong and his advisers could do nothing. The mayor, a good merchant, was a bad politician. He could not stay on either side of the police board war, nor could he hold the two parties together, and he had not the strength to call for resignations.

"Say," said Schmittberger, "we'll be beaten and Tammany'll come back." Often he said it, and there was alarm in his tone and eyes. He was afraid of what would happen to him when his old crowd came into power.

"You go right on," I advised him. "Dr. Parkhurst and I will be here all the time, and we'll take care of you."

I could tell him that, and some few others, but I could not reassure all the police officers and men that came over to our side, and most of them slowed up. T.R. could not hold them. Other heads of departments failed likewise to get bold, steady service from their men. The explanation is simple.

Policemen and the rank and file of government officials are either born or brought up in an environment of unbelief. They know facts; they know how things are really done; they don't develop illusions as I did in my protected youth, and their surprises are at unexpected good, not, like mine, at unexpected evil. They know that good is rare and short-lived. The New York police force did not vote for, they voted pretty generally against, reform; and they forced votes for Tammany. When the reformers won the police were astonished, and since the victory had been won at the cost of police exposures they were prejudiced and afraid. Of course. But what counted with them was their belief that reformers are no better than others, that they lack the knowledge, efficiency, and machinery to establish permanent reforms.

"Reforms, yes," said a cautious reform chief of police whom Parker got T.R. to choose. "They can find a Colonel Waring in the army to clean streets; they can appoint a man that can clean tenements; they can do a lot of little things, but they cannot make any real change in conditions. I am willing to play up with T.R.

but I cannot help keeping one eye on the signs of the failure of reform and the return to Tammany. Tammany is not a wave; it's the sea itself; and I am not going to fall out altogether with what stays to follow a bunch of climbers who pass on to Albany and Washington. I have a career to make, too, only mine is right here in New York."

Like Schmittberger, this shrewd, street-schooled policeman, whom T.R. called "bad," had the strength to be of as much service to good government as bad. There were many such; there are many such. There are outlawed criminals whom I would like to have in office under me if I were a responsible mayor or governor; as a voter I would prefer certain bold, intelligent bandits to a "good man" like Mayor Strong or a "good-natured" general like Commissioner Grant. T.R. himself and Parker were all right, each in his own way; but they should not be asked to work together on the same job, especially if the job be police reform. The public knew that Roosevelt was confused, when his announced policy of enforcing the law because it was the law was challenged by the citation of hundreds of statutes too ridiculous to be enforced. Parker would have enforced some laws, ignored others, keeping in his own mind his private aim, first to train the police to habits of obedience, and second to reform the town, gradually. Either would work; both have worked temporarily, but separately.

Reform was beaten. Tammany did come back. The police and other cynics were right. And as they predicted, the reformers passed on up, T.R. to the navy and the army, the governorship at Albany, and the presidency at Washington. But the reform policemen had to stay and face Tammany Hall, their friends the saloon men, gamblers, and all the rest of the people who had felt the clubs on their heads or the business losses caused by—reform, yes; but at the hands of—traitors on the police force.

I passed on up, too. My city editor, Wright, and Seymour, the publisher of the *Evening Post*, went over to the old *Commercial-Advertiser*, a paper with some two or three thousand circulation— nothing in a city like New York. They proposed to carry out there the news policy they had not been able to work out on the *Post:* to print all sorts of news. The assistant city editor, Milholen, was made city editor of the *Post*, and he called me to be his assistant. I left police headquarters, therefore, but I was too interested in the police story and the predicament of my friends there to forget them. When Tammany came in and I heard the underworld saying, "Now we'll get the cops that soaked us, and first Schmittberger," I wrote and printed their intention, suggested editorials, and prompted Dr. Parkhurst to warn Tammany.

"Now we'll see who are the honest men on the force. Tammany will point them out to us by firing them."

I saw Croker, too, and I appealed to his political sense. "Don't give yourself away." He said it was none of his business; the new administration had to deal with such details. But he wondered what they could do with Schmittberger if they kept him. "Doesn't Tammany ever have use for a broom?" I asked.

He reflected a moment, smiled as if he had an idea; and, "We'll see," he said.

I don't know what his idea was, but Schmittberger was kept, and the use made of him was the same as the reformers': to clean up. Wherever there was a precinct backward in payments or subject to some recalcitrant political leader, Democratic or Republican, the Tammany administration sent Schmittberger there, and he shut off the graft, closed up the vice business, till the disobedient came to terms. Then the terrible captain was transferred to the next precinct that had to be brought into line.

"I'm playing their game," said Schmittberger to me, and he did not like it, but his face cleared when I bade him never mind. I think he consulted Dr. Parkhurst also and was similarly reassured. Thus he became an institution under Tammany and had no more troubles until another reform administration came in, with the police job to do all over again.

The effect of the exposure and reorganization by the Roosevelt board of police was to reform the methods of corruption and graft. The reformers did not learn much, but Tammany and the vice interests did; they saw that it was foolish and dangerous to let so many in on the graft. Patrolmen, sergeants, captains, inspectors, chief—everybody had his rake-off. With so many knowing so much about what was going on, it was inevitable that the facts should become public property and that, under pressure, some individuals would be caught, weaken, and expose the system, dragging down Tammany Hall and hurting business. Tammany, therefore, centralized the graft, cut off all subordinates (leaving them nothing but tips or "pickings"), and arranged to have protection granted and payments made and received by a few men chosen for their nerve and reliability. These men were never identified except by rumor; the whole business of police protection for law-breakers was resumed, and the results, a wide-open town and a corrupt police force, were all the public saw. But these were enough. The next reform administration elected, that of Mayor Seth Low, found the police the most urgent and obvious problem. The mayor appointed General S. V. R. Greene, a military man, who had been the head or front of the infamous asphalt trust of Philadelphia. By that time I was muckraking for a magazine, was working in Pittsburgh, knew something of Pennsylvania politics, and so believed that Greene was—what the asphalt trust was. When I received telegrams from Dr. Parkhurst and, through my wife, from Schmittberger that the captain was in danger, I was not surprised. I hastened to New York, prepared to fight. My wife and Schmittberger, awaiting me at my home, showed me a newspaper clipping: a list of police officers to be promoted as acting inspectors and chief of police. Schmittberger was not among them; few "honest men" were on that list; most of them were shrewd crooks. Schmittberger came in and broke down: "Now they'll get me, all right; might as well quit." I asked him to wait and see. I went straight over to General Greene's pretty little old house and was received at once.

Too excited and indignant to be even polite, I threw the clipping down on the general's desk before him, exclaiming, "Do you mean to appoint that list?"

"Yes, I did," he said coolly. "I threw it out to draw comment. If you have any to make, I'll be glad to hear what you know against those men."

"Well, they're mostly crooks," I said hotly. "Your first task is to win the belief of the police force that you are 'wise,' that you know who is who and mean to promote honest men. You will be judged by the cops you appoint, and the police know, as we police reporters know, that this is a list of crooks that has been put over on you."

I was standing, he was sitting; I was angry, he was quiet, attentive, thoughtful.

"What do you know against these men?"

"Know!" I flamed, and I told him some things, but I cut my-self short with the savage inquiry, "But what's the use? What I know is what you know when, in command of troops, you advance some men and keep others where they can do no harm."

He was watching as well as listening, and he was slow. After a long pause he asked me whom I would promote in his present state of inexperience of the force and the urgent emergency. I named a list, including Schmittberger.

"Schmittberger?" he inquired. "Do you think that a man who is guilty of the crimes he has confessed—"

He did not finish. I walked up to his desk, leaned over it, and said in his face, "Do you, who have been the head of the asphalt trust, ask me that?"

I afterward heard in Philadelphia that General Greene had been put at the head of the trust as a front, to lend it credit with his undoubted honesty and ability, and that when he learned what he was representing he resigned. Anyway, I was wrong in my estimate of him; the Philadelphians convinced me that General Greene had a perfect record. And his police performance was proof of it. His deportment that evening in his house when I insulted him might have shown what he was.

"I will try Schmittberger," he said.

I almost collapsed with astonishment and relief.

"Yes," I said, "put him in the worst district you have and have him watched. Let his enemies, let some of those crooks on your list, shadow Schmittberger and report to you. You ought to have a squad of detectives anyway, to furnish you information."

He nodded, reflecting.

"Let me have your list, by the way," he said.

I gave it him, he rose, and—in a few days most of my list was appointed, including Schmittberger. When it was published in an evening paper the new acting inspector came running with it to my house, crying, "We're made, we're made."

He was tried, permanently promoted, and finally became chief of police, where he served honestly till he died. And among his proudest possessions were written letters of high praise from all his reform commissioners from Roosevelt to Colonel Arthur Woods, and none was so explicit and complete as that of General S. V. R. Greene.

X I V

I MAKE A CRIME WAVE

EVERY now and then there occurs the phenomenon called a crime wave. New York has such waves periodically; other cities have them; and they sweep over the public and nearly drown the lawyers, judges, preachers, and other leading citizens who feel that they must explain and cure these extraordinary outbreaks of lawlessness. Their diagnoses and their remedies are always the same: the disease is lawlessness; the cure is more law, more arrests, swifter trials, and harsher penalties. The sociologists and other scientists go deeper into the wave; the trouble with them is they do not come up.

I enjoy crime waves. I made one once; Jake Riis helped; many reporters joined in the uplift of the rising tide of crime; and T.R. stopped it. I feel that I know something the wise men do not know about crime waves and so get a certain sense of happy superiority out of reading editorials, sermons, speeches, and learned theses on my specialty. It was this way.

The basement of the old police headquarters was a cool place in summer and detectives, prisoners, and we reporters used to sit together down there and gossip or doze or play cards. Good stories of the underworld were told there, better than are ever printed as news. They were true stories, and true detective stories are more fascinating than the fiction even of the masters. Sometimes a prisoner would give his version of his crime and his capture after the detective who had caught him told his. Sometimes the stories were dull, technical, so to speak, and therefore interesting enough to the participants, like ex-soldiers comparing notes of a battle after the war.

One day I was dozing away, bored by a long dispute as to whether it had happened on a Thursday or a Friday night, when a fresh voice broke into the debate. The speaker was evidently bored too.

"Ah, say, cut that," he said. "I'll tell you a good one on two cops up on Murray Hill. They were talking at the corner of Fortieth Street and Madison when a wagon drove up to a house, a swell residence closed for the summer. The family was away and a caretaker was in charge. The caretaker was Billy Bones, that Chicago house-buster who has no business to be in New York anyhow, and the driver of the wagon was our own well-known sneak, Mr. Busy-Bee. They had planned a clean-out of that house; Billy had got the job for that super-purpose, not to take care of the house, but, as I say, to clean it. It was dusk, the hour they had agreed upon for the job, and they were a bit troubled at the sight of the cops on the corner. Busy-Bee pointed 'em out when Billy Bones answered his ring and came to the door. Billy felt of his face to feel if his chin was clean-shaved equal on both sides; it was; so he says, 'Oh, well, they're not Chicago bulls; they're only New Yorkers. If they come up we'll ask 'em to help us. See?'

"The Bee has no local pride, no loyalty. The traitor says, 'All right, Billy. We'll try it; I don't want to hire the wagon twice for nothin'. Let's get some heavy things down on the sidewalk so as to give them something to do.' They did that. They brought out more and some bigger things than they ought to have taken. The sidewalk was a mess when the cops parted at the corner and one of 'em comes down to see who was cluttering up his beat so that honest citizens could hardly pass. He came up to the Bee, who was sweating more than he would have if he wasn't scared.

" 'Why don't you get some of those things into the wagon,' the cop ast him, 'instead of cluttering up th' right o' way this away?'

"Because the Bee had to swallow before he could speak, Bones comes down the steps with a trunk and explains that, as th' caretaker, he wants to get the things out and close the house as soon as possible; that they meant to load up afterward, but everything was out now, and if the cop would lend 'em a hand they'd clean the sidewalk in two shakes. The cop didn't like the work.

"What did he join the force for? he asked Bones, and Bones didn't answer that. 'Couldn't of,' he told me. 'I couldn't no more of explained that than I could of told why the force joined th' cop.' All he says was, 'Ah, come on, be a sport an' give me a boost with this trunk.' The cop boosted that trunk; he boosted other trunks; he put the parlor clock in himself. Say, that cop did more of that crime than the Bee did. The Bee apologized afterward to Bones for layin' off. He wasn't malingerin', he said. He simply wasn't used to workin' on housecleanin' with policemen. And Bones adds to me—to me, mind you, a plain-clothes detective sergeant— Bones adds as a postscript to the Bee's reflection on policemen, 'He means policemen in uniform.'

"Well, anyway, that burglary was done with police aid and protection. When the wagon was loaded Bones got his coat, locked the front door inside, came out by the service entrance with his coat and hat on, and thanking the cop, got up on the seat with Busy-Bee, the driver, and drove off with a selected load of pictures, furniture, clothes, and odds and ends, which amounted, the owner says, to about ten thousand dollars! Why, Bones and the Bee alone got eight hundred for it from Barny Levy, the fence."

There was some laughter, a little comment, and the conversation passed on to idle gossip again. Pretending to wake up, I stretched, rose, and idly walked out. In my office across the street I wrote a news story of that robbery, but only because the victim was the well-known family of a popular Wall Street broker. I could not give away the source of my information; it might exclude me from the basement. I did not repeat the joke on the cop who helped the thieves. The *Post* having it alone, however, the morning newspapers printed the "beat," and Riis was asked by his editor the next day why he did not have it. In the course of his irritated reply he said that he could get all he wanted of that sort of stuff, and his editor answered, "All right, get it, then."

That afternoon Riis reported a burglary which I knew nothing about, and it was my turn to be called down. My editor wanted to know why I was beaten.

"I thought you didn't want crimes in the *Post*."

"No, but a big burglary like that—"

All right. I called on my assistant, Robert, and told him we must get some crimes. We spent the day buttonholing detectives; I sat an hour asleep in the basement in vain. Nothing but old stories. Robert saved the day. He learned, and I wrote, of the robbery of a Fifth Avenue club. That was a beat, but Riis had two robberies that were beats on me. By that time the other evening papers were having some thefts of their own. The poker club reporters were loafers only by choice. They could get the news when they had to, and being awakened by the scrap between Riis and me, they broke up their game and went to work, a combine, and they were soon beating me, as Riis was. I was sorry I had started it. Robert or I had to sleep in turns in the basement, and we picked up some crimes, but Riis had two or three a day, and the combine had at least one a day. The morning newspapers not only rewrote ours; they had crimes of their own, which they grouped to show that there was a crime wave.

It was indeed one of the worst crime waves I ever witnessed, and the explanations were embarrassing to the reform police board, which my paper and my friends were supporting, in their difficult reform work. The opposition papers, Tammany, and the unreformed police officers rejoiced in the outbreak of crime, which showed that the reformed police and especially the new detective service could not deal with criminals in a city like New York. This criticism had a point which pricked the conscience even of Roosevelt himself. He had got rid of Superintendent Byrnes, the most famous of New York's detectives, removed Byrnes's self-trained inspector, and put in a captain who would have no dealings with professional criminals. The old system was built upon the understood relations of the crooks and the detective bureau. Certain selected criminals in each class, pickpockets, sneak thieves, burglars, etc., were allowed to operate within reason; the field was divided among them by groups, each of which had a monopoly. In return for the paid-for privilege the groups were to defend their monopoly from outsiders, report the arrival in town of strangers from other cities, and upon demand furnish information (not evidence) to the detectives and return stolen goods. This was called regulation and control, and it worked pretty well; more to the glory of the police, who could perform "miracles of efficiency" when the victim of a robbery was worth serving, but of course it did not stop stealing; it protected only citizens with pull, power, or privilege. There were many crimes done within and without the system, which depended for public sufferance on the suppression of the news, as any detective system does. But Byrnes had taught New Yorkers to report their losses to the police, never to the press.

"If you tell us your troubles we have a chance to detect the criminal," he said over and over again. "If you tell your friends or the press the thieves are warned and run away, and we can do nothing."

If citizens would reverse this method and report both to the press and the police they would learn something; they would soon find out how many crimes are committed in a day, how few are "detected," and force the police to detect many more. And as for warning the criminals, these wise men know that the police always are told of a crime and that detectives work hardest on a case that is in the papers.

Roosevelt's chief of detectives was appointed because he hated the old system, held it to be useless, and declared that he had a better way of dealing with the crooks. He asked leave to run the old crooks out of town, to watch for and arrest at the railroad stations new and known arrivals and to drive them away by threats of holding them as fugitives from justice until he could obtain evidence against them from the cities where they had been working. This method was succeeding so well that Commissioner Parker, who was watching it, was satisfied with the progress made, and T.R. believed all was well till the crime wave rose and frightened him. He suspected Parker anyhow; the detective chief was Parker's choice, and the outbreak of crimes all over the city so alarmed him that he was almost persuaded that the opposition was right in its criticism: that the police reformers, knowing nothing of crime, criminals, and police work, technically, had blundered in changing the system, the good old Byrnes method of handling this, the real business of the police; not to interfere with business and sport, but to catch and punish house-breakers and other law-breakers. He called a secret meeting of the police board and was making one of his picturesque harangues when Commissioner Parker interrupted him.

"Mr. President, you can stop this crime wave whenever you want to."

"I! How?"

"Call off your friends Riis and Steffens. They started it, and—they're sick of it. They'll be glad to quit if you'll ask them to."

Roosevelt was perplexed, as Parker meant him to be.

"I don't understand," he said.

Parker, who was "wise" and liked to mystify, explained that when the crime wave was running high he inquired into it, not as the editorial writers did, and the jurists and the scientists; he asked for the police records of crimes and arrests. These showed no increase at all; on the contrary the totals of crimes showed a diminution and the arrests an increase. It was only the newspaper reports of crimes that had increased; there was a wave of publicity only. He turned therefore to the newspaper boys and asked them about it—"not your friends Riis and Steffens, but the regular fellows, the poker combine. They explained it. They said that the morning newspapers got their crimes from the courts where only arrested prisoners are tried or held for trial, and that their own, the evening papers, got their stories by hard detective work, which they hate to have to do. But they must continue as long as your friends, Mr. President, keep up their fight. They started it; the other reporters didn't know where they got the dope from; they thought some inside office detectives were squealing."

T.R. adjourned the meeting, sent for Riis and me, and bang! "What's this I hear? You two and this crime wave? Getting us into trouble? You? I'd never have believed it. You?" Up and down his room he strode. Betrayed he was, and by us whom he had trusted? Who, then, could be trusted? And for what? Why had we done it? Why?

"And you laugh!" he blazed at me. I couldn't help it. But Riis saved us. He was contrite; he looked ashamed, and T.R. saw it.

"You, Jake," he said, "you tell me about it."

Riis told him about it, how I got him called down by printing a beat, and he had to get even. And did. "I beat the pot out of you," he boasted to me, his pride reviving. "And I can go right on doing it. I can get not one or two crimes a day; if I must I can get half a dozen, a dozen. I can get all there are every day.

"But"—he turned to T.R.—"I don't want to. So I'll tell you where my leak is, and you can close it up. I have had it for years, seldom used it, but—you can stop it for ever."

And Riis, the honest, told us how the reports of all crimes of high degree against property were sent in by the precincts to the heads of inspection districts and then were all compiled in a completed list which was filed in a certain pigeon-hole in the outer office of the chief inspector. Not he, but his boy, Max, had observed the making and filing of this list one day long ago; he had reported it to Riis, who resisted temptation to some extent.

"I told Max never to pry into that pigeon-hole—except in emergencies. And we never did, except in emergencies. But when you"—he blazed at me—"when you got so smart, I got so mad that I told Max to go to it, and, well—" He turned back to "Mr. President, that file is in the extreme left of the third row of pigeon-holes from the bottom. It should be kept in the inside office."

"And you?" T.R. whirled upon me.

I had to tell him about my naps in the basement among the gossiping detectives. I did not want to give up hearing the gossip, and I asked, and T.R. and Riis agreed to grant me, leave to go there on condition that I would use it only to collect local color for fiction or data for the scientific purposes of my studies in sociology and ethics.

Thus the crime wave was ended to the satisfaction of all. T.R. took pleasure in telling Parker that he had deleted, not only the cause, but the source of the wave, which was in Parker's department. He would not say what it was; sufficed that it was closed for ever. Parker had to resolve that mystery by learning from the chief of detectives that the president had ordered the daily crime file removed from the public to his inner office—for ever. Both commissioners, separately, promised that the wave would soon recede; and it did. When Riis and I ceased reporting robberies the poker combine resumed their game, and the morning newspapers discovered that the fickle public were "sick of crime" and wanted something else. The monthly magazines and the scientific quarterlies had some belated, heavy, incorrect analyses of the periodicity of lawlessness; they had no way to account for it then. The criminals could work o' nights, honest citizens could sleep, and judges could afford to be more just.

I INHERIT A FORTUNE

AMONG the foreign news cables to the *Evening Post* one day was a personal message for me from the German Consulate at Naples: Johann Friedrich Krudewolf had died there, leaving instructions immediately to inform me, the residuary heir and the sole executor of his will. I felt as a bird must feel when it is shot on the wing. I remembered my promise to Johann to stop whatever I was doing to go to Germany and carry out his wishes when he died, but I did not want to be stopped then when I was in full career. Remorse, too, I felt, not only sorrow. I had long known that my old university chum had to die young, but I had almost forgotten it, and him, too. I had answered his letters, but not promptly and with not much interest in his painful labor to keep alive and carry on his researches in art history. So far as I could recall them my letters were full of my own selfish, healthy interest in my vivid, purposeless life. Ashamed and depressed, I went home early that afternoon, got out some of Johann's recent letters, and they also were full of me and my doings; they were answers to mine and, therefore, about me. Always me: as my mother had always said.

My wife, to turn my thoughts, suggested that maybe some of the money left me was really for me; and I had been wanting money to use in Wall Street. That made it worse, and my mother-in-law, Mrs. Bontecou, remarked that Johann must have loved me.

"More than you loved him," my wife added.

"That was his gain," said Mrs. Bontecou.

"And my loss," I answered.

"You will always be loved more than you love," said Josephine. I felt that to be true, but I thought she was thinking of herself.

She may have read my mind, for she said, "Look at your parents—"

This was an old grievance of hers. I had not reported our marriage till I had made good in New York, was earning my living, and, with my wife's novel published, we were independent. I had accepted financial aid from my mother-in-law and would not heed my wife's plea that my family ought to have shared the burden. And then, when my father and mother did come to New York to attend our wedding, they were hurt to hear that we had been married several years.

My mother wept, and my father asked, "Why?" Josephine answered out of her anger at me that when I received my father's letter advising me not to come home but to stay in New York, go to work there, and learn the practical side of life, I had declared that I would not only do that; I would never again ask him for money or other help.

"But," he protested, "if I had known you were married—"

"There," Josephine triumphed. "I told you," she said to me.

She had told me always when fear seized me—whenever I felt that the circumstances of life and the conditions of journalism would make of me what I saw it make of old reporters and editorial writers, a Greek slave in Rome, a writer of the master's opinions—then my wife had reminded me that there was my father to lend me the money to buy my liberty. And he would have done it. He said at our mournful wedding funeral in New York that he had cast me off only to try me out, and he offered then again to buy me an interest in a San Francisco evening newspaper. Josephine besought me to accept, and when I refused she declared I was selfish both as to them and as to her. And she punished us all for my obstinacy, me, my parents, and my sisters, who soon after came home by way of New York from three years at Göttingen. I think she thought I would refuse to take Johann's money, too.

Johann's money was different. It was probably a small sum; Johann was through with it, and, as Mrs. Bontecou and I recalled, he had bound me when I last saw him to do something with it for him. He had spoken of founding a scholarship. One of the shots that wounded me and my selfishness was the obligation I was under to interrupt my work to go to Europe to do this something

with Johann's money. My wife liked that, and she had us ready
to sail when the letter came from Johann's attorney, W. Lorenz,
giving details.

W. Lorenz wrote that the estate would be valued at somewhere
around 100,000 marks or $25,000. There were many bequests, both
to persons and to institutions. The attorney had ordered the body
of the deceased to be shipped home and would direct the funeral
and burial, but I must come to choose a family plot, where I had
to gather from many places the bones of other members of his
family. When all was done, W. Lorenz estimated that my inheritance, the residuary estate, would amount to some $12,000.
Nothing about a scholarship, no special duty such as Johann's
solemn pledge had implied. Why, then, had he left the money
to me? What was I to do with it for him?

Now the seat of this modest estate, the home of the Krudewolf
family, was Lehe-bei-Bremerhaven, and Bremerhaven was the
harbor for Bremen. We took a North German Lloyd ship, therefore, and on the way up the narrow channel to Bremerhaven,
passed and looked with a curious personal wonder at the small
village, Lehe, which only the captain and members of the crew
knew or had ever heard of. Some of the crew lived there; it was
indeed a seaman's village, and my steward, whose wife and children waved to him from the shore, wondered what in the world
we two foreigners were bound there for. And so at the dock in
Bremerhaven porters, officials, ticket-takers could not believe that
we wanted to "go back to Lehe." There, straight ahead, was the
way to the train to Bremen; everybody else always went from
the boat to the train and so on to Bremen and Berlin. It was something of a fight to get ourselves and our baggage out of the stream
to Bremen, and then, when we did escape to the street in Bremerhaven, it called forth all our German and some rage to convince
the porter and the carriage driver that we were to go through
Bremerhaven back to Lehe. "Nobody goes to Lehe"—"there is
nothing to see in Lehe"—"it is nothing, Lehe"—"even Bremer-
haveners never go to Lehe." Our final release came from a by-
stander who explained it all in a muttered sentence of which I
caught but one word, "*verrückt.*" I knew the rest; so did the
porter and the driver. We were crazy Americans and so were allowed to drive out through Bremerhaven on one long street which

became, at a wave of the driver's whip, the main street of Lehe also. My house was No. 32.

My house! It was a neat, white shop, tight up against and exactly like the shops on both sides, which, in turn, were of a solid block of similar business houses running a mile or so both ways. It did not look like mine, and I did not think of it as mine till our carriage stopped and three women and a man rushed out of it at us, crying joyously, "*Wilkommen, Herr Hausherr*," to me, and a more formal, less joyous greeting to "my gracious lady."

They were Frau Hamel, the mother, two daughters, and a son, who leased the ground floor of the house and ran the shops, the two shops, one on each side of the main entrance to the three-story house. The driver was so astonished that he could only sit up on his seat and exclaim, "So, they *live* here. *You* live here!" The family had to take our baggage, and they did it merrily, laughing and talking, greeting and explaining. They swept us and our baggage into the hall, up the clean stairs to our *Wohnung*, the family residence for many years of the Krudewolfs, Johann's, his father's, his father's father's, and so on. It was ready for us, neat and white, polished, dusted, furnished—just as it had always been kept—as homelike a place as I have ever seen.

"We'll serve you supper here in half an hour," said these amazing tenants, leaving us to clean up after our journey. We looked into the closets, bureaus, chests in all the rooms, and my wife exclaimed. Space had been cleared for our clothes, but there were drawers and chests filled with fine old linen for beds and tables, stuff enough for several such houses, and some of the chests were beautiful old carved, rare boxes.

"All yours," said the three tenants when they came up with the supper, and "Look here!" They unlocked a great box in a back room; it was full of funny old heavy silver sets. "Three complete services," they said, "most of it, like the linen, never used."

"But why? Whence?" we asked.

"Every bride brought something rich, silver or linen or both, and such things are kept; not used. You use ordinary things."

That was the custom; that was the tragedy of our inheritance. As we looked over the items of the property left to me, a foreigner, by the last of the Krudewolfs, houses, lands, stocks and bonds, furniture, clothes, and miscellany of all sorts, we heard, and we

saw in the accounts, the story of slow growth and thrift—the savings of sacrifice—for generations—all for us, strangers, who had
had no part, little sympathy, and nothing but pity for the lives
that had given up so much for us.

"Why did Johann leave this all to me?" I asked these kindly
women, who seemed always to have been tenants and servitors, too,
of the family.

They did not know. They looked at one another as if the
question had never occurred to them, and the mother cast it
aside. "All we know is that he did." That was enough for them.

"And why do you serve us supper?" my wife asked.

"Oh, we always served Johann when he was home, and his
father before that."

Was it included in the lease? No. Yes. Maybe. They would let
me see the lease if I wished, but it really didn't matter. They
would buy our food for us, anything we liked, and present the
bill, but we could not cook and prepare the table or clean the
rooms. That was their part; it had always been so. The *Mandatar*,
W. Lorenz, would explain everything, but—with looks of amiabil-
ity—they hoped there would be no changes.

But, why, by the way, had the attorney not called that first
evening?

Oh, they answered, he said that he would save the cost of a
useless visit. He charged for each and every service, and if he
came that night when we were tired we could do no business; so he
was coming in the morning, when he not only could greet us but
would have time to show us the accounts and make it worth our
while.

He came in the morning after our breakfast in the pretty garden
back of the house. He was a tall, dried-up professional man in an
old professional long black coat—with flat red hair, a kind old smiling face, and a lame left arm, like the Kaiser's. He often mentioned
that, "like the Kaiser's"; it turned the defect into a decoration.
He used it to hold his brief-case tight against his ribs. He greeted
us, as the tenants had, with a "Welcome, Mr. Landlord and
gnädige Frau," but he swept the table clear, laid out his papers,
and wanted to go to work.

I wanted to ask some questions: why had Johann left me his
property? But W. Lorenz was reporting, while piling his papers

in order, what he had done since Johann's death and my succession to the estate, how he had got the news, opened the will in court before witnesses, and begun at once to obey its directions, ordering the body shipped, preparing for the funeral, which he described in business details. He would show me the grave, unmarked, which I was to put a stone on. His report was completed, with prices paid, for which he showed me the bills.

My difficulty was to realize that this was my business, that I was the master he regarded me as.

"But, *Herr Mandatar,* why did Johann make me his heir? What does he ask of me?"

"I am coming to that," said W. Lorenz, and he drew out the will, read it with all its many small bequests and requests—nothing for me to do; nothing, I mean, that this, his old family attorney and agent, could not do. I said so.

"But you have to see to all these things," he answered. "I will do them if you bid me do them, but you are responsible for me and for my correct performance of them." He read the figures of the added-up column of bequests, but the sum was only about half the value of the whole estate. What was the rest for?

"The rest is for you," the matter-of-fact old man answered. "I read you the clause—" He was going to re-read it.

"No," I interrupted. "What I want to know is why Johann left the rest to me, a foreigner? What did he ever write or say to you to indicate why he gave it to me?"

"Ah, that! He never said anything—he would not write anything like that to me. I am his agent; I may say that I am a friend of the family, though that might be presumptuous. I would not ask, I would not permit myself to ask, that question. Only an enemy or—or an indignant relative or a malicious neighbor would question a will."

Were there indignant relatives and malicious neighbors?

W. Lorenz fingered his papers, looked up and away, before he answered.

"The will has been filed for probate," he said, "and no one has entered a protest. If they do the will gives all to you."

It was no use pumping the *Mandatar.* He talked business, not gossip; he took account of laws, documents, and legal acts, not grumblings and emotions. We went on to arrange in order the steps to be taken to execute the will, item by item, and to settle the estate, which he assumed I proposed to turn into money. It was not dull, any of it, as W. Lorenz discussed and did it. It was all so actual; my appearances in court and at public offices were insights into a Germany I did not know; an orderly, smoothly running machine, which worked as well for me, a foreigner, as for any one else—hard, precise, but impersonal and efficient.

Josephine had a still more interesting side to attend to. She had to see the relatives remembered in the will, mostly children, and their parents let her feel that there was some resentment. They did not say much, and Josephine thought to placate them by gifts of clothes, silverware, and furniture. The Hamils approved this "generosity," but W. Lorenz shook his just red head.

"You should be careful about that," he cautioned me. "The will of the deceased gave, but also it withheld, and what is withheld is of the very essence of the document. Johann may have made you his heir partly because he wished to deprive his relatives of the inheritance."

Did the kind old man know more than he would tell? Was there a story back of this strange will? No, he said, he was only studying the document to interpret the will of the deceased.

"But these are properties that I do not want and will not sell," I said, pointing to the bridal linens and other family heirlooms.

"Give them, then, to the children that are named in the will," the old man advised. "Them our dead friend had no feeling against, but all others whom he overlooked you should not give to."

To try him out, I offered him some little things. He refused them. "I am not named, except as an attorney," he said. "If he had meant me to be a beneficiary he would have given me something himself."

So just and so loyal was this impersonal professional friend of my friend. All I could persuade him to take was a lot of old German guidebooks to Europe. He saw them, evidently coveted them, and when he felt my disappointment at his refusal of more valuable things he said one day that he would take *one* of two guidebooks to Switzerland.

"I have always wanted to travel in the Schweitz," he explained.

"Good," I answered quick. "Take the Baedeker's Schweitz and

take also the Germanies which you will have to use to get to Switzerland." And he did. He hesitated; he seemed to be resisting a temptation; it was too much for him; he suddenly reached for the books, gathered them under his lame arm, and hurried away with what turned out to be a prize—to him, a treasure that became an occupation for the rest of his life and, by the way, the key that unlocked his professional character and let me into his human being.

W. Lorenz became a traveler. His sisters told me about it; they "consulted" me about it, for they were alarmed. They said that that night when he came home with the guidebooks, he sat right down with them and a sheet of legal cap paper to plan a trip to Switzerland. He worked late on it, and the next night he took it up again, this journey which he was making. The two old maiden ladies, who adored their brother and lived his regular life, were mystified and frightened by the change wrought in him by those guidebooks.

"He plans tours all the time," they whispered, "expensive tours which will ruin him. He has always been so saving, hardly enough to eat, and now—he wants us to go with him. Yes. He asked us the other day if we would go. We refused, of course, absolutely, indignantly. We said we could not afford any such extravagance, and we meant that he could not afford it either. But he said—do you know what he said? He said, 'Oh, *then* I can do it.' "

They were thrifty, too. They were too thrifty to waste their slow-growing, neat little substance on riotous travel, and the brother profited by their refusal to accompany him. This he revealed to me one night when I went up to his house to see him about some business that had turned up unexpectedly. His sisters purposely slipped me in upon him as he was at work on one of a pile of sheets of paper on the dining-room table under a center light. He looked guilty. He kept his hands down on his maps as he stood to receive me, and his parchment face seemed to blush. He answered my question and waited for me to go—no invitation to sit down.

"What are you doing?" I pried, nodding at the papers.

"Oh, nothing," he answered, "just planning a journey."

"Fine. Where to? Anywhere I've been? Show me."

Reluctantly he lifted his hands, and shyly he said he was revising a tour of Switzerland. I pulled his neatly written sheet of paper around to me and saw that it was an itemized plan from Lehe-bei-Bremerhaven to and through Switzerland and back. It was complete. There was the carfare to the Bremerhaven station for a train at 6:50 A.M., the cost of a third-class ticket to Bremen, carfare to the hotel there, which was named, with the prices for lunch, supper and bed, light, service, and tips. There were fees to museums and sights, all listed in order with the time of entrance and exit. He started from Bremen the next morning early, after coffee, fifty pfennigs, and carfare to the station, with the price of a third-class ticket—and so on and on across Germany to Switzerland, day by day, hours, prices, meals, hotels, fees, all blocked out by stops, with the costs listed and summed up each day, each week, and a grand total at the bottom of the right-hand side of the sheet. There were several sights and side-trips canceled.

"Why?" I asked. I had made them, one with Johann, I said, and they were worth while.

"Too expensive," he swallowed.

"And this plan?" I pointed to another sheet with a complete plan for the same general tour with more stops.

"That was too much too. I can't afford it."

"And this?" I drew out another, a smaller one.

"Well," said Lorenz, with a slight cough, "that was an itinerary I drew when I thought my sisters were going along; it left out many places I wanted to see, but I could not work them in; I felt pretty bad till it occurred to me that maybe my sisters would not care to suffer the fatigue of travel at all. So I asked them, and sure enough, they did not want to go, not anywhere."

His relief shone out of his face, it had to break through a cloud of shame or shyness or something, but—he was glad.

"When they refused to leave home to travel—anywhere," he said, "why, then I was free to make this big plan that was too big; but now this last one, this is possible." He stopped, hung his head, fussed with the papers. "I don't suppose I'll ever go; it costs an awful lot, but—well, I can. It's within my means. I can do it—if I'm careful; if the books are correct."

I understood. All of a sudden I knew that W. Lorenz would never make a tour of Switzerland, never meant to travel at all except on paper. And I understood that the same thrift which would keep him home would keep him traveling on paper with precise care for each item of expense, and all within his means. I remembered my boyhood when I used to play I was Napoleon or a trapper or an explorer and played out my make-believe secretly, in detail, and practically, well within the possibilities. And I remembered, too, the grown-ups who caught me making believe and did not laugh at me, but confessed that they also were really something else than what they appeared to be and so entered into my game and took me into theirs. Their behavior and mine—the shyness, shame, and sneaking persistence—it was all just like the embarrassed manner of W. Lorenz. So I gave him one long, understanding look, which he returned—the look, not of man to man, but of kid to kid, and I broke in.

"Sit down," I said quietly, "and I'll show you something."

He sat down, relieved, happy, eager, and I showed him how he could make his Swiss tour and include all the places he had left out and more. He did not know that he could save money by buying at Bremerhaven a round-trip ticket (*Rundreise*). He was amazed, he was thrilled, as I read from the general hints in the guide-book about the system which cut the whole cost of train travel by just about one-third. We worked his itinerary over together, and when I rose to go I had promised to bring up, and he was impatient to accept, other guidebooks—Austria and Italy, France and Spain, and Norway and Sweden.

"Why, we can travel all over Europe!" he exclaimed as he saw me out of the front door. He said it so loud that he looked back into the house to see if his sisters had heard. "They would never understand," he whispered, and then he said aloud again, "I can go anywhere, almost."

"Why not?" said I. "If you take your time, learn all the tricks of travel, and look out for the smaller items, like food, carfare, and tips, you can see one by one all the countries of Europe, and right, too."

"Yes, and within my means," he rejoiced with a joyous clasp of my hand.

XVI

I BECOME A CAPITALIST

W HEN W. Lorenz let me into his scheme for the secret
satisfaction of his two great, apparently conflicting pas-
sions, first to save all his savings, and second to travel all
over the world, he was bound to let me in also on the true story
of his client, our friend Johann. He might conceal some of his
own secrets; he did, in fact. I discovered one day that he proposed
to do some traveling fourth-class, "only on long dull day
stretches," and only to save enough money to visit places off his
general itinerary, places double-starred in the guidebook. I opposed
that economy. He was too old and frail to stand the discomfort
of a box car without seats, among soldiers and tramps. He gave it
up finally. At any rate he laid that plan aside and took up another, which he went to work on, cutting hotels and meals to
save the equivalent of the difference between third and fourth
class.

Meanwhile my wife, sorting over the heirlooms of the Krudewolf family with Frau Hamil and her two daughters and consulting with them as to the disposition of the things we did not
want, had crept into the confidence of these good women and so
heard their version of the Krudewolf saga. These two stories unlocked my memory till I could recall and understand remarks
Johann had made to me when we were students at Heidelberg and
Leipzig—remarks which, pieced together in the light of the gossip
of Lehe, gave me his own story and some inkling of the purpose
of his strange will.

A pretty little basket held all the elements of the tale. My wife
discovered it in the attic one afternoon. W. Lorenz and I had
been selling bonds and stocks, odd pieces of land, and when we
had some money on hand, we went to Bremen and other places

in between Lehe and Bremen to gather up the bones of certain ancestors whom Johann required in his will that I bring and bury together somewhere. I was making a plot in the Lehe cemetery and had ordered a fine bust of Johann, by a sculptor he had spoken well of, to crown the graves. I had left the inventory of the house to her, and she had worked her way slowly, conscientiously, up to the attic, which was the most fascinating of all. She and the Frau Hamil and the Fräulein Hamil spent days there over the old dresses, hats, toys, schoolbooks—everything that an old family attic should contain. But the Hamils had house and shops to attend to; they could not be always there, and my wife was alone when she called me up and showed me the pretty little flat basket. As I stared at it, wondering why she was so interested, she lifted the lid and disclosed two crowns of artificial flowers, some trinkets and cheap jewelry, a long, thin book in brown paper, which looked like a butcher's book, and, on top of all, two yellow third-class tickets to Bremen *und zurück* that had never been used. What did these mean?

My wife called Frau Hamil, who, at sight of the basket, called her daughters, who closed the shops and came and stared. They all looked into the basket, at one another, back into the basket, and at us, and they seemed to communicate and decide something.

"Those two wreaths," Frau Hamil said, "were the bridal crowns of the two sisters who married Herr Krudewolf; the jewelry was theirs. The book I don't know. But the tickets I know. They were found clutched in the hand of the second wife when I came up and saw her lying there dead."

I had been fluttering the pages of the butcher book. It was the roughly kept accounts of the growth of the family fortune for some seven generations. It began in an illiterate hand with the evaluation of a small farm, worth a few hundred thalers, and the dower of a bride. Another such hand added a few bits of land and a bridal dower. Another and another added dowers, a few hundred thalers and then a few thousand marks. Then there was the sale of the farm, all but a few pieces of land, and a record of the price, over 50,000 marks. This, I reckoned, was in the hand of Johann's grandfather. The next hand was more modern, and it added a large sum in money, 20,000 marks, and two bridal dowers, 10,000 each. It was a record of thrift; there were no losses or big expenditures; there were small profits. The increases came with the wives.

"This book," I said, "is the history of the sacrifices and savings of the Krudewolf family."

"Ah," Frau Hamil answered, "of their success."

"Yes, over seven generations. But those return tickets to Bremen, what are they?"

"Sit down and I'll tell you," said Frau Hamil, and we sat down on the boxes and old chests.

"Herr Krudewolf, Johann's father," she began, "was a good man, but hard. He was a sea-captain; he went to sea as a lad, studied, and worked up till he commanded ships that sailed all around the world. He sailed to America, often, and he learned something there that made him give up the sea; or maybe it was when his wife, Johann's own mother, died in giving birth to her baby that the father retired from the sea. Anyway he bought the house with the shops, which he meant Johann to have a big business in. Everything was for Johann, who was to be a great merchant, like they are in America. He was too old to become a business man himself, but Johann—the baby could learn.

"But the father could not bring up the baby; he asked the mother's sister to do it, and he married her. He loved her, too. Ah, yes, he loved his wife. He could not help loving his wife. She was an angel; we all loved her, and Johann adored her. She was his mother, the only mother he knew, and she adored Johann. And *der Herr Kapitän*, he loved his wife and his child, too; he lived only for them. But—"

Frau Hamil looked at her daughters, who looked at her till she looked away to continue.

"We think that Herr Krudewolf was made hard by the sea and the seamen he had to command. It is said that he was terrible on board ship; sailors who lived here in Lehe and sailed under him tell how he ruled them without mercy. They, too, these sailors, were hard men, strong and terrible; they feared nothing and nobody, neither at sea nor ashore—nobody but the *Herr Kapitän*, and him they feared always, even at home here, even on the street. They cursed him behind his back, but to his face, when they met him, they were afraid. Johann's father was a hard, hard man. He loved his wife; he loved his son; and he was good; he was honest and just; but he was strict; and he commanded his wife and his son, his relatives, and—us, his tenants, as he ruled his crews at sea."

Frau Hamil rested a moment; she looked at no one. She looked into the basket, touched the crowns, the tickets.

"Frau Krudewolf became ill. She was not strong, to begin with; she had the weakness in the chest that her sister had, and she was frail. And she was gentle, so gentle. Her voice was low and very sweet; when she bade you do something she seemed only to plead with you to do it. And when she answered her husband you could hardly hear her. She respected her husband, of course; she was a good wife, but her happiness was in the baby, the little boy who grew and was quiet. He talked to his mother. He couldn't talk much to his father, because he was a dreamy boy with wild ideas and wishes, and his father would not listen to his prattle about traveling and studying and learning and writing. But the mother did. She would sit and listen, or later, she lay on her bed and let Johann talk and imagine things; she loved it. I think that she wanted what Johann wanted, not what her husband wanted. There was some trouble; I think it was over Johann's being apprenticed to the merchant. Johann cried and cried and cried, and his mother, too, but he did what his father said. He was a good boy, an obedient son.

"And then the tickets. I must tell you about them. As Johann grew up and became a young man, when he went to work in the business to learn, the mother became worse. Captain Krudewolf did not believe she was very ill. She had always lain a good deal on her bed, but by and by she stayed in bed; she did not get up any more, and finally, one day, she was very ill, a hemorrhage. Even then the captain was not concerned, but he called a doctor. It was the doctor who made him believe. He came downstairs and, drawing the captain aside, whispered something to him. I heard only what the captain said. He said, 'Die!' He shouted it, and that was the only time I ever saw him weak. He ran upstairs; I followed, and I heard. He went to his wife's room; he went in, and he knelt down by her bed, and he asked her if she felt bad. She said she didn't. He asked her if what the doctor said was true; she said she thought it was. And he cried. It was awful to see that strong, terrible, good man cry; just like Johann. He wanted to know if he had not been a good husband to her; she put her hand on his bent head and said something. I could not hear.

" 'Haven't I given you everything you wanted or could want?' he asked her, and before she could answer, he asked her if there was anything in the world that she wanted that she did not have, and she said, 'Yes, there is. *Ich möcht' a 'mal die Welt anseh'n.*' She wanted to see the world.

"He sprang up, that broken, weeping man; he came out, ran downstairs and out of the house. When he came back he had those two tickets, and he took them upstairs and he showed them to her —to Bremen—and back; he put them into her hand, and she clutched them, she clung to them, till she died. We, Herr Krude-wolf and I, we found them; we could hardly get them out of her hand."

"Did Johann himself put these things in that basket?" I asked the women. They said that he did; when his father died Johann had gone over everything, put all in order, and must himself have made up that little basketful of keepsakes. "I did the gathering and packing," Mrs. Hamil said, "and I never saw that basket."

So Johann had seen the relation of the bridal trinkets, the butcher-book, and two return tickets to—the world. I carried off the book; I showed it to W. Lorenz, who was interested enough to cast up the figures, making corrections, and to draw a moral from it. "So are family fortunes saved up, bit by bit."

"Bride by bride," I commented bitterly.

"Not only," he corrected. "There was careful saving in all that."

"What for? For me?"

He nodded. "Yes, as it turned out. But to the men who saved it the fortune was capital for a business."

"Which Johann did not want. Why did the father insist on his boy's doing something he didn't want to do?"

"Johann's father," said Lorenz, "was a stern, strong man. He learned in America—he said that there was money in shops, there was money in trade, but there was no money in sailing ships. He learned that there was more money in trade ashore; so he came ashore. He was too old; he was too impatient with people; he was spoiled by the sea for business ashore. But he had a son. He brought up Johann to be what he could not be. He bought the house with the shops for him; he apprenticed him to a merchant; he would put his money into his son's business. It was a good plan; it is too bad Johann did not follow it. He had queer ideas of traveling and studying, and his mother listened to him, and I think she encouraged him. Anyway she listened as a mother will to the dreams that a boy will have."

To my direct questions Lorenz answered that he thought she interceded with the father for the boy, but without effect.

"Even after her death?" I asked, thinking of the father's remorse and the two yellow tickets. Lorenz was silent a long moment.

"Johann did not give up his place in the shop till his father died," he said, and as I sat there taking in the meaning of this, the *Mandatar* added gently, "Johann's father was a very determined man."

We were in the *Mandatar's* dark little overloaded office, he at his desk, I in the one client's chair. Our easy labors over the estate that were coming to a close had been suspended, and I knew Lorenz wished to get on with the settlement. I had proposed to pay all the bequests, free of taxes paid. He approved. I could do whatever I pleased for the schools, the city, the city park, and the relatives named. But when I suggested giving money or goods to any other relative he objected. There was something back of his resistance. I must know what that was. I recalled aloud things Johann had said long ago to me. He had loathed business in any form. He resented the power of parents over children. He had asked me if my father had any fixed idea of my education, future, and general welfare. When I said, "No, not fixed," he declared me fortunate. "My father," he said, "knew what was good for his son. My whole family did, all except my mother."

"Did Johann's relatives," I asked, "back up his father?"

"Yes, they did," said Lorenz that day.

"Hard?"

The *Mandatar* squirmed, but he let out his professional secret to the full.

"After the old man was buried and Johann took over the estate, he quit his position in the business. He announced his plan to go away to study, and there was a row. The relatives held that he had no right to squander in study, travels, and pleasure the family savings of generations."

"Then that is the reason why he has cast them all off, all but the children," I said, relieved.

Lorenz nodded. "That," he said, "is why I think you should not give anything to them."

"Why haven't you said so before?"

"It is not so stated in the will," he answered, "and he never said it to me or you. I go, and I think you should go, by the will."

"I will," I said.

"By his will," he said, "not his ill-will, not his hate."

Then the just, wise old attorney told me of some kindnesses I could do. The Hamils wanted to buy the house. "You can get more for it in the open market," he said, "but they were good to Johann; they served the family always; they are sweet people. They have a little money, and they can add a sum which they can borrow from the institutions Johann has given money to: the exact amount of those bequests." I agreed to that. "Good," he said; then he told me that a relative Johann used to find amusement in, a man who had lived long in Brooklyn and come back home well-to-do but full of America and American superiority—this old uncle wanted to buy at a low but sufficient price a piece of land between two separated pieces of his land. "The other relatives hate this man," said Lorenz, "but Johann rather liked him." I agreed to that. I agreed to several such arrangements, and he went out, and I sold the land. I saw why the relatives hated the buyer, but I saw, too, why Johann found him fun. He did "rub in" Brooklyn, where he had lived unhappily; he had hated it, been homesick, but as something to talk about that would make Lehe and Bremerhaven and even Bremen look small, he found Brooklyn, to say nothing of New York, very useful.

The Hamils had the happiest day of their lives, I think, buying their house from me. They set the table in the garden for the bargaining, which Lorenz drove hard for me and the estate, only to be glad every time I took the buyers' side and went against him.

The business was settled with smiles; the daughters literally danced with glee. The only day to compare with that day was the day of the payment, the actual transfer of the money. And that was a day I shall never forget. Everybody dressed in his best for it, and I soon saw why.

The moneys we had collected from sales and settlements were all deposited in cash in the savings bank. Lorenz, in his Sunday best, called for me, with some money to deposit—gold. We turned it in at the bank, drew out some 42,000 marks in gold coins, which we carried in bags to the three institutions which got it in three sums, counted out on large tables. The recipients, accepting these sums, came with us to the Hamils' house, where, in the parlor, they counted out the money, which was united in a loan to Frau Hamil. She gathered it up, held it a moment, and then counted it out with her additional cash, also in gold coins. We counted it again, and Lorenz swept it into his bags and back we went, alone now, to the bank, where we redeposited the same coins we had drawn out a few hours earlier.

"Why not use checks?" I asked, and the answer was that that system had been tried and found unsafe. I had to make a very slow, elaborate deal with a Bremen bank to get what was coming to me into the form of a draft on New York. However, that was done, and all was settled except the bill for professional services of W. Lorenz. He was slow about rendering it. It was a long, detailed, complicated bill, he said, and I could well believe that. He had been doing practically nothing else than my business for three or four months, and I expected a big bill; I had kept in cash a large amount to meet it, and as he worked on it nights, I began to fear I had under-estimated the amount. He himself was embarrassed when he ushered me into his office to present it, and I was shocked by the length of it, many foolscap sheets. But the items: carfare downtown, 10 pfennigs (he walked back); appearance in court, 1 mark; argument in court, 1.50. So it went; every single service done was entered, but at such rates as these; and the total? One hundred and sixty-four marks, twenty-five pfennigs! About forty dollars.

I counted out exactly that amount, down to the pfennigs; he gave me some small change to make it exact. Then I handed him a few hundred marks.

"What's that for?" he asked.

"Oh, for a trip to Venice."

"From Switzerland!" he exclaimed, receiving it, delighted.

"But"—he clouded—"I can go on to Rome with all that," he said.

"Yes," I answered, "but you can't get back."

"Let's see." He hoped, and he rose to go to the dining-room where the guidebooks were kept.

"No, no, Lorenz, not now," I protested. "There's something else I want you to do for me. Tell me why Johann left his money to me. He said once that there was something he wanted me to do with it. What was it? What did he want me to use it for?"

Lorenz dropped back in his chair. He trifled with his papers. "There is nothing on record to bind you at all," he said. "But I think that he wanted you to be free."

"Free?"

"Yes, free of your father, free of your family, free to do what you might want to do, study or go into business or—travel—"

"To Rome."

"Yes," he mumbled. "I think so."

"Yes, and I think so too," I said. "I think that's it." For I remembered once when we were making a foot-tour of the Saxische Schweitz that Johann had said that money was liberty. We were discussing whether to go on and see Prague or to return to Leipzig.

"Money is not money," he said; "it is liberty."

And that's what Johann's money has been for me. It was only some $12,000, but I knew how to make it more. I had not been a reporter in Wall Street for nothing. When I got back to New York my father wrote, asking me what I proposed to do with the money. "Speculate," I answered, and he, frightened, straightway wanted to borrow it all from me. He said he needed it just then; I suspected that he wished to save it for me, but I lent him one half of it, and with the rest, to his amazement, I slowly, surely, easily made enough money to make me free for life, as my friend Johann Friedrich Krudewolf willed, free even of Wall Street.

XVII

REMAKING A NEWSPAPER

A NEWSPAPER is indeed like a woman or a politician. When it is young, honest, and full of ideals, it is attractive, trusted, and full of the possibilities of power. Powerful men see this, see its uses, and so seek to possess it. And some of them do get and keep it, and they use, abuse, and finally ruin it. The *Commercial Advertiser*, the oldest newspaper in New York, looked like a wretched old street-walker or a used-up, ex-"good" governor, when "we" got hold of it in 1897. It had a circulation of some 2500, no influence, and it must have cost its keeper the income on a small fortune to make up its losses. But there is a difference between a fallen human being and a painted prostitute. A newspaper can be saved—to sell again, as we discovered.

"We" were Henry J. Wright, the city editor of the *Evening Post*, who became the editor-in-chief of the old *Commercial*; J. S. Seymour, the publisher of the *Post*, who took the same position on the wreck; Norman Hapgood and myself, whom they brought with them from the reportorial staff; and later, Joseph B. Bishop, an editorial writer. Hapgood had the theaters, I the city department, and he and I went to work without any instructions except to be careful about spending money. Editorially we were free, and I think Wright and Seymour were free, from any requirement beyond that of making the bankrupt a profitable property, which meant, at that stage, a good newspaper. Anyhow that was the spirit in which we went to work in the news department, and the result was a busy, happy, progressively successful period of four or five years.

My inspiration was a love of New York, just as it was, and my ambition was to have it reported so that New Yorkers might see, not merely read of it, as it was: rich and poor, wicked and good, ugly but beautiful, growing, great. I had no policy that went very deep. "We" inherited from the *Post* an opposition to Tammany and corruption, but I really liked Croker and the "bad men" I knew more than I realized, much more than I liked the reformers "we" consulted and supported.

"He's a crook," I would tell a reporter, "but he's a great crook," and I think now that I meant he was a New York crook and

BEFORE "WE" TOOK IT OVER

therefore a character for us and all other New Yorkers to know intimately and be proud of.

My reporters liked our attitude. They were picked men and women, picked for their unusual, literary pose. I hated the professional newspaper man; I had seen him going down, down, down, and I dreaded his fate. I remember once how one of them came to me for a job at the beginning of our enterprise when I needed reporters. I recognized the type; I smelled it on his alcoholic breath, read it on his cynical lips. To stall him, I asked him what experience he had had.

"Experience!" he echoed. "I have been Washington correspondent of the *Herald*, city editor of the *Tribune*, London man for the *Times*. I"—he waved his arm contemptuously out over our long, big city room and concluded—"I have been the editor of this shebang."

"Then there is no place here for you now," I cried at him, my hands up in horror.

"What am I to do then?" he asked bitterly.

"Go out of this office," I answered, "turn to the left till you come to the corner, then turn right and go—go till you come to the dock."

"And then?" he questioned. "What then?"

"Go on," I finished. "Don't stop. Keep right on."

It was astonishing, my outburst, and I must have shouted it at the poor wretch, for some one asked me as I came back to my desk why I had been so loud and fierce. My answer surprised me. I said that to have that man on my staff would have been like seeing the ghost of my future constantly before my eyes. I had not realized till that moment the subconscious fear in which I was working, the depth of my dread of becoming a professional newspaper man. I wanted none on my staff. I wanted fresh, young, enthusiastic writers who would see and make others see the life of the city. This meant individual styles, and old newspaper men wrote in the style of their paper, the *Sun* men in the *Sun* style, *Post* men in the Godkin manner.

There were professionals on the staff I inherited, of course; there were no others at first. I discharged some at once, and I was discharging the rest so fast that Mr. Wright remonstrated. Shouldn't I wait till I had found substitutes? I did not want to; it was only Wright's insistence that made me keep the few men that stayed, luckily. There was a Wall Street man, who was no expert, and a political reporter who was an expert but so bored that he wrote dead stuff. He was of use only for tips; other men wrote the stories he thought he had covered. There was Miss Josephine Meagan, who did the woman's department; she was a young woman but an old trained professional who soon proved indispensable. The most useful to the staff was John Weier, a young man but a newspaper man who saved our amateur lives many a time by his quick, knowing skill and amiable willingness to help any one out of a hole. The most useful to me personally was the assistant city editor, Charles Lachaussee. I did not know it, but I was not an editor nor any other kind of executive. Lachaussee was. He carried on the routine and filled in wherever I was neglectful, forgetful, and incapable. This he did so tactfully, so quietly that I think nobody remarked at the time and I myself came only later to recognize that whatever of completeness and steadiness there was in our city news service was due to this modest, experienced wheel-horse. I kept, I clung to, Lachaussee by instinct, and I can see in memory reporters going also instinctively to him for the needed instructions I did not give them.

The rest of the old staff were dismissed suddenly—and their places were filled by utterly inexperienced writers. Hutchins Hapgood, a brother of Norman, was one of the first. He, too, loved, if not New York, then life and people and ideas. Soon after him came Neith Boyce, an unsentimental, pretty girl, who ran a romance through the city room by editing Hutch and his copy till he fell in love with and married her. Another New Yorker taken early was Abraham Cahan, an East Side Russian socialist, later to become editor of the Jewish *Daily Forward*, who made incessant propaganda among us for the Marxian program and for Russian realism; but he had published a novel and in the paper wrote fact stories direct from the news, just as Hutch Hapgood picked up philosophy from artists, bums, and thieves. In the main, however, the *Commercial* reporters were sought out of the graduating classes of the universities, Harvard, Yale, Princeton, and Columbia, where we let it be known that writers were wanted— not newspaper men, but writers.

My verbal advertisement and my announced rules drew the right kind of young men. I would take fellows, I said, whose professor of English believed they were going to be able to write and who themselves wanted to be writers, provided, however, that they did not intend to be journalists. "We" had use for any one who, openly or secretly, hoped to be a poet, a novelist, or an essayist. I could not pay them much in money, but as an offset I promised to give them opportunities to see life as it happened in all the news varieties. No one would be kept long in any department; as soon as a reporter became expert in one branch of work, he would be turned into another. This was not only for their sakes, but for ours also. When a reporter no longer saw red at a fire, when he was so used to police news that a murder was not a human tragedy but only a crime, he could not write police news for us. We preferred the fresh staring eyes to the informed mind and the blunted pencil. To express if not to enforce this, I used to warn my staff that whenever a reporter became a good all-round newspaper man he would be fired. And to encourage each man to form and write in his own style, I declared that if any two reporters came to write alike, one of them would have to go. There was to be no *Commercial Advertiser* style, no *Commercial* men. So also there were no rules about promptitude, sobriety, accuracy; no lists of friends or enemies of the paper; no editorial policy; no "beats"; and best of all, there was no insistence even upon these rules, which were broken at any one's convenience.

My practice was to take as many university graduates as came each year after their Commencement, and trying them out in the summer when the older men were on vacation, select in the fall those that we liked, "we" being myself, Lachaussee, and the other reporters, who were harder judges than I was. Most of the men who made good were from Harvard. Other colleges sent us candidates who were elected. Walter S. Edwards, from Columbia, was one of the most sensitive reporters I ever knew. He "covered" Dick Croker, the Tammany boss, with an affection which this lovable man deserved and returned—Edwards covered him with love and with (unintended) ridicule. But music was Edwards's gift, not literature. Mr. Wright got from Columbia a young man, George Wharton, who created a school news department which was a model. From Yale came Larkin G. Mead, a nephew of Mark Twain, who could not spell, punctuate, or keep within the rules of primary grammar, but he had a sensitive eye, red hair, and freckles, and drove words like nails. There was the copy desk downstairs and the typesetters upstairs to make his living English correct. "Red" Mead of Yale was one of our stars. On the desk, besides Neith Boyce, was Pitts Duffield, who had taste and a gift for the appreciation and ordering of other writers' writings. He became a publisher.

Eugene Walter, who became a playwright, worked for us for some time and suffered all the time. He was one of those men who wanted to write, was sure he could, but had not yet found his form. He was not a success as a reporter, but when he turned to the stage he did brilliant things. Harvey J. O'Higgins came to us for a job, but, as Carl Hovey put it recently in a letter, "We didn't think he was any good; so we allowed him to work on the telegraph desk, but he practiced writing on our Saturday supplement." Edwin Lefevre reported Wall Street for us, but he had the newspaper man's sense of news. He wrote the bald, important facts for the publication and then, after the paper went to press, told us the stories which, under the drive of our scorn, he afterward wrote and published under the title *Wall Street Stories*.

The Harvard men who stayed and gave character to the city news were Hutchins Hapgood, Carl Hovey (afterward editor of the *Metropolitan Magazine*, now a Hollywood editor and writer), Guy H. Scull (who has since died), Robert S. Dunn, a novelist—all writers; and there were others, like Humphrey T. Nicholls, who were not naturally gifted but could report, because Harvard somehow taught her students that there is such a thing as the beautiful in this world and that there is an art in writing. I think now that one member of the Cambridge faculty, Professor Copeland, had a great deal to do with our success with Harvard men. He understood what kind of students we were looking for, and he was wise enough to send me that sort and no others. I say "wise," and I might say "extraordinary," for most men and most of the professors of English I was in touch with thought only of getting some young friend "a job," any job. Professor Copeland knew that that was worse than useless; it was harmful to put a young man in a position he was not fitted for and so start him off with a failure. Nor is it a service to the employer. Mr. Copeland considered both his students and me; he sent me only the fellows he was sure could see and express the beauty in the mean streets of a hard, beautiful city. Every one of his men made good. But I have always given credit for that to Harvard in general. That university gave, and I think gives, something of what is called culture and made its students aware not only, like other American colleges, of what men know, but of that also which men do not know and have to discover of "the True and the Beautiful."

We talked of such things on our paper. We dared to use such words as "literature," "art," "journalism," not only in the city room itself, but at a fire or in the barrooms where the Press drank. The old hacks hated it and ridiculed us; we were the freshmen of Park Row, and our tittle-tattle was sophomoric. But we did not care what the old bums said, and as for the star men of the other papers, we could see in their printed stuff that they likewise were laboring at the art of telling stories. Cynicism was a pose in the journalism of those days, and my staff did not take it. They meant to be writers, and they did not pretend to be working only for money. How could they on the miserable wages I paid, $12, $15, $20 a week? My contract with them was to pay them in opportunities, to see actual tragedies and comedies and to report them. They were not held accountable for news beats; Lachaussee and I with the city news service of the Associated Press could take care that we were not beaten; my young writers were expected to beat the other papers only in the way they presented the news. The flash of a murder would come in. I did not rush a man out to get the news first; Lachaussee would write a short bulletin for the next edition while I would call up, say, Cahan; I would ask him to sit down and then, without any urge, tell him quietly what to do.

"Here, Cahan, is a report that a man has murdered his wife, a rather bloody, hacked-up crime. We don't care about that. But there's a story in it. That man loved that woman well enough once to marry her, and now he has hated her enough to cut her all to pieces. If you can find out just what happened between that wedding and this murder, you will have a novel for yourself and a short story for me. Go on now, take your time, and get this tragedy, as a tragedy."

Our stated ideal for a murder story was that it should be so understood and told that the murderer would not be hanged, not by our readers. We never achieved our ideal, but there it was; and it is scientifically and artistically the true ideal for an artist and for a newspaper: to get the news so completely and to report it so humanly that the reader will see himself in the other fellow's place.

Our theory was not generally accepted even in our own office. No ideal was unchallenged there. It was a place of constant debate. Any answer ever offered to the question, "What is art?" was disputed, and hotly, too. This may have been Cahan's influence. He brought the spirit of the East Side into our shop. The Ghetto and the Russian Jews, a disputatious lot, were splitting just then into two parties over the question of realism in the arts. Cahan took us, as he could get us, one by one or in groups, to the cafés where the debate was on at every table and to the theaters where the audience divided: the realist party hissing a romantic play, the romanticists fighting for it with clapping hands and sometimes with fists or nails. A remarkable phenomenon it was, a community of thousands of people fighting over an art question as savagely as other people had fought over political or religious questions, dividing families, setting brother against brother, breaking up business firms, and finally, actually forcing the organization of a rival theater with a company pledged to realism against the old theater, which would play any good piece.

I rejoiced when this East Side controversy flowed over into my newspaper. I had enjoyed and profited by my police reporter's interest in the picturesque Ghetto, and I knew it was good—good journalism and good business—for my reporters to follow and report the happenings over there. It increased our circulation; the Jews read the *Commercial,* and it broadened the minds of the staff and of our readers. Norman Hapgood reviewed the Yiddish theaters or let Cahan and other reporters write criticisms of their shows; he often put their plays and performances at the head of his column, where they often belonged. The Yiddish stage was about the best in New York at that time both in stuff and in acting; some of their players went on to the English-speaking stage afterward.

Whatever it was that did it, whether it was Cahan and the Ghetto or my encouragement, the *Commercial* city room had ideals and flaunted them openly. There were clashing notes. Neith Boyce used to smother the sentimentality of Hutch Hapgood when he became too soft. He brought in one day an interview he had had with a broken-down tramp on a park bench. Hutch saw in it philosophy and pathos, and he wrote it so. I sensed in the tender way in which he handed it to me that he felt it to be a sensitive manuscript, which meant that he would fight against any editing. I turned it over to Miss Boyce, who edited it as freely as if it had been an advertising write-up, and sent it up to the press room. When it appeared in the paper it was under her heading, "He Lost His Grip," a title which changed the whole meaning of the story. I saw Hutch hold it up like a wounded bird, almost with tears in his eyes. He said not a word, however, and I (alone, I think now) did not understand why he stood such treatment from Miss Boyce till one day when he came in late and unhurried with an important bit of news. I jumped on him only to have him hold me and, pointing to a sun-ray lighting upon the girl's red hair, ask me if it was not beautiful to have such a touch of color in our dingy old city room. Then I understood all that had happened and foresaw what was going to happen. For Neith Boyce was as romantic in her way as Hutch Hapgood was in his way, and as idealistic and ambitious as any one on the staff, as her novels and other writings have proven since.

XVIII

A HAPPY NEWSPAPER STAFF

IT is fun to make or remake a newspaper. It is work, too, hard
work, and the sport of it appears best as one looks back at it,
but we of the *Commercial Advertiser* saw the humor of it at
the time. Neith Boyce helped us there, she and Harry Thurston
Peck. They were irresponsible enough to see it objectively as a
game and to play the useful part of fans. Peck was a professor at
Columbia University and the editor of *The Bookman,* but he was
one of those tireless geniuses who never have enough to do. He
had accepted also the editorship of our book department. With a
stenographer and an assistant editor he carried on pages and pages
of book reviews, literary notes and news; he had his *Bookman* and
his lectures to attend to, but he used to sit in his stovepipe hat and
white spats in "the culprit's chair" beside my city desk and watch
us collect the news of the city, watch and wonder and ask questions.

"But how do you know there's a fire there?" or "Will the mayor
answer such a question? Won't he throw the reporter out?" And
later, as he learned the business of news-gathering, he would raise
the order of his questions: "So they really do such things? Take
bribes and steal?"

Neith Boyce sat directly behind me at the copy desk, quiet,
golden, sharp, quick, and whimsical. She saved my nerves from
explosions. I sent Guy Scull, a yachtsman himself, to the dry dock
in Brooklyn to get and telephone the official handicap measure-
ments of the two yachts about to race off Sandy Hook for the
international cup. The figures came in, but not from Scull, and another man, who was reporting another angle of the race prelimi-
naries, was asked to find the lost reporter. He came back to the
office after the paper had gone to press with Scull humbly in tow

and reported, "I found him on a pile of lumber in the Navy Yard writing poetry."

Neith Boyce laughed just in time to make me see my ridiculous staff of writers as I see them now, all gathered around Guy Scull and debating whether his lines were merely verse or really poetry. The measurement of the yachts was editorial business, not literature. And Peck, the literary editor, sympathized with me, and said so to the staff, who only stared at him, and went on talking "over my head," as he put it when he came back beaten to me. But the editor of *The Bookman* was reconciled to my staff and to my policy of using inexperienced writers when he saw the results of some of the general assignments "we" gave: to look for one instance of gayety in New York, with the promise to report it in the paper as conspicuously as a murder. All the reporters joined in that search, and though none of them brought in an account of pure gayety, we did have, and we put on the first page with stud heads, two or three instances of merriment. Peck agreed that "mere gayety" does not occur in America. He was most enthusiastic, however, over a joint report by the whole staff of "How Grief Is Expressed." Reporters often see tragedies, deaths at fires, injuries in the streets and in falling buildings; they see the relatives find their injured and killed, and they carry the first news of disaster. I had asked everybody to observe directly the actual expression of sorrow, and the reports did not bear out the stage and the novels; there is more blowing of the nose in real life. Peck suggested other such studies: manifestations of indignation, real and pretended, of rage, surprise, cunning, etc., and I soon had my writers reporting in their daily news stories such close and correct observation of the details of demeanor that artists and professional men began to take notice. William Dean Howells, the novelist, once said that no writer or artist could afford not to read the *Commercial Advertiser*, and Professor Peck was as pleased as if Howells had recommended his columns of book reviews. There was nothing narrow about Harry Thurston Peck, and that's why he made *The Bookman* what it was, the authority on the literature of his day.

He and other editors entered into some of our games. One of my test assignments for a new reporter was to go and see and write the difference between Fifth Avenue and Broadway or Thirty-sixth and Thirty-seventh Streets. Norman Hapgood tried one of these, and everybody on the paper "did" the parade at Easter; we printed them all, a whole page which probably no one read through except the men and women on the paper. What of it? The readers got the results. The concentration of the staff on the technique of writing made them better reporters; yes, and got us "beats."

Carl Hovey outwrote all the reporters in New York one day when Archbishop Ireland came into the harbor from Rome with some news. The wise old prelate would not tell his news—"not a word," he said to the reporters, "not a single word." They were all balked but Hovey, who told us how the archbishop refused to talk. He reported how he looked, how he waved his long, canny finger, smiling, as he warned the reporters not to make up a fake; and how he came upon the crowd lying on the deck, their heads together, trying to fake up something—the fine old priest came up, cast his shadow over them, and startled them with his "Now, now, now, what are you all up to?" Our readers *saw* that happen, and they saw the archbishop and the kind of dignified, humorous, fine human being he was; and that was half the news of that day.

Carl Hovey, after he made the *Metropolitan Magazine*, became an editor on one of the most successful of the big movie lots, where I saw him recently. Just for the fun of it I asked him what the art was of making photo-plays. He answered quite seriously: "It's just what we learned on the old *Commercial*; you go and see something interesting and then you show it interestingly, that's all."

Yes, we used to talk art, and we tried openly, shamelessly, to practice it on that good old newspaper, all of us, even Robert Dunn, who would not himself recognize literature and broke up every conversation he could butt into about it. He began with his first day, when he came to us fresh from Harvard. The moment he was accepted on the staff, he turned and by his sarcasm damped a group of art talkers. "Bah!" he said. "There is no such thing."

One by one those reporters stepped up to me, and with Neith Boyce laughing, they begged me not to keep Dunn. "He'll spoil the spirit of the paper," they said. "We'll see," I answered, and the next morning I sent him off to a near-by one-alarm fire. He saw and he described it; Miss Boyce and I read, and without a change, sent it up to be set. It was in our first edition, and as the other reporters came in with their stories to write, they glanced at the paper and they read Dunn's short sketch of that fire. The first was Cahan, who was most against Dunn; he came up to me with his finger on the story.

"Who wrote that?" he asked.

"Dunn," I answered.

"Oh-h-h," he groaned. "We'll have to keep him, won't we!"

Dunn could write and Dunn could bite, and he bit and wrote his way through with us for months. He had no respect for anybody or anything. Some friend of his family told me that his method of conversation was to draw people out till he discovered what they held most sacred and then to "spit on the emblem thereof." He certainly spat upon us, all of us, and all our emblems. He would have split up the staff if he could have let any one follow or take sides with him. But no, he scoffed at those who agreed with him and soon had no one to speak to. I did not want to discharge him; I explained the situation and besought him to make it up with the other reporters.

"You mean that you want me to speak"—he looked around for an example, and seeing Cahan, he continued—"actually talk with Cahan?"

"Yes," I said.

"All right, I will, just for you," he said, and he walked up to Cahan and asked him, "Say, Cahan, why is it you East Side Jews never bathe?"

No use. I had to fire Dunn, and the staff hung around and regretfully watched it done. The boy came up, handsome, defiant, and stood there eying me as I told him how sorry I was to lose him.

"You can write, Dunn," I said. "The gift is in you, and you are sincere in the exercise of it. Your scorn of literature is affected; your contempt for seriousness and for the rest of us is—"

"Contempt for talk and talkers," he broke in. "Writing is all right, but talking about writing is—talk."

"A pose," I said.

"Every Harvard man has a pose," he sneered the circle of Harvard men around, "except me. And that's mine: to have no pose."

No use. I repeated that he could write, and I erred by remarking that he could be made a great reporter. I could train him myself if I were willing to abuse him, but I did not care to spoil my disposition, cuss him out, and discipline him; so I had decided to let him go, with a bit of advice. He laughed.

My advice was that he go out and find out who was the worst city editor in town, the meanest, the most first-mate-like martinet in the business. "Let him treat you rough for a while," I said; "take his medicine and learn to report; then, when you think you can be decent, come back to me, and I'll give you a job again."

"And finish making me a newspaper man!" he added. "Fine," he said. "But how do you know that I want to be a newspaper man? I've seen him; I've seen you all. Suppose I became one, suppose I should do what you advise and succeeded, suppose I rose and rose and rose beyond the utmost possibilities of the reporter's dreams and became—let me say—became finally and triumphantly a—say—a city editor—"

His handsome, honest, fearless face was twisted into hateful contempt as he paused, looked around at the listening staff, and so back to me.

"I'd rather clean streets," he finished.

And I admired and liked him more than ever. "Never mind, Dunn," I said, "I was not thinking of making you or anybody else a newspaper man; you know I prefer writers and ask you all only to report, to write what you see and hear, as you, for instance, can't help doing. You go on and do what I say, and I repeat my promise. If you will then come back to me I'll take you on again."

"Never," he said, and he marched proudly down the long room out and away. Proudly, I say; Dunn was pride in person. He went away and did exactly what I advised. He found the most terrible city editor in town and asked him for a job. And the most terrible started right in on him.

"Dunn," this fierce man said. "Experience: Harvard and the *Commercial Advertiser*. That means you can't write anything but literature. No matter. I have desk men that can write newspaper stuff. I'll take you on. You can do Harlem on the dead watch, midnight till daylight, and you needn't ever come to the office. Telephone your dope, and I'll have a reporter write it for you."

Dunn accepted, did Harlem all one winter, telephoning his news and letting it be written for him by the hack desk men. He went to the office once. The city editor called him up on the 'phone one night and called him down; he roasted Dunn so outrageously, with such insults to him, Harvard, and his family, that Dunn hung up, saying, "Wait. I'm coming down to lick you."

He didn't have to. That city editor, like me, really admired and liked Dunn. He also respected the unbroken spirit of the boy, and—there was no fight. There was no relaxation of the discipline, either.

One afternoon in the spring Dunn appeared, badly dressed in dirty old clothes, but head high, at the entrance to my office. I saw him sweep the office boy aside and come on slowly toward me. He seemed to me to be kicking himself up that long aisle, forcing himself to trample on his pride, and sensing the struggle, I jumped up and went to meet him.

"Have you come back to work, Dunn?" I asked, and he stopped and looked wondering at me.

"Say," he said, "will you take me back after—after what I said?"

"You bet I will."

Well, he did not want just then to come actually on the city staff. He had spent his vacations from Harvard exploring in the north, Canada and Alaska, hard, dangerous traveling, with little equipment and few companions. He knew the books and the technique of exploration, and he had an aunt who financed all such "follies," as his family called them. A great woman, she must have been; I never saw her, but I have somehow a picture in my head of Dunn's aunt, who taught me something about young men.

"My aunt," Dunn said that day, "my aunt is putting up enough money to start me on a trip into an unexplored area of Alaska, and I'd like to write about it for you, to make enough to get back."

I said I'd pay him double space-rates for all he would send me, and when he got back, give him a job if he wanted one. This he agreed to; he made his trip; he nearly lost his life, but he wrote us many perfect prose reports; and in the fall he rejoined the staff, who were as glad as I was to have him and his stuff on the paper. It was all so true; Dunn simply could not lie. I used to assign him to report reform meetings; most of my men so disliked reformers that they could not write fairly about anything they said or did. Dunn was the most prejudiced and always threatened to ridicule such a meeting; he meant it, too, but, pencil in hand, this born artist had to report things as they were.

It was this observation about him that prompted me to have him taken along on Dr. Frederick Cook's first attempt to climb Mt. McKinley. I had seen a good deal of arctic explorers, read their books, and heard their gossip, which revealed to me that no book in that field had told it all; they all left out the worst of the wranglings and depressions which were an essential part of the truth about human nature in such tests. Dunn went with Cook on this expedition; he wrote what I regard as a classic on exploration, *The Shameless Diary of an Explorer;* and I think now that it was his presence that caused the failure to top the mountain, and the second expedition. I mean that Cook too must have seen that he could not trust Dunn to stand for a lie and so went and reported the "top" later without this shameless explorer. But the odd thing about Dunn is that he was the most literary of the writers he affected to despise, the most idealistic. Dunn has written novels, or rather he has overwritten—book after book of beautiful truth. He and he alone of them all was an artist for art's sake.

XIX

GETTING OLD BILL DEVERY

THEODORE SCHROEDER, a well-known New Yorker who was spending his life and his livelihood fighting for liberty, halted me on the street one day to tell me with the glee of a collector that he had "come upon the most beautiful tyranny you ever heard of." He related the story, but I hardly listened. I was enjoying his esthetic joy in his discovery of a wrong to set right. We of the *Commercial* were like Schroeder.

A newspaper, to advertise itself and build up circulation and power, has, now and then, to do something besides print the news: help elect or defeat a party, force a public improvement through or stop an outrage, bring to justice some public enemy or rescue a popular hero from the machinery of the law. The *Commercial* rejoiced in the most beautiful opportunities to increase our growing circulation. There was the Cuban war, the Boer war, and best of all—Tammany was back in power.

The reform administration, which some of us on the *Evening Post* had helped to elect with the ammunition supplied by the Lexow police exposures, had failed somehow. William L. Strong, the good business man chosen as mayor to cast out the devil of politics and give us a good business government, had appointed Colonel Waring, an army officer, to clean our streets, and T. Roosevelt's bi-partisan board of non-partisan police commissioners to clean out the police department. These men did clean both the streets and the police force as they were never cleaned before, never. Many other departments likewise were scrubbed till they shone with polish and businesslike order and efficiency. "We" (meaning chiefly myself now) were shocked almost into thought when this good government was beaten and the old gang turned back into power. The only considerable failure I noticed was one that revived for a moment my old student interest in ethics.

Mayor Strong, the good man in business, was a bad man in politics. Some critics put it that the good business man was a bad politician, and that, too, was true. Mr. Strong tried to play the political game; he was pledged not to, but he found that he had to, and—he could not. His moves were technically wrong. But what struck me was that this business man and his business ethics were immoral in politics; his word was not good; his resistance to pull was so weak that he sought by compromise to satisfy everybody; and his ideas of integrity, ethical perhaps in a merchant, were downright dishonest in government.

This observation in the reform mayor, confirmed by the conduct of other business men in his administration and contrasted with the queer and attractive candor of the "honest crooks" I knew in politics, led me to a tentative theory which I noted in my old notebook on morals: "Ethics are professional; they differ in different occupations; and an ethical practitioner, formed and fitted in one profession, trade, or business, is apt to be disqualified thereby for another occupation morally as well as technically."

This I noted and passed on. There was no time to think. Newsmongering calls for action, not reflection, and Tammany, hungry and irritated, was providing us with a world of public enemies to hate and unconcealed schemes to expose, all in the familiar field of our experience on the *Post*. The only obstacle that troubled us was that we did not hate, we rather loved, our enemies, who rather liked us.

For instance: the Tammany mayor appointed as director of the Aquarium a man who knew nothing about fishes. The experts, proud of their famous collection, asked us to interview this ignoramus and show up his ignorance out of his own mouth. Fine. I sent down, fully instructed, a reporter, one of our best college graduates, who came back, not with the incompetent director's hide, but with the glad news that he had discovered "a character." The interview which he wrote and we ran did indeed expose the character's ignorance; out of his own mouth came the cheerful confession that he had never before met a fish face to face except cooked upon a plate or hooked upon a line. But he had taken the reporter out to the tanks, talked about the fishes there as if they were human beings, read into and out of their facial expressions and behavior such motives, sentiments, and thoughts that you felt that the new Tammany director, however scientifically unknowing he was about fishes, was an expert on men and life, reporters, newspapers, and the public. Now this was all very well as literature, but the unscrupulous writer who was supposed to be a reporter on an anti-Tammany newspaper wrote the wise things this bad man said as if his genial wisdom were a fair substitute for technical ignorance, and "we" went right on making this bad appointment seem good in the eyes of the world by printing other interviews with him on the fishes' views of politics, art, and—whatever came up in the news. We used him as he should have been used, not as Tammany used him. We used him as a commentator on the news of the day, as what the Greeks would have called a comic voice in the chorus, what the newspapers now dub a columnist. But the effect upon the unthinking readers must have been to welcome his appointment as a fish man.

We were clearer on William S. Devery, who was made chief of police to reform, not the department, but the system of police graft, as he understood and told me when I called to congratulate him on his appointment, renew our old acquaintance, and warn him that I meant to "get" him.

"Good," he said. "We both been appreciated and promoted, you to city editor, me to chief of police; you to be a head for headless reporters, me to be the same for a lot of flat feet and glad hands. We'll have a fight, and I hope you'll enjoy it as I will. I'll win, you know, and it'll be a credit to you and the rest of the reformers. For you learned me the business. Honest. I never knew it was so good till you showed it all up in black and white. All the matter with the police business was that it was mismanaged, too democratic, every cop in on it, somehow. I'm a-goin' to fix that. Concentrate it. I'm a goin' to fix this police graft so as you squealers won't get nothin' to squeal at."

"Nothing but you," I interjected.

"Oh, say," he said, "there is me. Sure. I forgot that. You can make a holler about me. But it's all right. That's what I'm here for: to be shot at. I'm the hero, see? You can bring your guns up here, station 'em out there in front of police headquarters, and shoot 'em off every day at me. I'll just shut the windows to keep th' noise out and go right along doing business just th' same. Better.

So long's you keep on making friends for me I won't mind bein' enemies with you."

It was easy for Dr. Parkhurst and the other Christian ministers to hate Devery and reproach us for loving our enemy; they never met him. I acknowledged and "we" reported, yes, and proved that he was no more fit to be a chief of police than the fish man was to be director of the Aquarium, but as a character, as a work of art, he was a masterpiece. Not only I myself—every reporter I ever assigned to roast the man came back smiling and put the smile in his report. Their excuse was the excuse Shakespeare would have offered if some contemporary critic had reproved him for creating such a lovely villain as Iago. The poet's eye in a fine frenzy rolling would have said, "Yes, but isn't Iago the most villainous villain you ever saw?" Or Schroeder, with his "most beautiful tyranny." It's the divine point of view: "Yes, Devery is—as you say—no proper chief of police, but speaking as one artist to another, wouldn't you be proud if you had created old Bill?"

I tried to prejudice my police reporter against the chief. His name was Robert E. Moran. He was an office boy, the most impudent, daring, get-there kid on the *Evening Post* when I, as a police reporter, asked for a "boy" like Jake Riis's Max. Robert was not like Max when he was first sent to me; he was not a seer of the heart of things; but Max, I, and the police soon made of him a police reporter. He knew what news was, understood and could tell (not write) it, and as for the police business, he became a master of that, inside and out. By the time I went over to the *Commercial*, "Bobby," as the police called him, was as "wise" as a bright, disrespectful Irish boy educated in the police school could be; so I took him with me to be my police man. His only fault was that he was, as he said, "dead on to Devery"; he liked him; they liked each other. I recalled seeing them once, the big policeman and the small boy, sitting hip to haunch on the headquarters steps, quarreling, to be sure, but quarreling as the Irish quarrel only when they love each other. To break up this unprofessional friendship, I told the chief that Robert was to be my eyes, and then I told Robert what the chief said.

"Huh, Moran! I ain't afraid o' him. He's Irish himself, as Irish as me."

Robert called on the chief to ask him if he had said that and what he meant by it.

"No," Devery answered. "I did not say that, not exactly. What I said was that you were an Irish bum, which I ain't, and that I could beat you at any game, crooked or straight, underground, overhead, or on the level. Get me? I said back of your back and I'll repeat it in front of your face—I says that I might 'a' been afraid of your boss, but of you—bah! Bah, I'm saying to you."

CAPTAIN "BILL" DEVERY

When he saw that the boy was firing up into a flame he laughed and added the truth. "Say, Bobby boy, honest now, just between us two crooks, I ain't afraid of your boss neither. Do you want to know who I'm askeered of? It's me, Bill Devery himself. Get me?"

Robert nodded; he really did see the menace Devery's honesty was to his crookedness, and that irritated the chief, too.

"Well, then," he said, "if you get me so easy as that, you can run along out of here, and say, don't you never forget that you and me's enemies—to the death."

The boy came out smiling, blown from behind by a huge laugh which followed him into the street, the laugh of the chief chorused by the laughter of the chief's police staff, aides, secretaries, and doormen.

Thus the fight began, and so it continued, the graft, the scandal, and the laughter all growing together. The chief was building up his system so boldly that the police understood and laughed about it. "Bad" men were advanced or transferred to "fat" precincts, "good" men were demoted or sent "up among the goats," to lean precincts. Robert telephoned, laughing, the reasons gossip gave for these moves. I could not use half that the boy reported—too libelous; but I could write enough to show that "we" knew, and Devery saw that and did not care because he read the smile in what I wrote.

One day Robert telephoned that the chief had decided to sit himself as judge at the police trials. The police commissioners had always heard, in turn, these cases which were complaints, by citizens or officers, of infractions of the police regulations by policemen of all grades. The newspapers paid little heed to these petty cases. Roosevelt had shone at them in his day, and Devery must have seen the chance they offered to teach the force his wishes, his policy. He was sitting in judgment the day Robert called me up to say that "it was a picnic; the chief was giving himself away in every case he tried.

"He tells a cop accused of kissing a girl in a dark hallway that he is fined, not for being off post, but for getting caught. Any man good enough to be a policeman would help a nice girl to a kiss, the chief says. 'I would kiss a girl myself; there's lots of things I'd do and do do,' he says, 'but I'll never get caught. And so I can and I do herewith fine you good and plenty for getting caught. Two days' pay.' "

So Robert reported, and his half-angry, half-laughing comment was that two days' pay was not good and plenty; it was nothing at all. And it was the same in all cases. The chief justice blustered and thundered, pretending to be a fierce disciplinarian, whereas he was "easy" and really encouraged misconduct.

"Red" Mead was assigned to cover the next week's police trials and show up this bad judge. I felt that I had erred in my choice of a Yale man while I was telling him what Robert had reported. Mead's rosy face lighted up; he grinned and hurried off to his task before I had finished my instructions, and sure enough, he came back that day with a humorous story. He did show up Devery; you could see the big fellow tight in his uncomfortable uniform sitting formally up there on the bench and handing out justice with a hard mouth and a laughing, sometimes a winking eye, to the cops who feigned fear and obviously rejoiced in the police Solomon come to judgment. You could hear—as well as read— the mocking chief imitating like a nigger the mouth-filling mind-emptying technical phrases of the law. You could feel—you did not have to read—that this jolly judge was teaching the bad cops to do, undetected, whatever they jolly well liked, so long as they did not butt into anything "touchin' on an' appertainin' to" police business. And—worst of all or best of all—although the whole scene made plain that there was police business and that police business was business and came first, therefore, with pleasure only second, the effect was to make our readers not indignant but happy; the Harvard reporters applauded the Yale man, and I, the one responsible reporter, after trying out other writers, sent Mead again and again to make a comedy of Bill Devery's tragic lynching of police discipline. Other papers followed us, sent their most humorous writers to get the chief's "wise cracks" in his blend of formal law language and the slang of the underworld. "Touchin' on an' appertainin' to" became a cliché in the language of New Yorkers. And meanwhile the evil grew.

"Say, boss," the chief said to me one day when we met on the street, "there's a question I got to ast you. Honest now, all jokin' aside. You know so much more than I do, specially crooked knowledge about crooked men and things, I got to ast you a question that's been botherin' me some of late."

He was holding me by both shoulders till, seeing he had my undivided attention, he put his troublesome question.

"What I want to know is, have you noticed any stray grafts runnin' around loose that I have overlooked?"

And then, without waiting for me to say "No," he laughed his good laugh, gave me a rude shove, and strode away.

"I don't like to ride," he said one day as he stepped out of his carriage to enter his office. "I'm more used to walking, and I feel better on my two nice big police feet, but it's the fashion in my set, when you're getting rich, to show it forth and not be hiding your light under no bushels, whatever in th' hell they are."

"We" did get him finally. In and about the chief's office were a couple of police officers whom I had served in my day. They would have gone to jail for me, as they said; and they did risk their rank and their living and their lives. For after all—all jokes aside— police business is business and there were men in it then, as there are men in it now, capable of doing murder or hiring it done. My friends were guilty of acts which would justify murder. They "tipped me off" on any of the chief's plans or deeds that they learned of, and they heard and saw quite enough. Unlike my reporter's gossip, these informers' stories I could print; if it came to a libel suit, they would testify. They didn't want to have to testify. They begged me to be careful, and I was. I wrote, usually without names, accounts of Devery's most intimate and secret agreements with gamblers, wire-tappers, and other law-breakers, with his instructions to captains and inspectors.

Devery knew I was getting it "straight." He laughed, but he worried. If I got something so dangerous that "we" could not "spread it," I would cut out the hidden paragraph and ask Robert to call on the chief, show it to him, and say that I "presented my compliments and begged very respectfully to ask what t'hell." Devery loved the mockery of form and always responded in kind. Robert would come away to telephone me something like this: "The Chief read your most interesting clipping and asked me to present his compliments and tell you kindly to go to hell."

One forenoon Devery had in his office a famous "reform" police captain, who said he was "tired of being out of it" and would like to get back in on the game. Devery, who took delight in the down-fall of reformers, told the captain that if he would return to his precinct, let certain men open poolrooms, and play fair with them and him for a month or so, he, the chief, would bring him downtown to a fat precinct. I had that agreement in the noon edition of the paper. A month or two later when the captain called again in the morning, reported, and was accepted into the fold, the chief ordered him transferred to the promised precinct. I had the transfer in the paper at noon, before the order was published. That afternoon, when Devery got back from lunch with the *Commercial Advertiser* in his hands, he sent for all the reporters and complained that he had no privacy.

"Look," he said, "I do something honest and fair at eleven

o'clock, and it's all in the papers at twelve as a piece of crooked corruption. What am I to do about it? What do you advise, Moran?"

Robert said he didn't know anything about it.

"Oh," the chief sneered, "I know you didn't know about it. You! Huh, the man that did that, the man that's doing it to me every day, is—well, he's the kind of a guy I'd like to make a policeman of, which I'd never make one of you. No, sir, I'm not looking for an innocent dub; I'm out for the guilty party that's got a leak in my office that I can't stop up."

"Well," said Moran, who knew that the chief despised plain-clothes men, "why don't you put a detective on the job?"

The chief exploded. "Detective! Detective!! Hell! What I need is a plumber."

Such sayings, though not all published, were passed around from mouth to mouth, from the under to the upper world, till the scandal of Devery grew with his popularity. Many newspapers found fault with him, the editorial writers criticizing him seriously. All righteous men deplored his happy, honest wickedness; he must be punished. The wicked deplored his shamelessness, which frightened them; they did not care to punish him, of course; he served them boldly, and it would have been all right if he had talked humorously with them in the clubs and barrooms, but to tell the world what he was doing was a violation of their code, and bad politics. Not only the righteous, crooked men also are hypo-crites. My impression, and I think Devery's, was that Tammany and a large body of his customers and the wisest of his police agents quietly turned against Devery. Anyway he had to go, and it was the system that "fired" him. The unofficial excuse of the firing officials was that Devery had made himself a scandal.

Devery had beaten himself as he feared he would, as he told Robert Moran he might. But he resented the disloyalty of his own kind. And by the same token he respected us of the *Commercial*, who had consistently distinguished between him as a person and as a chief of police. I think that we never printed a para-graph against this crook that did not betray our involuntary lik-ing for his honesty, courage, and character.

When the order for his retirement was published, Mr. Wright, the editor of the paper, came down to my desk and remarked that we ought to have a photograph of the chief to print the day of his departure. I reminded him that Devery never gave out his picture, and Wright knew that, but he thought that "somehow we ought to be able to get one for such an occasion." The smiling manner of his hint gave me an idea.

"I'll get one," I said, and he crossed to the other side. "How?" he asked.

"I'll get it from the chief himself."

"I'd like to hear your conversation with him."

"You can," I answered, and I told him to go to his 'phone and listen in while I talked to Devery. He did.

"Hello, Chief," I called affectionately. "This is the city editor of the *Commercial*."

"The hell it is," he replied amiably. "What can I do for the city editor of the foremost paper in New York?"

"Lend me your photograph for publication."

"What!" And I could hear heavy, indignant breathing. I hurried.

"Yes, Chief. Listen. I know that you never give out your face for publication, and I can guess the reason. But also you are enough of a politician to understand that when a paper like the *Commercial* has spent years trying to get an official fired from his job, it likes to hang up his picture with a boast, 'William S. Devery, the unspeakable chief of police, whom the *Commercial Advertiser* has finally succeeded in ousting from—' "

The heavy breathing grew to gasps. I changed my tune.

"No, Chief, but honest, now, we have given you more space than we have given to any other public man, and I really think that we ought to have your picture and have it alone."

He burst. "Well, Jesus Christ! Of all the good God-damned gall. Send up your man."

And then, when he was all packed up ready to leave his office, he called in all the reporters at police headquarters, and Robert reported that his farewell was as follows:

"Gentlemen, I have summoned you to bid you good-by and to ask you politely to tell your editors to go to hell; all except you, Moran. Give my compliments to the city editor of the *Commercial Advertiser*."

We were, and we remained, friends as long as Devery lived.

He retired to his own home ward a rich man and set out to be the political boss, the Tammany leader, of that district. When Tammany opposed and beat him he was amazed, and he used to talk with me about it. His theory, his experience, of life had taught him that all you had to do to succeed was to get money, and that then, when you had "the stuff," you could buy with it anything you wanted. This he believed; that was his philosophy and his religion. His last chapter in life proved to him that it wasn't so, and Devery tried to think it out, change his mind, and the effort was in vain. It broke his heart; that and the queer mix-up of disloyal friends and loyal enemies.

"You, f'rinstance," he said one night on his favorite corner, "you been a good friend o' mine, and you ain't my friend at all. I mean —oh, hell, I don't know what I mean; do you?"

X X

THE CUBAN WAR AND T.R.

G LANCING back over the last few chapters, I see that I have
presented fairly well the conceit of myself and of my
staff of local reporters. "We" knew it all; we knew how
to tell it; we were "making" the paper, which was, indeed, growing in circulation. H. J. Wright, the editor, let us think that we
were doing it. There were other departments, on which he worked
hard, but we rarely noticed them and nobody asked us to. Even
the business office did not bother us much. Now and then the
publisher, Seymour, hoping to bring in a new advertiser, would
'phone me to send one of my "best reporters" to some shop to
write up some advertisement.

"What!" I would answer. "Let one of my writers write a reading notice? No, sir. We do news, not dirty work."

He would come frowning upstairs to see Wright. No doubt
he complained, but I never heard a word of it from the editor.
The write-up appeared in the paper, written, and well written,
too, by Josephine Meagen. We of the city room came to admire
this quiet little trained reporter of fashion news, even though she
was not in our department; she was almost in our class.

Sometimes an advertiser who thought he owned the paper would
telephone direct to me. He had a piece of news which he wanted
a good man to report. "Oh," I would answer, "you are a business
man. Well, you have the wrong number. This is the news department. We have a business department that attends to business.
Call up the publisher."

In a few minutes Seymour came running upstairs, and giving
me a look of indignation, disappeared into Wright's office, whence
I heard the angry noises of his resentment and the soft purring
of the editor. The matter was smoothed out somehow; they hired

a Russian named Mendeloff, who was charged to my salary list but took orders mainly from Wright and Seymour. He did the commercial journalism for the business department after that. The city department heard no more of the advertisers' influence on the local news policy of the paper.

There was other news than city news. There was state, national, and foreign news, but we ignored it. It may have been important in the world's history, but it was not well written, and, you understand, we were writers; I was a newspaper man, temporarily, but my staff were writers, getting the news as material for poetry, plays, or fiction, and writing it as news for practice. The reporters on the other papers sneered at us, and the profession would have cut us; only we cut first, and being the youngest journalists, we could outdo their contempt with our pity. Those were times when a *Commercial* reporter met and praised some fellow like Richard Harding Davis for some story which we had analyzed and found pretty well written. Our applause did not improve our standing on Park Row, but we did not see that until later, too late. By that time we were old enough to realize that neither our talents nor our egotism were extraordinary and that an affectation of modesty was better than honesty as a policy.

Among the news of our day were a presidential election and the Cuban and the Boer wars. We used the presidential election to further our interest and purposes in the city election that occurred with it. The Cuban war served as a smoke-screen under which we played around in the city news, developing our cubs into reporters. We reported the local preparations for the war and the formation of the Rough Riders and other units of the army. We saw just enough of the commercialism of the business of supplies to agree that the place for a war correspondent to go was not the front, but the rear of a fighting army. There was a good deal besides canned beef to show up and protect the troops from. About the only reporting we did of the front was a long series of letters from Captain Theodore H. Low, a Marine officer on the battleship *Iowa*. He must have spent all his spare time writing those volunteer letters which pictured in detail everything that happened on a fighting ship just as it happened, the bombardment of San Juan, Porto Rico, in much the same tone as a frolic of the idle sailors. There was no more order than there was emphasis in this correspondence, but Pitts Duffield gave the letters form. Duffield had his work to do editing local copy, but his love was Captain Low's stuff. He kept it in a drawer, and whenever he had time he pulled it out and worked on it, cutting and piecing, weaving and connecting it up into copy that looked like embroidery. Day after day it ran, and "we" were proud of it as about the simplest, truest reporting done in that war. Other papers copied it enough to confirm our superiority in and to the Cuban war.

When the Boer war came we had an opportunity to appear at the front with a full-fledged war correspondent. Guy H. Scull wanted to go. He said he would pay his own expenses if we would give him credentials that would enable him to pass the British War Office. Scull arranged in London to write also for the London *Telegraph*, and his correspondence was a success in London. To us in New York it proved only that any of us could go anywhere in the world and write beautifully about anything. Any of us. True, Guy Scull was a gifted writer, but we did not then regard him as any better than the rest of us, and Carl Hovey recalled recently that upon Scull's return, covered with credit for battles pictured and soldiers characterized, he sat down and wrote a weather report like any ordinary reporter.

But the Cuban war ended in the city department. The army—all that was worth while of it, Colonel Roosevelt and the Rough Riders and some other regiments that had stood out in the war news—landed at Montauk. We all took turns going down there to report the scenes, types, and incidents of that camp. This was in accordance with the contract with my reporters that, in lieu of fair salaries, they were all to have equal chances to see and report —life. Also it was in accordance with our theory of journalism that anything that interested any of us would interest our readers and, therefore, would be news if reported interestingly. Unprofessional, this; the current theory which has prevailed on both newspapers and magazines is that the reader is a dub and that the editor must guess what the dub likes or will stand, give him that and nothing else. We knew nothing of the law of demand and supply; so we had a column from Montauk on a trooper treating two guests to fly-decked pie and eating all three portions himself.

This trooper, Edwin Emerson, was the bane of Colonel Roosevelt's short Army life. He had been a colleague of mine on the *Evening Post* and was fired for guessing wrong the verdict of a jury in a criminal case. When I became a city editor he offered to report for me, and needing a friend, I took him on. He came to my house for dinner one night when he should have been working and told me he had the news I expected; he got it by telephoning to the mounted police station. The next day, when he handed in his report and I told him it was wrong, that that new police station had no telephone, he laughed heartily. Edwin Emerson was a happy chap; he asked me to get him another job. The *Evening Sun* took him and fired him, as he said himself, "because, you see, they had three lists: names never to be mentioned; names never to be mentioned without praise; and names never to be mentioned without a roast. I couldn't help it. I specialized in mentioning the unmentionables, in roasting those to be praised, and in praising those to be roasted. So—can you help me to another job?"

I couldn't, but Seth Low, the ex-president of Columbia University, persuaded the secretary of the Woman's College to take Emerson as his secretary. When he turned up to ask for another job, he explained—happily, of course—"Well, you see, it was this way. The secretary of the Woman's College had a theory of education which I think is bad. I discovered it by accident. He was away on a vacation, and his children, coming home from school with my children, called for me and I began telling them (and my children) fairy tales. The children had never heard any fairy tales; they were hungry for them. Well, as you know, I know all the fairy tales of all the nations of the earth, and I make up more. So when the secretary of the Woman's College came back he found that his children could tell him all the fairy tales of all languages and were able themselves to make up more. Since his theory was that children should be taught nothing but facts, and principally scientific facts, he felt that his experiment on his own children had been interfered with and his children's minds ruined. He dismissed me. I don't mind that; I can see those hungry little children eating up my unscientific but lovely literature of childhood, and—well, say, can you give me a letter of introduction to T.R.? Judging by the kind of men he is choosing for his Rough Riders, I feel I am born for his regiment."

I gave Emerson a letter in those terms, saying that the bearer was peculiarly fitted to be a Rough Rider; and when the regiment came back to Montauk with Emerson (happily) in irons and T.R. roared at me his remonstrance, I bade him read my letter and see that I had told him the truth. The Colonel yelped with rage and laughter and let Emerson escape for an hour to show me the camp (and the Rough Riders' pie stand). He really liked Emerson, too; all Emerson's friends and victims liked this soldier of fortune and professional correspondent, all except the secretary of the Woman's College and another correspondent who alleges that Emerson once undertook to sell a horse for him and forgot (and was sorry for and never ceased to apologize to) the horse, which must have starved to death in the gulch where Emerson hid him.

T.R. gives some space to Emerson in his work on the Rough Riders or, as Mr. Dooley named it, *Alone in Cubiia*. He said that he put him under arrest for writing "a description of the personnel of his regiment," and when I objected that that should not have been a crime, the Colonel changed the subject.

"Say," he said, "they are talking me for governor of New York. Should I run?"

Now Roosevelt did not ask one such questions as that for the sake of an answer. They were merely questions he was asking himself out loud, but it was fun to reply as if he were putting them to you. I answered this question promptly and firmly.

"Yes, sure."

Astonished and diverted, he whirled upon me with another question: "Why?"

"Oh," I said, "it will make Platt and his machine so mad."

He lost his temper, but we were standing just inside the flaps of his tent and two ex-cowboys of his regiment came racing and yelling down through the crowded camp, and T.R. ran out to wave his hat and give the cowboy yelp. That eased him till I asked if it wasn't against orders to tear through camp like that.

"Yes, it is," he said, and he sneaked into his tent out of sight.

"Don't you enforce the law any more?" I asked.

"Yes; no. Oh, well, the war's all over. But honest, now, what is your real reason for my running for governor?"

"So that I can have the inside track on the political news and get a beat a day."

He turned his back on me, declaring he could never draw any

serious advice from me. But I asked him to observe that my answer implied that I believed he would be elected. "And you will," I said, reasoning that the reluctant willingness of Senator Platt, the Republican State boss, to support Roosevelt, suggested that this knowing politician knew that election was sure to follow the nomination of the war hero. There were obstacles, however. T.R. as police president and as a reformer had always opposed the boss, and it would be embarrassing for him now to deal with and accept his indispensable aid. T.R. sat on a box in his tent, wagging his head.

"We'll see," he said at last. "Meanwhile I'll get on with my book." And he resumed the dictation to the waiting stenographer. I knew T.R. well enough to feel sure that he would run for governor; which was news, even to T.R.

COLONEL ROOSEVELT AS GOVERNOR

THE colonel of the Rough Riders wriggled out of the army at Montauk as he had wriggled into it, fast. He said he had to get to New York to consult his friends and others about running for governor.

"I don't know whether I can get the nomination," he said, "and I don't know whether to take it—if I can get it."

"You don't think with your brains, do you?" I answered, and to meet the look of astonishment on his over-expressive countenance, I added that he had decided in his hips or somewhere not only to take the nomination but to go and get it, if he must, and to be elected.

His outthrust jaw drew slowly back, and he laughed. "That's so," he said. "How did you know it before I did?"

"You don't know it yet," I answered.

I didn't know how I read his mind. Having to watch him for news all those years at police headquarters, I had learned to guess what he meant while I listened to his answers to our questions, as a sailor looks for the weather in the sky and the sea. All reporters look as well as listen when their news sources are talking; how else do the newspapers report so correctly the news gathered out of lies! Roosevelt's lies were unconscious. He was an honest man; he could not tell a lie until he had made himself believe it. He did not know that day at Montauk, even when he acknowledged that I did, that he meant to be governor of New York. He did not deny my assertion that he "didn't know it yet." He turned away, then turned back, and named out loud to himself the men (and women; his sister Mrs. Robinson was one of them) whom he had to consult.

"And Platt?" I asked.

"No, never," he answered.

Senator Thomas C. Platt, the Republican State boss, was the counter villain of Richard Croker; he was the anti-Tammany city boss. The reformers hated them both, and Roosevelt was a reformer. He did not really hate bosses; the make-up of his regiment—dudes and athletes from the east and gunmen from the west—showed what his hips preferred. Only his mind ran with

Life

"LIFE'S SUNDAY SCHOOL CLASS"

Present: Teddy Roosevelt, Willie Bryan, Tommy Platt, Jacob Riis,
Booker T. Washington

the reformers, who were already asking, under the lead of Godkin in the *Evening Post*, whether Teddy would surrender to Platt, call on and make a trade with him. And Roosevelt did not have to yield to the boss. He returned from Cuba as Lindbergh later came back from Paris: a hero. When he lighted on Montauk Point, the colonel of the Rough Riders could have been elected to anything; Platt sincerely hated him, but the Senator was a politician, and he knew that his best chance of carrying the State was to have Teddy lead his ticket. My information, from the political reporters, was that Platt would not ask Roosevelt for any pledge; all he wanted was a formal acknowledgment of his leadership and some outward sign of the "united front" so dear to machines. This I reported to the colonel, who did not understand himself.

"You don't have to see Platt," I said, "but you will."

"Will I?" he snapped, and though he was standing inside his tent his lower jaw seemed to protrude beyond the flap. But it soon went indoors.

"Why will I?" he asked, and his curiosity about himself was as sincere as his rage at my presumptuous prophecy.

"You're a practical man," I answered, and I used the phrase as we reformers used it, contemptuously, and T.R. seized it straight.

"I am, you know," he said. "I'm a practical man." And he repeated it several times then; he repeated it again and again during his very practical political career. "We are practical men," he wrote once to a railroad president, and the newspapers played it up as news. Roosevelt was a natural politician.

He called in New York on Senator Platt. After consulting with all his friends, after many meetings of the family, with advice for and against the step, the colonel sneaked over and called on the boss of the Republican State machine. There was no bargaining; Platt exacted no pledges. T.R. came back with his pride up, his jaw out, and his fist clenched. He had not yielded one iota of his independence.

"None was asked, was there?" I questioned.

He was pacing, like a fighting man, up and down the dining-room of his sister Mrs. Robinson's house, and my question seemed to hit him like a blow. He stopped, stared angrily at me, and then answered meekly, "No."

"But"—he advanced upon me furiously—"they are accusing me of surrendering to Platt."

"Oh, it is the reformers you mean; it is their bodies you are walking on, their eyes you are pummeling."

He laughed. "Yes. Nobody saw me call on Platt, but the news of it has leaked out. How? How? How?"

"Platt," I suggested. "That's all he got out of it: your recognition of his bad eminence. He must have that known."

T.R. stood rocking a moment. "Of course," he said. "Of course. He didn't care to see me; he wanted others to see me see him. Of course. So he— Come with me."

He darted for the hall, grabbed his hat, and with me after him, he tore over to a room, a sort of office, where he was making his headquarters. There was no one there.

"Now," he said, "you've got to help me. I have to deny that I 'saw' Platt. The reformers are making bonfires of my call, and I must put them out. I must write a denial. You do it. Sit down there at that desk and write a correction."

"But," I protested, "it's true. You did see Platt."

"Yes, yes, I know, but there must be some way to make a statement that will—cover the case."

"That is a job for a statesman, not for a reporter."

He lost his temper, accused me of joking all the time, even in emergencies; I was no use, not in a charge. This was no joking business. As his wont was, he satisfied his rage completely in words and came out quiet and reasonable.

"I'll tell you what to do," I grinned. "You sit down at that desk, write out your statement like a reporter, and I like an editor will read copy, pass or reject it as plausible, and maybe edit it a bit."

He did that. He sat down, wrote painfully a short statement, and handed it to me. I read it and must have smiled.

"I know," he said. "That won't do, but it can be done, and I'll do it." He wrote another denial, offered it hopefully, and as I read the copy and he read my grin, he knew again. "I know, I know, but wait—we'll get it."

He wrote and wrote, one statement after another, till the desk was strewn with rejected sheets. It was late. I had to go home to dinner; he had other things to do.

"Look here, Colonel," I suggested. "We can't go on all night at this one job, and it isn't necessary. There is no known literary form for denying a fact without lying, and that you don't want to do. Why not pick out one of those statements, destroying all the others, set the selected one up on your desk, and read it before and after meals, till, in a day or two, you'll come to believe it yourself? Then give it out. It will be true then."

He looked up at me; I suppressed all signs of joking, and he muttered, "I *can* do that; I can *do* it. Which one shall I keep?"

I picked up at random one copy; he shook his head. "No, this is the best," and he held up his choice. I agreed. We destroyed the others, and I stood the chosen one on the lid of his desk, saying, "Now then. Read it twice before breakfast, once after; once before luncheon, twice after; and so on till bedtime. Read it on going to bed till you fall asleep. That's the principle of prayer. Some morning you will find that it's true."

"Good night," he said abruptly, and he hurried me away.

The demand from the press for a statement from T.R. was becoming irresistible. Knowing that one existed, I wanted it first. I had told my office about the written statement, and they wanted it first. After waiting two days I asked our candidate for it. I put my question wrong.

"Well, Colonel," I said, "have you got that lie so that you believe it yourself?"

He was furious. He leaped up from his desk where the statement stood and yelled at me that I "would spoil anything"; he was just getting so that he could have given out the statement, and I, by my insulting question, I had set him back, probably a day or two.

"And it ought to come out," he complained. "Everybody's after it, and there it is. Why should I hold it back?" But he would not give it to me. "Not on your life," he said.

The next day I read it, not in my paper, but in the morning newspapers, and my office was disgusted with me. Some of them suggested that it might be better for me to stay at my desk, mind my own business, and let reporters do the reporting. But I liked reporting better than editing; so I went on reporting. When I had the assignments all given out I sent myself up to see the Republican candidate for governor.

"Well," I said that morning, "I see that you did finally get where you could believe and publish that—statement."

"It's true, that statement," he exclaimed. "That statement is absolutely and literally true."

"Sure," I said. "I told you you'd come to believe it yourself."

He stood there at his desk, looking as he often looked: as if he had half a mind to beat me up. He never did; never got more than half a mind. I was lucky.

"Say," he said one day during that campaign, "things aren't going well up the state. I must try a new tactic. What'll it be?"

"Why not an old one?"

"Which?"

"Oh," I said, "go up there and eat dirt. Confess you're wrong on something, made a mistake, committed a sin, or were about to."

"But I'm not," he answered grimly.

"I'm talking politics," I said, "not facts."

He charged across the room, charged back, and stopped in front of me. Boring his eyes defiantly into mine, he said, "You think that's a joke, don't you? Well, it isn't. That is politics, good politics, and—"

"What's the difference?"

"There you go again. Think you're funny. But I tell you that trick will work, and I'm going to work it. It'll make the people see that I'm just like them; one of them."

He did it; it worked; and all through his career he showed that he knew when to make or confess a blunder. Yes, T.R. was a very practical politician, and it was partly from watching him sympathetically that I lost some of my contempt for politicians and practical men generally.

And I did watch T.R. Doubleday, Page and Company contracted with me to write his life, and I contracted with T.R. to tell me his story and give me the documents. Not a line of it was ever written; it was too hard a job for me to do while I was city-editing. We started it, however. T.R. was finishing his book on the Rough Riders and running for governor; he could do a lot of things at once.

"Come on," he would call after some political conference. "Let's walk and talk."

Darting out of his house at Oyster Bay, he would jump a fence and crash into the woods, telling me, who came running breathlessly after him, how, when he was a child, his father—

"My really great father—a gentleman and a sport—he was the first American to drive four horses handsomely through New York—in style, in the good old English style, with everything that belonged—he worked for, he saved, my life. I was a weak-lunged, asthmatic child, and I remember—I think I remember—him carrying me in my distress, in my battles for breath, up and down a room all night. Handsome dandy that he was, the thought of him now and always has been a sense of comfort. I could breathe, I could sleep, when he had me in his arms. My father—he got me breath, he got me lungs, strength—life."

I remember this because I was all out of breath when I heard it; I was chasing along behind the once asthmatic athlete who was taking a rest from his politics by tearing through the brush of those Long Island woods for fun.

"I wish," I remember saying to him, "I do wish, Colonel, that you would be a father to me as your father was to you."

"How?" he stopped to demand.

"By carrying me in your arms till I can get my breath."

"Oh," he said. "Don't you love to run like a deer through the timber?"

"Maybe," I answered, "but not like a bull moose, not like a hound after a bull moose."

The pretense of taking his *Life* was kept up for a few years; it was a good excuse to be near him when he was a source of news, as governor and as president. Many a good story came out thus, and I did write some magazine articles about him. I could stand well the stuff he poured out of his memory and his reflections, but I could not stand the cross-country walks which were runs to me, running and jumping over plowed fields and high fences.

When he was governor he let me in on his most private political plannings, conferences, hesitations, and decisions. They were all news to me. I mean that I heard and saw what the governor said and did from the merely professional point of view of a newspaper reporter. A few years later I would have had a more philosophic attitude; I would have had theories and opinions and purposes of my own, and I might have tried to influence the man in power that I was so close to. At that time I had no theories beyond those of the ordinary reformer. Roosevelt's governorship, his Legislature, and the situation in the State and city of New York were a mere spectacle to me, interesting, dramatic, comic, but taken all in the day's work, as a matter of course. The meaning of it came out later, when I was seeing other governors at work in other States.

I could see that the bosses and the business interests were willing to use up Governor Roosevelt as they are wont to destroy the political possibilities of the presidents, governors, mayors, and legislators they find they can use for their purposes. Roosevelt used to tell how they came to him with their extravagant demands for privileges, holding out offers of contributions and backing for the U.S. senatorship and even for the presidency. And he did some things for the interests. But T.R. was a practical politician; he saw that he must stand in with the powers that govern our government, but that he could not, for his sake and for theirs, give them all that they asked.

"They want the earth," he blurted one day, "and they would destroy me and themselves and the earth itself to get it."

His habit was to spend the middle of the week, while the Legislature was in session, at Albany, and on Friday, when it adjourned, he would come to New York to stay till Monday afternoon or Tuesday morning. I met him at the station when he arrived in New York, kept in close touch all the time he was there, and saw him off when he took train for the capital. We had an understanding that I was to know all the political acts that he was contemplating, with his reasons for them. At Albany we had a man, Larry Graham, a charming, handsome fellow whom the governor liked, who acted as Albany correspondent. Graham did not know New York politics very well; he had had no experience in that field as a reporter. He was not a "wise" old newspaper man; he was, like the rest of our staff, a fresh, young, open-eyed observer; he differed from the others in that he was not a writer. He rested while I worked week-ends, and he returned with the Governor to Albany with instructions, not to write and wire, but to telephone me, when the news we both expected and understood was released by T.R. I wrote it, and I wrote it as one having authority. This was most unprofessional, but it was amusing, and as T.R. said, "It worked." T.R. was rarely quoted; no other authority was cited. As we were sure of our news, it was stated briefly, firmly, positively, upon our own authority. The result was that when we had a beat, other papers had to say that "the *Commercial Advertiser* said," which had the effect of making people think the paper was an authority, on the inside, especially as our news was so regularly confirmed by executive and legislative acts. When we were beaten, when some other newspaper reported something that we had overlooked, we used to say, "The *Sun* reports so and so.

This is correct." It was impudence; it was an annoyance to the *Sun* men, and other newspaper people made disagreeable remarks about us in Park Row. But we of the conceited *Commercial* enjoyed it all, and we made the whole street laugh with us before we were through.

One week-end when Larry Graham was in town he reported to me with some embarrassment that Franklin Clarkin, the city editor of the *Evening Post,* had made him an offer of $75 a week to quit us and cover Albany for him. "What shall I do?" asked Graham.

"Take it, of course," I answered. "We're paying you only $35; you have a family behind you and a career ahead. Go to the *Post,* sure."

"But—" Graham did not want to go. He liked our crowd, and he realized that Clarkin did not know that he, Graham, was not writing all his dispatches. But he consulted with the staff, and they all saw the humor of the situation; they made me promise to take Graham back any time he wished to come, and then they—"we"— all pushed our Albany correspondent over upon the *Post.* A few weeks later I met Clarkin on the street.

"Say," he said, "what sort of a gold brick is this that you have sold me?"

"Graham is no gold brick," I answered. "No man on the *Commercial* is a gold brick; they are all bricks and pure gold, but they are not gold bricks."

He backed up. He liked Graham, felt his charm, and got the results of his popularity with the governor and the legislators; Graham got the news all right, "but," said Clarkin, "he does not write it; he wires it in bulletin form, like notes, and there is no force in it." I explained that that was the way we had taught Graham to report—short bulletins which I took and rewrote *ex cathedra* in the tone and style of the All-Wise.

Clarkin walked along, silent a moment; then he smiled. "What shall I do?" he asked.

"Oh," I said, "keep Graham and hire a good city editor, me, for instance."

But this was bluff on my part. I was not so superior as I pretended. It was just about that time that my wife was having me examined by a physician who wagged his head and told her—not me—that I "could not keep it up." I was on the "verge of nervous prostration." And I happened just about that time to overhear one man in the business department say to Wright, the editor-in-chief, that I was all in. "We've got out of that man just about all there ever was in him."

T.R., approaching the end of his term as governor, was saying what he saw ahead—and among these was, to use his own winking word, "Washington."

"There'll be something for you and Graham, too," he hinted. But I was not interested. I remember that I answered that all I wanted was a sinecure, "a well-paid job with no work to do."

"Find one and you shall have it," he promised, but the very energy of his promise depressed me. I was emptied of energy— done, for once. If I had been told I was to have "seen" sixteen other cities as I had seen New York, and eleven States, I would probably have died.